Designing Democracy in a Dangerous World

ANDREW REYNOLDS

OXFORD

UNIVERSITY PRESS

OXFORD

UNIVERSITY PRESS

Great Clarendon Street, Oxford ox2 6DP

Oxford University Press is a department of the University of Oxford.
It furthers the University's objective of excellence in research, scholarship,
and education by publishing worldwide in

Oxford New York

Auckland Cape Town Dar es Salaam Hong Kong Karachi
Kuala Lumpur Madrid Melbourne Mexico City Nairobi
New Delhi Shanghai Taipei Toronto

With offices in

Argentina Austria Brazil Chile Czech Republic France Greece
Guatemala Hungary Italy Japan Poland Portugal Singapore
South Korea Switzerland Thailand Turkey Ukraine Vietnam

Oxford is a registered trade mark of Oxford University Press
in the UK and in certain other countries

Published in the United States
by Oxford University Press Inc., New York

© Andrew Reynolds 2011

British Library Cataloguing in Publication Data

Data available

Library of Congress Cataloging in Publication Data

Data available

Typeset by SPI Publisher Services, Pondicherry, India
Printed in Great Britain
on acid-free paper by
MPG Biddles Group, Bodmin and King's Lynn

ISBN: 978–0–19–959448–1 (Hbk)
978–0–19–959449–8 (Pbk)

1 3 5 7 9 10 8 6 4 2

Contents

Acknowledgments

Completed books lay in the comfort of a latticed hammock where each thread and knot is a person who gave something to the author along the way. Without the interweaving of each individual piece of advice, data, correction, and encouragement, the work would never come to fruition.

My mind is more befuddled than most and thus I am bound to leave out some names whom I should be thanking heartily—for that I am truly sorry.

At the University of North Carolina (UNC), I am indebted to the assistance of Ali Yanus with the statistical work in chapters 4 and 6. Alison Garren, Desiree Smith, Maggie McDowell, Jeff Saltzman, William Dupont, Meghan Staffiera, Olivia Burchett, and Catherine Kannam all provided invaluable research assistance at some point in time. The Institute for Arts and Humanities at UNC has supported and nourished me in so many ways—not least as a faculty fellow when I was deep in the writing of this book. I thank John McGowan and Ruel Tyson in particular.

In addition, many friends and colleagues in the field of democracy were especially helpful—foremost among those, Pippa Norris, Michael Gallagher, Dan Posner, Matthew Shugart, John Carey, Mark Crescenzi, Don Horowitz, Ben Reilly, Rob Richie, Nigel Roberts, and Charlie Kurzman. My mentors have consistently supported me through the fifteen years since leaving grad school—Arend Lijphart, Bernie Grofman, and Larry Diamond. Their wisdom and support continues to be my foundation.

For the last eight years, I have taught a First Year Seminar at UNC titled "Designing Democracy." Over the years, these students have probed, criticized, and molded my ideas as much as any other group. Teaching the class has been an inspiration and I thank them for that.

Designing Democracy in a Dangerous World was researched and written in Chapel Hill, North Carolina, and in the field during advising trips to Afghanistan, Burma, Guyana, Indonesia, Kenya, Jordan, Lebanon, Nepal, Pakistan, Sierra Leone, South Africa, Sudan, Yemen, and Zimbabwe. This is how I learn—on the ground, glimpsing some of the realities. I am indebted to all my employers and hosts. In particular, Peter Erben, Hermann Thiel, and Paul Harris of the International Foundation for Election Systems; Susan Stigant, Peter Manikas, and Shari Bryan of the National Democratic Institute; Lauren Ploch of the International Republican Institute; David Carroll and Therese Laanela of the Carter Center; Horacio Boneo, Carina Perelli, and Richard Gee of the UN's Electoral Assistance Department; Andrew Wilder of the Afghan Research and Evaluation Unit; and Alex Thier of the US Institute of Peace.

This book rests on a discussion of many countries. To understand in greater depth such a diverse pool of cases, I have relied on the advice and teaching of a host of experts. A few I need to single out as they are crucial to my empirical knowledge: On Burma, Aung Naing Oo, Zaw Oo, and Win Min; Zimbabwe, Peter Godwin; Afghanistan, Alex Thier and Andrew Wilder; Sudan, Ray Kennedy and Riek Machar; Namibia, Susan Glover; Fiji, Brij Lal, and Jon Frankel; Kenya, Yash Ghai.

Oxford University Press has been a dream to work with as always – notably, Dominic Byatt and Sarah Parker. I am so proud that this book is being published in the Comparative Politics series edited by David Farrell. David is a longtime friend and someone who I respect greatly for his incisive research and human decency. He accepted and shepherded this manuscript into production and for that I will be eternally grateful.

Last, my family. I am so proud of each of them in their own ways. They are spectacular people and they surround me with the love which makes everything else possible: My wife Layna Mosley, my son Atticus (born 1995), and my daughters Madeline (born 1997), Cecilia (born 2007), and Tess (born 2009).

Andrew Reynolds
Chapel Hill, NC, USA April 2010

List of Figure and Tables

Figure

Tables

List of Appendices

1

Designing Democracy in a Dangerous World

> The art of progress is to preserve order amid change, and to preserve change amid order.
>
> Alfred North Whitehead

INTRODUCTION

This book seeks to shed some light on a question which lies at the heart of contemporary world politics: how does one craft democracy in a fragile and divided state, a nation ripped apart by conflict and buffeted by unrelenting political and economic storms? The question is not simply one of governance and rights but one of stability and peace: stability for the nation-state at hand and peace for the region it rests within and ultimately the world beyond. While many fragile nations have sought to democratize over the last half century, success has been uneven at best. In many fledgling democracies today – most notably Iraq and Afghanistan – spiraling conflict was driven in large part by the missteps of democratic design in the immediate post-conflict period. The hopes for peace and stability in those cases, and most others, rest in large part on crafting a well-designed political system which brings legitimacy to elected leaders and reassurance to minority groups.

The debate over how to promote democracy abroad has captured the attention of policymakers, scholars, politicians, and activists, throughout the world. The American and British governments placed democratization front and center in their justifications for military intervention in the Middle East in the early 2000s. Along with other Western nations, their foreign ministries spend huge amounts of foreign aid on promoting democratic institutions, elections, and an emerging civil society in Africa, Asia, Eastern Europe, and the Middle East. The mantra of "democracy brings stability" echoed across the ideological spectrum from American Neo-Conservatives to European leftists. Multilateral donors, private financiers, human rights advocates, and multinational corporations all pay heed to the belief that "good governance" is democratic governance and that without free elections and accountable leaders, nation-states are likely to be fractious and be bad neighbors in their region.

The constitution lays out the ground rules of the democratic game, and thus I shall use the terms "constitutional design" and "democratic design" interchangeably, although the constitution will speak to issues beyond the scope and derivation of the institutions of governance. A good constitution is a foundation of communal harmony, but it is only one pillar. Even when the constitutional designers do well, the new state can be thrown back into violence and chaos caused by regional conflict or meddling neighbors. But when it comes to building stability and managing ethnic conflict, well-crafted political structures are the best way of dealing with the communal conflicts that exist within nation-states. A suitable democracy can lay a foundation that assuages minority fears and alienation and provides the majority with the incentives to accommodate.

DOES DEMOCRACY MATTER?

It has to be noted that not all observers of political tides in the developing world are democracy evangelists. As Diamond notes, "in the wake of the Iraq debacle...cultural arguments about the limits to democracy are fashionable again" (Diamond 2008: 20). The foreign correspondent and author Robert B. Kaplan has been at the forefront of skeptics for well over a decade and articulates the strongest refutation of the democratization mantra of any of democracy's critics (see Kaplan 1997). Kaplan does not merely argue that liberal democracy has, and will, fail in the poor parts of the world, but that democracy promotion merely has become a way of transforming such governments into new authoritarian regimes: some more efficient that their dictatorial predecessors, others less so. He argues that democracy in sub-Saharan Africa has weakened institutions and services in many places and competitive elections often lead to chaos. Contrary to conventional wisdom, Kaplan (1997: 58) believes that Russia began to fall apart because it became more democratic, and China "may be succeeding in part because it is not."

So what is the mechanism? How does democracy make things worse for people in the developing world? Kaplan offers three suggestions. First, there is the "Museveni" argument. President Museveni of Uganda justifies his suppression of democracy with the argument that elections cause conflict and poor states are too fragile to survive such conflict. "If one forms a multi-party system in Uganda, a party cannot win elections unless it finds a way of dividing the ninety-four per cent of the electorate (that consists of peasants), and this is where the main problem comes up: tribalism, religion, or regionalism becomes the basis for intense partisanship," says Kaplan (1997). Second, Kaplan (1997: 61) believes that the sharing of power has to be settled *before* elections, a divided state will collapse if it invests electoral democracy with the task of sharing out the national pie:

Democracy often weakens states by necessitating ineffectual compromises and fragile coalition governments in societies where bureaucratic institutions never functioned well to begin with. Because democracy neither forms states or strengthens them initially, multi-party systems are best suited to nations that already have efficient bureaucracies and a middle class that pays income tax, and where primary issues such as borders and power sharing have already been resolved, leaving politicians free to bicker about the budget and other secondary matters.

Third, Kaplan suggests that successful leaders in the developing world are ones not dependent on voters, or accountable to majorities, but rather those dictators, or pseudo-dictators, who act like Thomas Hobbes' enlightened despot – leviathan. He would rather have a Moin Qureshi (Pakistan), Lee Kwan Yew (Singapore), or Alberto Fujimori (Peru) in power, than an elected parliament full of "corrupt, bickering, ineffectual politicians whose weak rule never had an institutional base to start with" (ibid.).

There are echoes of Kaplan's democratic pessimism in the writings of Fareed Zakaria (see Zakaria 1997, 2003). In 1997, Zakaria argued that the conventional wisdom of the early 1990s – which maintained that electoral democracy was the first point of call on a march to stability in the developing world – was deeply misguided. Rather than deepened participation, democratic transitions were entrenching illiberal elites who were just as authoritarian in their behaviors as in days of old, but now were protected by the cloak of electoral legitimacy. Zakaria preferred the idea of Hobbes' enlightened despot, along with economic and legal liberalization, preparing the ground for electoral democracy over a not inconsiderable intervening period. Richard Haass has more time for engagement than Kaplan or Zakaria but advocates a more measured approach to "regime change" than was followed by the Bush administration. Haass (2005) believes that diplomacy can act as the liberalizing balm which eases the way to political openness. "A foreign policy that chooses to integrate, not isolate, despotic regimes can be the Trojan horse that moderates their behavior in the short run and their nature in the long run."

It is also questionable whether democracy actually guarantees peace. Fully consolidated democracies may be less likely to go to war with their neighbors but emerging ones have a higher propensity to be involved in extra-state violence (see Mansfield and Snyder 2005). A well-constructed democracy can be a tool of internal conflict management but there are many examples of poorly crafted democracies which are no less fractious than their authoritarian neighbors. Paul Collier (2008) argues that "at very low levels of income, democracy does not appear to enhance the prospects of peace...but instead it seems to make them more dangerous. And in post-conflict situations elections appear both to increase and to shift the risks of a resurgence of conflict, sharply increasing them once the election is over". Nor is democracy a guarantee that sympathetic pro-Western moderates will take power. In places that have historically antagonized the North Atlantic powers, democracy can be hard to swallow when the "bad guys" win.

Politically "ugly" governments have come to power through free elections in Palestine and Iraq, the Muslim Brotherhood gathers strength as democratic windows are opened in Egypt and Jordan, and Hamas slowly grows more powerful in Lebanon. Algeria's government cancelled elections in 1990 when it became apparent that radical Islamists were going to win.

Ian Bremer's "J Curve" theory of *openness* and stability has some overlap with *democracy* and stability but, as he notes, fledgling inchoate democracies are considerably more vulnerable to immediate instability than entrenched authoritarian regimes (Bremer 2006). Nevertheless, the initial phase of building democratic institutions and holding competitive elections may be the most dangerous to a fragile state. As democracy becomes increasingly entrenched, shocks to the system are less likely to cause catastrophic consequences – but first elections are surgeries which take place when the patient is weakest and most susceptible to collapse. This leads Bremer to argue that "demands for far reaching political change should be fully supported only in those states that have a fighting chance of surviving the passage through the depths of the curve" (from authoritarian to open).

While Zakaria, Haass, Collier, and Bremer offer serious and reasonable cautionary tales about the trajectory of democratization, in his absolutism Kaplan fails to see the big picture and is too quick to dismiss appeals to "moral arguments" as being ephemeral and indicative of the lack of substantive appeal democracy may have. An argument that democracy is a "moral" good is an argument that democracy brings substantive good, because morals are rights and benefits. The decency of democracy comes through its potential to protect and enhance and dignify the individual.

HOW DOES DEMOCRACY MATTER TO "THEM"?

This book trains its focus on fragile post (and ongoing)-conflict cases. But even if, on balance, democratic rule would bring significant benefits, is it really wanted in the countries which face massive challenges to survival let alone building intricate democratic institutions? Well yes, it is. A wealth of evidence now refutes the tired thesis that developing world citizens are lackluster in their desire for democracy. *Democracy* may be articulated in different ways but at the core millions of "regular" people in Africa, Asia, Latin America, Eastern Europe, and the Middle East, when asked, strongly say they want to choose their leaders, hold them accountable, and live under a rule of law that treats them justly. We know that most people want democracy because of three things. First, more and more countries are democratizing, often in large part, because of people pressure. The trend of democratic diffusion fluctuates, but 27 percent of nation-states were "electoral democracies" in 1973 and 63 percent by 2006 (Diamond 2008). Second, international laws and norms increasingly reflect worldwide governmental acceptance of democratic principles. The UN, European Union, African Union, Organisation of American States, Organisation of Security and Cooperation in Europe, and Association of South-East Asian Nations have all adopted pro-democracy policies and incentives of varying impact. Third, for the last decade people who live in the developing world have been telling pollsters that they want democracy. On every continent between 81 percent and 92 percent of citizens agree with the proposition that "democracy may have its problems, but it is better than any other forms of government."[1] In a comparative survey of twelve African nations two out of every three citizens said that democracy was always preferable to nondemocratic forms of government,[2] the East Asian barometer found widespread support for democratic values in 2002,[3] and World Values Survey data (again in the early 2000s) showed that support for democracy in the Arab world was as high as in any other region (Jamal and Tessler 2008). Of course there are significant exceptions in all three areas but the trend of increasing public desire to control of government is overwhelming.

It is not uncommon to hear the criticism that ending violent conflict in a failing state has little to do with institutional design at the center. Why should the humanitarian disaster of eastern Congo which reignited in October 2008 be affected by government type in Kinshasa? A new National Assembly and President were elected in 2006 but that did little to dampen instability in the jungles of the east. But the success of national democratization does matter deeply in such places because ethnically rooted and regionally manifested violent conflict happens when there is a vacuum of legitimacy at the center. A stronger national government has the capacity to either incorporate the outliers politically, or defeat them militarily, without alienating the component parts of the central government. President Kabila's government in Kinshasa has scant ability to stop the Tutsi insurgency in Eastern Congo because they are weak, isolated, and seen as illegitimate by the large minority groups shut out of power.

When it comes to the question of whether economic growth is enhanced by democracy, the evidence is mixed. Przeworski, Alvarez, Cheibub, and Limongi find that while wealth clearly sustains democracy it is not clear that democracy per se is the driving force behind economic growth (Przeworski et al. 2008). Nevertheless, it is clear that democracies do a better job at averting, or at least managing, humanitarian disasters that have economic roots. Amartya Sen notes

---

[1] World Values Survey 1999–2001. www.worldvaluessurvey.org
[2] http://www.afrobarometer.org/papers/AfrobriefNo1.pdf. Data based on surveys taken in 2001.
[3] http://www.asianbarometer.org/newenglish/introduction/ProgramOverview.htm

that democracies are far less likely to have famines, and economic development is enhanced by the openness of decision making which is the cornerstone of liberal democracy (see Sen 1999).

Ultimately democracy is about individual dignity and collective decency: that is why a well-designed democracy is the very best construct for managing a plural society. When various ethnic groups are segmented into very separate divisions of private life, that is, by and large they do not work together, live together, play together, worship together, or go to school together, then the public (political) sphere becomes the chief, if not only, place of interaction. If there is no democratic and inclusive forum there is no place for leaders to talk through the compromises that must be made. If there is no place to talk then history shows that violence is the default method for settling disputes. There are strong arguments that every effort, both domestically and internationally, should be focused on helping to support democracies that work and endure. This is an imperative that becomes even more prescient when it becomes clear that democracy remains under threat in much of the world (see Diamond 2008; Carothers 2006).

WHY DOES DEMOCRACY ELSEWHERE MATTER TO "US"?

Thomas Carothers (2006) notes that the commitment to promoting democracy abroad has ebbed and flowed throughout American history, and the same can be said of Western European efforts. During the Cold War a belief in the universalism of democratic principles took a far backseat to the *real politik* of playing off superpower proxies in Africa and Asia against each other. The United States was more than happy to support compliant dictators like Hastings Kamazu Banda in Malawi if he towed the American line. But later in the early 1990s the credo became one of democracy promotion, rooted in the belief that democratic regimes in the developing world would be sympathetic to the United States and more stable internally. A paradigm which proved to be equally flawed. Over the last twenty years American foreign policy has articulated strong support for democracy promotion (not least in Iraq and Afghanistan post invasion) but has been inconsistent in substantive follow through. At any given time nondemocratic regimes have been supported in Pakistan, Nigeria, Kazakhstan, and much of the Middle East. Now the Obama administration is wrestling with the dilemma of an electorate who want their troops out of Iraq and Afghanistan. But US withdrawal may leave those fragile pseudo-democracies even more susceptible to collapse. There is even less popular support for a substantive expenditure of time, money, and resources in other failing states (e.g., Sudan, Somalia, Burma) further to the edges of the public's radar screen.

However, if it is true that well-designed democratic institutions do help strengthen fragile nation-states (as this book argues) and violent anti-Western groups breed in the primeval swamp created by despised authoritarian regimes, then promoting democracy (in the right way) becomes a crucial tool of national security. This theory applies to Iraq and Afghanistan, but also beyond. In those two countries the failure of fledgling electoral regimes would bring to power leaders who would threaten Western security and harbor renegades whose *raison d'être* would be to attack American interests at home and overseas.

But it is not just Afghanistan and Iraq which require our monitoring. Kaplan would have us write off smaller "basket case" states like Liberia, Somalia, or the Philippines (Kaplan 1994), but the globalization of communication and terror means that imploding small states, out of our sight line, can be as dangerous to our interests as anywhere else. Surely that was the lesson of Afghanistan in 2001. The UK Commission on National Security in the 21st Century, chaired by Paddy Ashdown (formerly leader of the British Liberal Democrats and Organisation for Security and Cooperation in Europe High Representative for Bosnia) and George Robertson (formerly UK Defence Secretary and Secretary General of North Atlantic Treaty Organisation), noted that Britain faced a greater threat from the rising number of weak states than from pre-existing strong ones. "Conflict, and the pressures of poor governance . . . are creating both 'swing states' in the struggle for international peace and stability, and the risk of ungoverned spaces that become havens for criminal and terrorist activity."[4]

Islamic terrorist groups thrive when democracy is under threat, notably in Sudan, Nigeria, Indonesia, Pakistan, the Philippines, and Somalia. Hoping to rely on a hard-line dictator to crack down on such groups bore no fruit in the past. In none of those six cases have authoritarian regimes eliminated or even reduced the threat against the West. What happens in Liberia, Sierra Leone, or Burma may not seem very consequential to Americans but their lootable wealth (diamonds, opium) is the currency and balm of terrorist networks. A stable Indonesia, Nigeria, and Venezuela matters to us because of our interest in the oil that they produce.

Democracy also aids the globalization of international trade and workers rights. All else equal, countries with democratic governments are more likely to be open to international trade than nondemocracies (Milner and Kubota 2005) and democracies have better labor rights than do their non- or semi-democratic counterparts (Mosley and Uno 2007).

Last, democracy in out of the way places matters to us because there *is* a moral imperative to politics and foreign policy. Those of us who have been fortunate enough to hear the call to prayer in Kabul, crunch the dirt in Juba underfoot, feel the blanket of heat of a Rangoon summer's day, or smell the open pit fires of

---

[4] *Shared Destinies: Security in a Globalised World*. London, ippr, 2008.

Lilongwe, feel a visceral sense of interconnectedness and responsibility. It has become passé in political science to be an advocate, a believer, but as unscientific as it may be, Martin Luther King sums up the moral imperative of promoting basic human dignity everywhere – without the freedoms, protections, and opportunities that democracy provides, there is no vibrant human dignity.

> As long as there is poverty in the world I can never be rich, even if I have a billion dollars. As long as diseases are rampant and millions of people in this world cannot expect to live more than twenty-eight or thirty years, can never be totally healthy even if I just got a good check up at the Mayo clinic. I can never be what I ought to be until you are what you ought to be. This is the way our world is made. No individual or nation can stand out boasting of being independent. We are interdependent.

CONSTITUTIONAL ENGINEERING

Over the past decade, the discipline of constitutional design has been rediscovered as both an academic field of research and practical means of managing conflict in democratizing nations. "Constitutional engineering" has rested at the heart of settlements as diverse as the Bosnian Dayton Accords of 1995, the end of apartheid in South Africa in 1994, Fiji's prosaic power sharing arrangement of 1997, Northern Ireland's 1998 Good Friday Accords, Kenya's post-2007 election pact, and Sudan's confederal arrangement between North and South signed in 2005. When ethnic competition is the language of discourse, the design of political institutions has been seen as a lever of interethnic accommodation and a means to political stability. The rules of the democratic game vary widely and the way the intricate moving parts of a nation's democratic institutions fit together will determine how successful the democratic experiment is. How is government chosen, who is represented in parliament and what is the division of power between the center and the periphery? Each element helps determine the stability and longevity of democracy.

Countless other nations – including Albania, Guatemala, Guyana, Indonesia, Lebanon, Lesotho, Liberia, Mongolia, Morocco, the Philippines, Romania, and Sri Lanka – have attempted to tweak electoral systems, offer autonomy to outlying regions, and allocate government ministries to minorities and majorities. All with the aim of including within the tent those in society who might wish to burn down the tent if left outside. Furthermore, debates over constitutional arrangements dominate discussions of what might replace the world's most intractable dictatorial regimes. Speculation about what comes next in places such as Zimbabwe, Sudan, and Burma are guided by issues of how to structure a new set of political institutions. While the results of democratic design efforts in divided societies have accumulated exponentially over history, lessons have not been learnt well. Mistakes are repeated time and again, and not only in high profile cases. As Francis Fukuyama (2006: 8) notes, "it is remarkable...how little institutional learning there has been over time; the same lessons about the pitfalls and limitations of nation building seemingly have to be relearned with each new involvement." Many fledgling democracies continue to adopt political institutions which retard effective government and harmony among disparate groups.

In Iraq, a vacuum on both the level of politics and security marked the first two years of the US-led occupation. Quickly establishing a legitimate domestic government might have constrained the sectarian violence which quickly spiraled out of control. A multi-ethnic Iraqi government slowly gathered some legitimacy after 2005, but its emergence was not quick or comprehensive enough to forestall the slide into anarchy as leaders played both public-democratic and private-paramilitary games. The process of democratic design in Iraq following the war of 2003 was characterized by a series of missteps, misreadings, and errors of judgment made by the occupying Coalition Provisional Authority (CPA) (see Diamond 2007). The first Iraqi Governing Council members chosen by the CPA proved to be impotent and entirely unrepresentative of Iraqi opinion. US advisors resisted early calls from Grand Ayatollah ali-Sistani for national elections and wasted fruitless months trying to engineer a parliament that would be selected by elite caucuses in major towns. The vacuum in legitimate leadership expanded along with growing political violence over the next three years. And despite the technical hand over of sovereignty to Prime Minister Allawi in June 2004, the election of a Transitional Assembly in January 2005 (virtually devoid of Sunni representatives), and permanent Assembly elections in December 2005, the situation *continued* to deteriorate. Technically, it is true that an elected assembly drafted the new constitution and that the document was approved in a national referendum, but Sunnis were effectively shut out of both processes, and the vagueness of the document when it comes to the details of power distribution left a troubling potential for future power grabs by the Shia majority.

In Afghanistan, widespread distrust of all political parties, especially those associated with the Communist era, and a misunderstanding of the implications of having given a single vote for individual candidates in large multimember constituencies triggered a series of unintended consequences. President Karzai changed a provincially based list PR system to SNTV by simply pronouncing that voters would select a candidate rather than a party, list, or block, and that candidates could not show party affiliation on the ballot. The system resulted in a great deal of voter confusion (in Kabul there were 400 candidates for the 33 spots up for election) and a spoiled ballot rate of 5 percent, as opposed to 1 percent in Iraq. The result was a highly fragmented parliament containing over thirty continuously evolving factions with shifting loyalties (in Iraq there are only four main blocs). Over two-thirds of all votes were cast for losing candidates, whereas in Iraq only 5 percent of votes were wasted in this way.

A misbegotten 1997 constitution contributed to democratic breakdown in the small and ethnically divided Pacific nation of Fiji. Constitutional designers wanted to move away from its communal voting system (in which indigenous-Fijians and Indo-Fijians elected representatives separately) to one using open seats that would force candidates to appeal to a multiethnic electorate. They also included the Alternative Vote form of preference voting, on the grounds that this would give candidates of one ethnicity a strong incentive to try for the lower-preference votes of citizens from the other community. The inclusion of minority – as well as majority – party members in the cabinet (power sharing) reinforced all these measures. These were all reasonable suggestions in and of themselves, but taken together they betrayed serious signs of misalignment. Aggravating this misalignment was the insistence of Fiji's existing indigenous-dominated parliament to allow only a third of the seats in the lower house to be open, leaving the other two-thirds still in communal hands and thereby destroying much of the incentive for multiethnic appeals. When the 1999 balloting resulted in an Indian-led party and two moderate indigenous parties forming a governing coalition, numerous Fijians of Polynesian and Melanesian extraction rejected it and backed a May 2000 coup. New elections held in 2001 restored Polynesian and Melanesian dominance: Ethnic hegemony had pushed out democracy.

Despite the intense study of a largely positive transformation in South Africa and the upheavals of post-Saddam Iraq, there remain significant gaps in our knowledge. First, systematic theories of constitutional design in the developing world are undeveloped, in part because lessons learnt are not easy to generalize. Second, we have a paucity of diagnostic tools when it comes to analyzing what ails a nation. How do we know that the problem is ethnic conflict as opposed to regional divisions, or class disparities, or elite manipulations? Is Sudan a conflict over religion or resources? Is Afghanistan a battle among ethnic groups, warlords and drug-lords, or interpretations of the Koran? When there is poor diagnosis of the problem, knee-jerk crisis management may do more long-term harm than good. In Bosnia, the institutions imposed to settle the war have split the nation into three exclusive ethnic units, now serving only to retard integration and nation building. How do the policymakers, both internally and in sympathetic Western governments, better understand the discipline of constitutional design to avoid the introduction of inappropriate institutions?

Designing Democracy in a Dangerous World aims to fill gaps in our knowledge in three ways. First, the book develops a theoretical framework for assessing what type of democracy will best serve a nation, taking into account its socio-economic and historical conditions. Second, it offers a behind the scenes look at the intricacies of designing democracy, drawn from the author's experience as an adviser during the last twenty years in nations such as Afghanistan, Burma, Iraq, Lebanon, Nepal, Sierra Leone, South Africa, and Sudan. Third, the book pulls together lessons for policymakers using a survey of successes and failures in democratic design over the last thirty years. The book's main contention is that there are very few places in the world today where the majority of people do not desire some degree of autonomy, accountability over their leaders, and the rule of law. The key is to craft a democracy that is appropriate to a given society.

INCLUSION AS THE FOUNDATION

If there is a single take-home message drawn from this study it would be: *the foundations of democratic stability rest on inclusion.* An inclusive polity is not risk free. Decision making can be gridlocked by minority vetoes, legislatures can be fragmented and chaotic, federal states can allow minorities to govern their own areas, but then oppress the minorities under them. Ironically the more the central state recognizes and devolves power down to minority groups there is a risk of making the whole ungovernable. Inclusion is a tricky balancing act between listening and leading. Nevertheless, there has not been a case of successful democratization in a divided society which did not, at its core, value the principle of inclusion in some important way. Perhaps even more tellingly failed, or failing, democratization attempts are uniformly characterized by their inability to include all significant groups (think of the exclusion of the West (Darfur) and East (Beja) in Sudan's "North–South" peace process which culminated in the 2005 "Comprehensive" Peace Agreement).

In a divided society there are two elements to building stability. First, each significant group must feel included and acknowledged in the running of the state. Second, the weaker groups and individuals (majority or minority) must be protected. It is quite possible for a state to include a minority in government but not protect that groups rights. Alternatively, a state can protect but not acknowledge the minority voice when making governance decisions. A state can have one without the other, but true accommodation requires both. Protections are ultimately legal, but inclusion is a characteristic of the political sphere.

Inclusion is both manifest and psychological and therefore it needs to be multidimensional. Being included in the process and act of representation is crucial to bring in groups which would be destabilizing on the outside. That means having both "descriptive representation" in legislatures and substantive impact in government. But being included in the running of the state also implies some degree of presence in the other wheels of the state; the bureaucracy, judiciary, military, police, and civil society. Inclusion in government may also be insufficient if previously marginalized groups do not share, to some extent, in the wealth of the nation. If the economic sector is dominated by the majority, or indeed minority, the sting of exclusion will be just as harsh as the exclusion from government. Such political and economic inclusion brings with it a share of rights in the nation. When minority representatives have significant say in the laws of the land and their business leaders control economic interests, the groups civil rights are far less likely to be trampled. All of these elements give rise to a state which has an inclusive ethos of citizenship: The nation is black and white, Muslim and Hindu, French and English speakers. Inclusion, if properly promoted, can make common nationalists of the most disparate cultural groups. So inclusion is a necessity. But the key is to then successfully identify *who* needs to be included in the process of governance and *how* that inclusion is manifested.

The "how" question has been powerfully engaged by Pippa Norris in her book *Driving Democracy: Do Power-Sharing Institutions Work?* Norris finds that both quantitative and qualitative evidence "reinforce and confirm the advantages of power-sharing institutions which have often been assumed, irrespective of which particular indicators are selected to measure democracy. Power-sharing arrangements increase the probability of democratic governance succeeding, even after controlling for factors such as economic development, ethnic heterogeneity, and colonial background" (Norris 2008: 211 and 214). Norris' "inclusive" power-sharing institutions are proportional election systems with low thresholds or reserved seats for minorities, federal and decentralized arrangements, parliamentary government, and an independent and pluralistic media. This book compliments *Driving Democracy* (and earlier works such as Arend Lijphart's *Democracy in Plural Societies* (1977)) by unpacking the way power-sharing institutions work in different ways in various combinations in different places. I show evidence which suggests that majoritarianism is rarely appropriate, in any fledgling democracy, but the precise framework of the actual inclusive (power sharing) arrangements required can vary substantially.

ORGANIZATION OF THE BOOK

Chapter 2 uses the lens of medicine to help us better understand how to help the failing state. Through the metaphor of an ailing patient, a framework is developed to analyze patterns of failure and success in democratic design and future treatment options. Failed political settlements often are born of poor diagnosis or inappropriate treatment. In Liberia, for instance in 1997, the diagnosis was simply that elections needed to be held and consequently the treatment was a simplistic winner-take-all race. This treatment did nothing to alter existing power structures already heady with corruption.

Chapters 3 and 4 engage the difficult task of trying to develop a contingent theory of design based upon the diagnostic principles which are outlined in chapter 2. I argue that most democratic design in fragile post-conflict states has been haphazard and idiosyncratic and failed to learn lessons from parallel experiences elsewhere and in earlier times. A contingent theory of design is not a one-size-fits-all straitjacket but rather an attempt to offer parameters of good practice based on what ails the nation. There is overwhelming evidence to show that in medicine algorithms based on previous case histories are much better at designing successful treatment plans than the individual case specific diagnoses that are dominant in the clinical field. In medicine, studies show that even a simplistic algorithm is usually better than an impressionistic diagnosis. When it comes to democratic design I argue that the goal is not to aggregate cases in a way which loses the nuance and cultural-historical peculiarities of a country, but rather to use comparative knowledge systematically to avoid reinventing the wheel. As Samuels and Wyeth (2006) note "each situation is highly specific and many factors may impact the choice of governance frameworks. However, such efforts essentially face comparable obstacles, and many recent post-conflict constitutions bear remarkable similarities."

As noted earlier, the ethos which underpins successful democratic design treatment regimens is one of inclusion. Thus, chapters 5, 6, and 7 of this book focus on the tools in the democratic designers' medicine chest, in which political institutions can be engineered to promote inclusion. Chapter 5 looks at elections and inclusion. Elections are a starting point and continuing focal point for democratization. They are flash points for failure and windows of opportunity for political actors to become involved and incorporated into solving their disputes through the ballot box, and not by the gun. I focus on the importance of electoral system design to the inclusion of voters and parties in parliament. Chapter 6 turns its attention to legislatures and inclusion and makes the argument that descriptive representation carries significant power to reassure marginalized groups that they have a place in the new democracy. To test this argument I analyze four dimensions of descriptive representation: women, ethnic minorities, diverse sexual orientations, and young adults. While there is a significant body of literature on the impact of women in elective office studies of ethnicity, sexual orientation and age are largely undeveloped.

Chapter 7 deals with how power and influence is apportioned within the political system beyond elections – in the executive, between the center and periphery, in the machinery of the state, and in the sharing of wealth. It considers the difference between a temporary power-sharing arrangement (such as Zimbabwe and Kenya) versus a permanent legally mandated power-sharing arrangement (such as Bosnia or Lebanon).

After describing the medicine chest of prescriptive options I seek to test out the theory of design on six paired and current cases. Chapter 8 analyzes patients in the intensive care unit (Iraq and Afghanistan), patients in the operating theater

(Sudan and Zimbabwe), and future patients which may (or may not) see fit to see a constitutional doctor in the future (Burma and Syria). The conclusion summarizes the evidence described in the previous chapters into ten core lessons for future democratic designers.

PATIENT CASES FOR STUDY

The chapters in this book draw on a wide range of case study data and experiences. The evidence of how various institutions have worked in new and old democracies is drawn from a universe of cases which includes rich and poor countries, from every continent. The analysis in chapter 5 on elements of inclusive descriptive representation, for example, draws on data from the entire globe. However, the majority of this book focuses on sixty-six "patients": sixty-four states which have attempted multiparty democracy since 1989 and two (Syria and Somalia) that might attempt conceivably one day. Some of the analysis is quantitative (see chapters 3, 4, and 6) while elsewhere qualitative patterns are analyzed (see in particular chapters 7 and 8). In sum, case histories are described, sicknesses are diagnosed, and institutional medicines are prescribed.

The pool of sixty-six cases includes the most significant, troubling, and surprising cases of democratization of the last quarter century. The countries include those which have attracted the vast bulk of Western democratic financial aid and material assistance over the last decade: Iraq, Afghanistan, Sudan, and Bosnia, and, to a lesser extent, South Africa, Lebanon, and Congo. The cases were selected on the basis of historical timing but also with Arend Lijphart's principles of good practice for the comparative method in mind (1971). The many variables, small "N" problem is reduced by choosing a large subset of democratizing post-conflict nations and backing those case histories up with broader quantitative evidence. The focus is on comparable cases and the key variables that affect each case's ability to stabilize and democratize. All of the focus cases are fragile and seeking to extract themselves from years of intercommunal hostility and violence. Many of the cases have been plagued by polarized forms of communal identity. Symptoms range from simmering ethnic hostility in places like Fiji and Burma to the large death tolls in civil wars in Bosnia, Congo, and Sudan. Most of the remaining cases fall somewhere in between these extremes. All cases have attempted democracy, in the form of holding multiparty elections. Some experiences have been brief (Burma in 1990), while other cases have held competitive elections for nearly twenty years (Mongolia has conducted five elections since 1990).

When it comes to variations, the patients range from the deeply poor and undeveloped (e.g., Afghanistan with a GDP PPP of $700 or Zimbabwe with $200 in

2008) to a case like Slovenia where GDP per capita levels are nearly 150 times higher than in Zimbabwe. The countries differ in size from the small populations of Timor Leste and Fiji to the massive size of Indonesia. On the dependent variable of democratization, in 2007 POLITY scored twenty-one of the cases between 8 and 10 (most vibrant democracies), twenty cases between 5 and 7 (partial democracies), four cases between 0 and 4 (inchoate and seriously challenged democracies), and seven cases as authoritarian nondemocracies (−1 to −10). The cases I include not scored by POLITY in 2007 include: Cape Verde, Sao Tome, Bosnia, Syria, Zimbabwe, Democratic Republic of the Congo, Afghanistan, Iraq, Somalia, and the Palestinian Authority (so leaning to the nondemocratic side of the pool).

In the medical sense this is a study pool for a clinical protocol that includes patients who share the broad ailment of communal conflict and political instability, but have gone through a variety of treatment methods, or no treatment at all.

## 2

Medicine and Constitutional Design

The first wave of democracy that took place in the early nineteenth and twentieth centuries (1828–1926) by Samuel Huntington's estimation (1991) gave rise to a couple of dozen liberal democracies that are, by and large, established democracies today. But the democracies that were born in Huntington's second and third waves in the mid- to late-twentieth century have had a less than stellar success rate. It has taken over half a century of deeply uneven democratic experiments in Africa, Asia, and the Middle East to reveal a glaring truth about designing democracy: that is, we do not really know what we are doing. Here the "we" refers to those who have some degree of agency in the process: politicians and scholars, domestic designers and foreign advisors, democracy-promoting western governments, and international organizations. The learning curve has been steep and onerous. Designers either think that the lessons of success and failure in other nations do not apply to their state (i.e., because the lessons from elsewhere are not transportable to their *unique situation*) or the community of practitioners and scholars have just not done a good job of learning and synthesizing what the lessons are. So how can the people writing a new constitution do a better job of understanding democratic design? As a starting point, it might help to at least recognize that there are lessons to be learnt from other places and from other times – even if ultimately such lessons are deemed to be irrelevant to the case at hand.

There are a surprising number of parallels between the *science* of medicine and the *art* of constitutional design, while of course there is some science in the sociopolitical and some art in medicine. Just as doctors seek to diagnose and treat sick patients with a variety of drugs and behavioral modifications the constitutional engineer looks on an ailing society and attempts to predict what institutional medicines might best stem the blood flow and provide the long-term foundation for a return to health and stability. Most social scientists nowadays accept that the discipline should be focused on the *management* of ailments rather than hoping to *cure* a bitterly divided society (see Harris and Reilly 1998), but political institutions and elections are key to dissipating ethno-political conflict when it gets out of hand. In essence, democratic designers seek to treat and manage nonfunctioning body politics.

The idea of seeing the political (and indeed nonpolitical) life of a nation in biological terms is an ancient one. Societies consist of complex interrelated organisms (individuals and groups) ideally functioning as a whole but in reality often disjointed and in conflict. Aristotle and Plato's ideal "mixed states" rested on the notion that balancing diverse social segments in a political sphere would forestall the dominance of any one segment, or what today we would call the positive side of governmental gridlock (Aristotle 1984; Plato 1992). For Aristotle healthy societies minimized excessive differences between rich and poor and neutralized disintegrating tendencies. Cicero based his conception of the good state on a type of true or natural law of the symbiotic nature of citizens within political society (Sherover 1974).

Later theorists such as Machiavelli and Rousseau (with his "common ego") extended the medical–biological metaphor (Rousseau 1974; Machiavelli 1988). Locke sought to understand complex political dynamics through an "atomistic" reduction of society down to its individual units (Locke 1960). The nineteenth-century English theorist Thomas Hill Green saw the state as composed of individual organisms in which each person has a function to fulfill. Green's organic nature of the state captured the interconnectedness of social networks and blocks which act as organs of the body politic (Sherover 1974). But perhaps the most direct philosophical precedent for such an approach comes from the works of Friedrich Hegel, who saw society less as a planned aggregate of self-interested individuals and more as the organic sum of complex interrelationships with interdependent economic, political, social, and legal structures giving rise to unitary natural growth. The society, as any living organism, grows, persists, and needs to guard against drastic sudden change (Hegel 1988).

Many of the failures of conscious constitutional designs, whether imposed from outside the country or domestically crafted, have stemmed from the fact that the political designers failed to maintain the basic precepts of good medical diagnosis and treatment. In countless cases (e.g., Iraq and Afghanistan) the seeds of failure were sown early on with a violation of the first premise of medicine – the Hippocratic oath, "*first, do no harm.*" Clearly, the missteps of postwar constitutional design in Iraq (as are alluded to throughout this book) violated the Hippocratic oath. The case of Angola in 1991 is also illustrative. After a fifteen-year bloody civil war (Angola's entire independent history) costing at least 1.5 million lives, international mediators brokered a settlement between the ruling MPLA party of Eduardo dos Santos and UNITA's Jonas Savimbi. While the peace settlement did give some hope to the numerically smaller UNITA, a presidential winner-take-all system was established which gave little incentive to the loser to commit themselves to the frustration of legislative opposition politics. In the elections of September 1992, Dos Santos won 49 percent to Savimbi's 40 percent. As a US State Department analyst noted at the time, when Savimbi lost the only prize worth having, it was inevitable that he would restart the civil war (Reid 1993: 2): A failed transition to democracy resulting in the deaths of hundreds of thousands.

WHAT IS IN THE MEDICINE CHEST?

When constitutional doctors open up their black bags what institutional drugs do they find? The key medicines consist of the broad macro democratic choices about who governs and how those rulers are chosen. Who forms the executive and what powers do they have? What role does the legislature have, how is it elected, and what form does it take? Is government decentralized or centralized, are there autonomies for distinct regions or minorities? There are of course a whole host of other institutional and more informal aspects of a democratic order that need to be robustly in place for democracy to flourish. Sometimes the key to conflict management lies not in elections and the diffusion of executive power but rather in how the judiciary is structured; whether land inequalities are addressed; in the sensitive and emotionally draining theater of truth commissions, education reform, and just modes of policing. Ashu Varshney has noted the powerful mediating role of civil society meeting places in parts of India where Hindus and Muslims develop bonds which make violent explosions less likely (Varshney 2002). But at the heart of the medicine chest lie the heavy building blocks of democratic government. But the macro institutions provide the foundation for governance regardless of how significant other elements are to democratization.

There are two opposing schools of thought on how democracy should be structured, each led by an prominent scholar of political institutions and ethnic conflict. The consociationalists are led by Arend Lijphart, and the incentive-orientated theorists led by Donald Horowitz. Consociationalism entails a power-sharing agreement within government, brokered between clearly defined segments of society which may be joined by citizenship but divided by ethnicity, religion, and language (Lijphart 1977). Examples of consociational societies have included Belgium, the Netherlands, Austria, and Switzerland. Cyprus and Lebanon are cited as countries which have had a more fragile relationship with consociationalism. The mechanics of consociationalism can be distilled into four basic elements. They are: (*a*) executive power sharing among the representatives of all significant groups (*grand coalition*); (*b*) a high degree of internal autonomy for groups that wish to have it (*segmental autonomy*); (*c*) proportional representation and proportional allocation of civil service positions and public funds (*proportionality*); and (*d*) a minority veto on the most vital issues (*mutual veto*) (Lijphart 1977: 25).

The argument goes that in bitterly divided societies the stakes are too high for politics to be conducted as a zero-sum game – the risks of governmental collapse and state instability are too great for parties to view the executive branch of government as a prize to be won or lost. Winner-take-all democracy might be fine in Britain and America because there exists a significant floating vote which determines whether Labour or the Conservatives take office in Britain and whether the Democrats or Republicans win the executive branch in America. But in plural societies, the segments competing for power are more clearly delineated and the floating vote is negligible. Therefore, alternation of power is far less likely than one dominant segment seizing power and never being obliged to relinquish it.

Consociational power-sharing structures are often seized upon as solutions in the most fragmented failing states but the theory is not without its critics. Jung and Shapiro argue that consociational systems of government do not allow for a viable institutionalized opposition. True democracy, in their view, depends on such opposition. If the constitution incorporates power-sharing arrangements at the executive level, opposition forces will be marginalized and eventually displaced from political discourse and participation (Jung and Shapiro 1995). Others complain that segmental autonomy over home affairs and territorial federalism merely encourage groups to seek further autonomy, possibly secession, and thus the eventual break up of the state. Open the door a crack and the minorities will run for the hills, metaphorically speaking (Nordlinger 1972). Last, there are those who say that consociationalism is the very last thing a new and fragile democracy needs at its time of most pressing need because its core principle is to block decision making in government. When majorities and minorities have to agree on every major issue the recipe is for immobilism and paralysis (Nolutshungu 1993).

The great value of consociationalism is that it offers powerful conflict-resolving solutions to those divided societies which show no hope of generating such interethnic political accommodation. It is the solution when all else fails. But if consociational structures are entrenched in plural societies which do show potential for the withering away of *ethnic voting*, then the very institutions designed to alleviate tensions may merely entrench the attitude that all politics must be ethnic politics. Consociationalism provides few incentives for political entrepreneurs to appeal for support beyond their own ethnic bases. Once you recognize and reify segments, as in Bosnia, you have preordained that all politics become segmental politics in the future.

On the other side of the aisle are the incentive-orientated theorists led by Donald Horowitz (1985, 1991, 2002). At its core, *integrative power sharing* (also known as *centripetalism*[1]) revolves around the belief that elites need to be given incentives to appeal outside of their primary and narrowly defined ethnic constituencies. The system should create the dynamic that the electoral advantage lies with the moderate multiethnic politician. To engineer such a spin to the system the theory often (although not exclusively) recommends that vote-pooling electoral systems should be used for the legislature, specifically the alternative vote form of preference voting (as used in Australia and Fiji).[2] This can be combined

---

[1] A term coined by Sisk (1996).
[2] See the important work on real case studies of AV by Reilly (2001).

with a directly elected president, chosen either by a national election on the basis of the alternative vote (as in Sri Lanka) or through a supermajority requirement where the winning candidate must win, not merely a national majority, but surmount a threshold in all regions of the country (as in Nigeria and Kenya). Last, comes federalism, which provides increased access points to power, thus mitigating the extremes of "winner-take-all" exclusion; promoting intra-ethnic political fragmentation; and encouraging the proliferation of parties. In conjunction with these institutional arrangements, the integrationists argue for socio-economic policies which recognize and advantage nonethnic communities of interests and reduce overall socioeconomic inequalities.

The trouble with the idea, and in contrast to consociational democracy, is that nothing within the institutions inherently guarantees that political power is shared between majority and minority groups. That is not to say that accommodation cannot take place under such institutional provisions, but such accommodation is dependent on the social and demographic context the institutions operate within. For the alternative vote to give parties incentives to behave in an ethnically conciliatory manner, constituencies must be heterogeneous with no one group holding an absolute majority of the votes – as noted later in this chapter this was the chief flaw of the system in Fiji. Similarly, in order to elect a president beholden to inclusive nation building, rather than ethnically divisive exclusion, no one group can be in the absolute majority if the voting rule is preferential (in Sri Lanka lower preferences have never been needed). The other suggestion, supermajority distributional formulas, might better ensure that the president has multiethnic support, but such mechanisms have been overwhelmed by other anti-democratic pressures in the cases of Kenya and Nigeria (see Suberu and Diamond 2002; Horowitz 1985).

THE SCIENCE OF MEDICINE, THE ART OF DEMOCRACY

There are six key components of the constitutional design/medical diagnosis and treatment metaphor which can help develop a methodology for establishing the appropriateness of distinct institutional designs for conflict management. The contingent theory of design is developed in chapter 3. The components are: (*a*) Failed political institutions in divided societies often result from a misdiagnosis of what ails the state. (*b*) There is a temporal aspect to constitutional engineering which follows the medical continuum of first aid, emergency medicine, convalescence, and longer term health management. (*c*) Within the constitutional framework, political institutions need to be holistically integrated and compatible, that is, that must be properly *aligned*. (*d*) There has been a history of discharging patients before they were healthy enough for democracy to endure. (*e*) There are limits to how much aid and protection constitutions can offer to a fragile and threatened polity. (*f*) Foreign nations increasingly advertise their preferred medicines directly to developing world consumers of political institutions, with mixed consequences.

MANAGEMENT VERSUS CURE

Constitutional engineering is ultimately doomed when designers seek to *cure* a plural society of its diversity. Within even the most conflictual state, divided by language, ethnicity, or religion, the seeds of difference are the things that germinate social progress. Thus, institutions need to be about managing and processing conflict rather than curing it. Inclusive structures do matter greatly but should help to constrain difference becoming a negative – from turning into a disease whose symptoms are violence and mistrust. If one seeks to *cure* a divided society, what one is aiming to do is flatten out identities into a single homogeneous block, that is, to integrate diversity out of existence. Not only is this a pipe dream but it is a dangerous thing to wish for. The elimination of cultural difference stultifies and retards social and political progress.[3] When political institutions are skewed so much against the recognition of ethnic or regional differences, they merely sweep the conflict out from the political sphere and into the usually destabilizing arena of extra-political mobilization.

The key to good institutional design is its recognition that conflict in itself is not a negative, per se. As Bloomfield and Reilly (1998: 17–18) note, "conflict is the interaction of different and opposing aspirations and goals... it is a necessary part of healthy democratic debate and dialogue, provided it remains within the boundaries of the commonly accepted 'rules of the democratic game' [it] can be the starting point for energizing social change and improvement." Indeed, "creating a national identity" to supersede the divisiveness of ethnic identities has uniformly been a byword for the suppression of minority rights and the hegemony of the majority. Examples proliferate from Hastings Banda's Chewaisation of Malawi to Houphouet-Boigny's "Ivoirite" logic of the Ivory Coast which marginalized northerners as *less pure* citizens and thus expendable from politics.

---

[3] As John Stuart Mill (1865) noted in *Considerations on Representative Government*, the way to include the greatest cross section of talents in the process of governing was to maximize social and intellectual diversity in the legislature; little social progress would be made if minority views were excluded from the discussion.

MISDIAGNOSIS

Poor diagnosis leads to inappropriate treatment, but one can understand the prevalence of diagnostic error when one notes that the symptoms of state failure can be similar for different illnesses (symptoms including everything from interethnic violence to governmental collapse). Misdiagnosis occurs when one believes that a given issue is driving the conflict but in actuality it is different problem. Are internal conflicts in Afghanistan driven by ethno-linguistic difference or by the competition between regionally based warlords for resources and economic wealth? Was the core illness of the six counties of the north of Ireland one of religious insecurity and intolerance or of economic disparity defined by a religious identity proxy?

There are many cases of poorly fitting political institutions but one case where the illness was clearly misdiagnosed occurred in the small Central African state of Malawi in the early 1990s. By 1994 the long-time dictator of Malawi, Dr Hastings Kamuzu Banda, had finally given in to domestic and international pressure and allowed multiparty elections to be scheduled. The opposition politicians, along with British and European donor countries, perceived divisions in Malawi to be rooted in a simplistic notion of Banda versus the rest, the dictator versus the democrats, and the old versus the new. They did not see identity politics as a necessarily divisive issue because language groups had over centuries become somewhat intermixed geographically and intermarried. Thus, all sides were outwardly content to carry over the structure of Westminster majoritarian institutions which had been inherited from British colonial rule, along with a strong presidency. However, a creeping and ominous new form of identity politics had been overlooked – that of regionalism, which cut across traditional ties of language and culture. Centuries of indigenous conflict, colonialism, and missionary activity, along with thirty years of Banda's autocratic rule had advantaged the center of the country and created second-class citizens of the Southerners, while marginalizing the educated Northerners to the third class.

In the first election of 1994 (a pattern repeated in 1999, and to some degree in 2004), a full 99 percent of the vote went to regionally rooted parties. The United Democratic Front cobbled together a majority in the legislature and took the Presidency (with just under 50% of the vote), but 75 percent of their total vote came from the Southern region. Banda's Malawi Congress Party took 74 percent of their vote from the Center and came in second with a third of the national vote, while 69 percent of the third-placed Alliance for Democracy's vote came from the North (see Kaspin 1995: 614–15). History had crafted a political system based on the politics of regional affiliation while the constitution parlayed that into blunt polarization and the exclusion from power of the "losing" two regions. Today Malawi wrestles with the massive trauma of institutional failure and political fragmentation not least because its political institutions do little to moderate the geographic cleavages which continue to define Malawian society.

EMERGENCY MEDICINE OR CONVALESCENT CARE?

It might strike the medical doctor as redundant to stress that different stages and severities of illness require different treatments but political doctors have demonstrated little appreciation for this core medical tenet. Constitutional designers have been either blissfully unaware or unwilling, or unable to project forward, to acknowledge that what may be good for immediate conflict crisis management may not be good for longer term care. Nevertheless, designing political institutions is as much a temporally defined task as is treating an ailing patient (see table 2.1). In the beginning the institutions negotiated and imposed are often about first aid – stemming the flow of blood and keeping the patient alive in the field (e.g., Bosnia in 1995, Sierra Leone in 1996, or Afghanistan in 2002). Then emergency medicine takes over – often encompassing enhanced provisions for power sharing, decentralization, or varying degrees of minority autonomy (e.g., South Africa and Kosovo, or even secession as in the case of Timor Leste and Indonesia). The next steps, medically, are convalescence and long-term care. However, it is rare that the institutions are then adapted and reinvented to

TABLE 2.1 *The phases of constitutional engineering*

Stage	Definition	Example	Institutional design objective
First aid	Peace settlement institutions brokered during conflict	Bosnia 1995	To end violence
Emergency medicine	Constitutions written or rewritten during a transition to democracy and at a time of post-conflict state fragility	South Africa 1994–9	Lay groundwork for free elections and the evolution of a state where conflicts are processed through elections and democracy
Convalescence	The early–medium period of democratic consolidation and enhancement. Electoral democracy has taken root but is not fully entrenched	Nicaragua 1996–	Consolidate democratic norms, the alternation of power in government, increase popular participation and support for institutions and the rule of law
Long-term health management	Electoral democracy is the norm	New Zealand 1996 Britain 1997–	Reforms are made to improve quality of democracy

promote the medium- to long-term care of the national state and its political stability – addressing the underlying sociopolitical divisions and helping to consolidate democracy. This continuum of medical treatment – *First aid, emergency medicine*, medium term (*convalescence*), and long-term care (*health management*) – is eminently applicable to the art of constitutional engineering but is almost never utilized theoretically or in practice.

Unfortunately, what often happens is that the institutions imposed during the first aid or emergency period are counterproductive for convalescence, long-term care, and the consolidation of a democratic political order. Two cases illustrate the point to varying degrees. In South Africa practical and political realities of the transition necessitated the use of a very simple, large district closed-list proportional representation voting system to elect the Constitutional Assembly of 1994. Centuries of colonialism and apartheid had led to a situation where district-based registration and delimitation would have disenfranchised millions of poor (non-white) South Africans (Asmal 1990: 17). The white minority would have been dramatically underrepresented had a district-based majority system been used: whites formed a majority in only 5 of the over 500 magisterial districts in 1994 (Reynolds 1993). Furthermore, other interested groups – coloreds, Indians, women, and smaller minority black language groups and parties – also would have been largely shut out of the process. Thus, what was needed was a highly proportional electoral system which succeeded in producing an extremely diverse and representative parliament along the lines of ideology, ethnicity, language, and gender. But the downside was that it was a system which detached representatives from their community and left wide power to choose and control legislative caucuses in the hands of party bosses. South Africans in the four elections since 1994 have been unable to choose a representative for their city or village or even region (below the huge provincial level), and they were denied the ability to differentiate between candidates of the same party. Nearly two decades after South Africa's transition to democracy there is widespread agreement that reforms bringing some degree of geographical accountability through the electoral process are needed, but the inertia of the *first aid* system and the politicians who benefited from it have proved difficult to overcome.[4] A political institution appropriate for the transition has become a block to the enhancement of participatory democracy and legislative accountability – two of the cornerstones of democratic consolidation.

The disjuncture between first aid institutions and what is needed for longer term health is even more pronounced in a case like Bosnia. The Dayton accords, signed in November 1995, finally brought a type of closure to the civil war which had raged throughout the territory of the former Yugoslavia since 1992 costing over 100,000 lives and the violent expulsion of over half of the Bosnian population

---

[4] A commission on electoral system reform chaired by Dr van zyl Slabbert ultimately favored a shift to an MMP system, but it went nowhere as the ANC was opposed to change.

from their homes (Bennett 1998:149). But the hopes for peace born in Dayton, Ohio, came at the cost of political structures which did all they could to separate, segment, delimit, and ultimately make all politics in Bosnia about ethnic identity and political–physical separation. Virtually no space was left for the evolution of moderate multiethnic parties which might lay seeds of a return to shared nationhood in the Balkans.

The Dayton accords divided Bosnia into two entities: The Federation (Bosniacs and Croats) comprising 51 percent of the land and the Republika Srpska comprising the rest. The national parliament has an upper house with five members from each of the three ethnic groups, while the lower house has twenty-eight members elected from the Federation and fourteen from the Serb Republic. There is a three-person national Presidency but Serbs elect the Serb member, Croats elect the Croat, and Bosniacs the Bosniac. Each community has an effective legislative veto over any matter they choose to delegate "destructive of a vital interest." The central state is relatively weak with powers over foreign affairs and trade; more power lies in the separately elected House of Peoples in the Federation and Republika Srpska Assembly which, it goes without saying, are chosen by Bosniacs and Croats, and Serbs, respectively. There is balancing at almost every level of government but it is rooted in ethnic identity and segmentation – elections are, by design, ethnic censuses in Bosnia.

This vulgar, identity-freezing form of consociation may well have been necessary to get signatures on paper in Dayton and to stem the blood-letting in Bosnia. But the preoccupation with *the first aid treatment* has meant that longer term integration and democratic consolidation is a much bleaker prospect. The institutions gave little incentive to parties to moderate their ethnically based appeals or work together once elected. In the first seven years the UN's High Representative had to assume a level of decision making far beyond what was envisioned to fill the vacuum left by recalcitrant politicians. The initially proposed Vance-Owen Peace plan had envisioned quite different structures with a nod to multiethnic representation and cross-community accommodation, but that plan did not have the will and force of the United States behind it. Elections in 1996 and 1999 were unsurprisingly characterized by the sight of all major parties crafting appeals on the basis of hostile and polarizing notions of ethnic community and difference. The elections of 2002 actually saw a swing to even *more* extreme nationalist parties in both the Bosniac and Serb entities.

Finally, as the patient convalesces, a good medical plan will check on progress through regular follow-up appointments, or, in more serious cases, discharge to a half way house. When supporting democracy in fragile states the wealthy nations would do well to not merely maintain the medicines of monetary aid, security help, and policy expertise but to encourage the state to undergo regular checkups to ascertain which parts of the body politique require most attention. Indeed, the state should build in mechanisms to revisit its democratic design. It is inevitable that overtime the constitutional provisions will need adaptation and reform to keep relevant to a changing environment?

HOLISTIC DESIGN

Just as in medicine, in constitutional design it is a mistake to treat a specific ailment (such as disputed elections) while failing to engage in a broader diagnosis which seeks to treat the patient as a whole (i.e., addressing the accountability of those in power, the efficacy of the judiciary, etc). The medical analogy would be sectionalizing the patient to treat individual ailments rather than seeing the body as a holistic entity. Different institutional prescriptions can work against each other in a harmful way, and exacerbate the illness, if the treatment regimen is not complementary for the whole. In medicine one drug may react with another and retard the patient's progress, or the treatment of one ailment may create new problems in other parts of the body. In constitutional design, for instance, a seemingly inventive electoral system (such as the Alternative Vote [AV] form of preference voting) may combine with a power-laden parliamentary executive to shut significant minorities out of access to power.

When the web of political institutions do not work in concert one can end up in a situation where political measures, which when taken individually seem appropriate and positive, combine to produce an outcome far less than the sum of their parts and in actuality make the situation worse than it may have been without intervention.[5] Holistic interpretations of political institutions are akin to the notion of *complementarities* between institutions that shape the political economy of a state. Hall and Gingerich define an institution as complementary to another when "its presence raises the returns available from the other" (see Hall and Gingerich 2009). For instance, politically independent central banks and centralized trade union structures interact to produce lower inflation. But one without the other can keep inflation unchanged, or even send it higher. In this conception of *holistic* I broaden that definition to one which both raises the sum benefit and precludes a negative loss in outcome when institutions interact.

Fiji's 1997 constitution is a good example of well-intentioned constitutional levers being applied in a non-holistic and non-complimentary manner. This contributed to the swift breakdown of the democratic order. The troubled Pacific island's design process of the mid-1990s was the academics' ideal type. A small three-person committee traveled around the world soliciting the advice of the leading constitutional design specialists on what rules might best serve their

---

[5] Carothers (1999: 345) broadens the notion of 'holistic' medicines to include the idea that socioeconomic aid must also be balanced with political aid.

divided nation. A nation in which the indigenous Polynesian/Melanesian (a fluctuating majority-minority) has long been adamant about its monopoly of government power even as the Indo-Fijians (descendants from the nineteenth-century transported plantation workers) surpassed them in absolute numbers in the 1980s. Two coups and the removal of the first-ever Indian-led government precipitated the constitutional rewrite which was aimed at reassuring both groups in this highly segmented ethnically bipolar state.

The Commission's report was a masterful summary of the constitutional engineering field and menu of options (see Lal 2002). It recommended a full press of human rights statutes, enforcing mechanisms, and judicial reforms. Importantly they argued that Fiji should move away from its communal voting system (where indigenous and Indo-Fijians elected their representatives separately) to one using open seats where candidates would have to appeal to a multiethnic electorate. They proposed the alternative vote form of preference voting with the rationale that this would force candidates of one ethnicity to appeal for the lower preference votes of the other community.

These were all reasonable suggestions in and of themselves, but when the parliament ultimately adopted a new constitution in 1997, they compounded some of the misalignment of the Commission's original construct with some misshapen cogs of their own. First, they retained two-thirds of the seats as communal ones, thus destroying any incentive for multiethnic bridge-building in these races. Second, they chose to leave the new preference voting seats as single-member district ones (and not multimember) which meant that because of their small size and the territorial concentration of indigenous and Indo-Fijians, there were very few districts that had an adequate multiethnic mix to give an incentive for one group to appeal to the lower order votes of another. The incentive was minimized even further by the electoral commission's decision to allow a straight party ticket choice on the ballot which left even less reason to look outside of one's ethnic group when voting. In 1999, 90 percent of voters took this option (see Frankel 2001).

Third, and superimposed on top of the Commission's structure the Fijian legislature added a grand coalition executive with all parties winning over 10 percent of the vote being offered seats in the cabinet (see Lal and Larmour 1997). But government decisions were to still to be taken by majority and thus there was no veto for minorities on legislative issues – even if they directly impacted the rights and needs of a given minority. In the elections of 1999, an Indian-led party formed the majority with the backing of two moderate indigenous parties. The new government, led by the Indian Prime Minister Mahendra Chaudhry, proved to be intolerable to large sections of the indigenous-Fijian community who tacitly supported a coup led by George Speight, an indigenous Fijian, one year later. New elections held in 2001 restored the indigenous Polynesian-Melanesians to political dominance and democracy was successfully subverted in favor of ethnic hegemony.

We might best think of institutions in terms of alignment – both with other institutions (horizontally) and the character of the society they seek to serve (vertically). For example, a presidential system might align with two-round election systems, but if the minority is concentrated politically and geographically then the social characteristics would be out of alignment with the consequences of the constitutional set up. The institutions would fail to mesh with the needs of minority incorporation and reassurance. On a theoretical level we can talk of broader bundles of institutions that are aligned. Consociational power-sharing schemes combine oversize grand coalition executives with minority vetoes, proportional representation, and forms of cultural autonomy. Indeed, underpinning institutional foundations of consociational theory are designed to reinforce and reiterate power sharing at every level of government. Integrative schemes partner preference voting for the legislature with presidents elected by distribution requirements and federal arrangements.

DISCHARGING TOO EARLY

During the twentieth century, development aid was forthcoming when the wealthy West recognized severe humanitarian crises in the developing world. But such altruism (or self-interest) was swiftly followed by the patient being given a clean bill of health and being sent on to cope largely unaided, despite the fact that most of these societies remained very sick and the underlying ailments had not been addressed. Economic upliftment and debt relief, often through the IMF and World Bank, sought to alleviate the worst of famine and disaster but did little to restructure the trade relationships so that poor countries would be less likely to suffer such crises again. Up until 2008 the credo increasingly became the *democracy imperative* – nations being told they should hold free elections and the rulers should be accountable to the people.

But even as the imperative shifted from the economic to the political the false economy of discharging the ailing society too quickly from care continues. The West supports transitions to multiparty elections sometimes with great generosity – there was a five-year $5.1 billion reconstruction plan in Bosnia administered by the World Bank, while the UN spent over $370 million on first elections in Namibia and $2 billion in Cambodia – but all too often the first election is seen as the end goal and Western powers pull out before any of the structural or civic foundations of multiparty electoral democracy have taken root.

At the other pole of a rush to discharge is the equally dangerous rush to surgery before the patient has been stabilized. Elections can be traumatic and require the patient to be stable; otherwise they represent a threat to any peace process. Nevertheless, there is consistent donor pressure to race to the holding of national elections regardless of whether the country is ready to go through such an upheaval (see Zakaria 1997). In post-conflict situations the infrastructure to facilitate legitimate elections is lacking and a climate which allows for free campaigning is often nonexistent. Elections were held in Bosnia on schedule, exactly nine months after the Dayton accords were signed, but this meant that they were a census of polarized identities rather than an expression of policy choices. The December 2001 Bonn Accords for Afghanistan ordained that elections be held within two and a half years – far too little time to guarantee security and the existence of viable institutions of the state and a new constitution, let alone free and fair elections. The presidential and parliamentary elections held in 2004 and 2005 failed to engender voter trust in the process or produce a coherent and legitimate government.

The rush to surgery – the quick holding of competitive multiparty elections – means that fragile political conditions often compel observers to fudge what a "free and fair" election is and make inconsistent pronouncements on legitimacy from case to case (see Elklit and Svensson 1997). The donor community rightly came down hard on Robert Mugabe's regime when they stole elections in Zimbabwe in 2002 but ignored Zambia's equally flawed election the year before, and positively encouraged President Museveni in Uganda who does not even allow multiparty elections. It did not help that South African observers ratified the 2002 Zimbabwean elections entirely on amoral grounds of political expediency. However, as Carothers notes this is not a new phenomenon, the democratic imperative has rarely been consistently applied. Up until the end of the Cold War all American administrations paid lip service to the notion of spreading democracy but compliant authoritarian and illiberal regimes were shielded from the pressure to democratize. In the late 1980s and 1990s Presidents Reagan and Bush sustained anticommunist dictators. Clinton's administration pushed the democracy imperative to the fore in foreign policy but even they were happy to ignore democracy movements in nations where US self-interest relied on the stability and compliance of an existing dictatorial regime (Carothers 1999: 4–5).

THE MEDICAL LIMITS

It is important to recognize the limitations of constitutions as levers of conflict management in fragile societies. Just as medicine cannot save the terminally ill, there are limits to what a well-crafted set of political institutions can do. With a patient there are a number of things that can reduce the effectiveness of treatment. An overwhelming external shock to the system, drugs that are insufficient in their power, or when a patient is unable to take the prescribed medicine – all these aspects hold true when it comes to constitutional engineering.

Lebanon's prosaic and segmented power-sharing scheme between Shias, Sunnis, Maronite Christians, Druze, and Orthodox held for nearly thirty years but collapsed under the weight of civil war and regional intervention in 1975 (Hanf 1993). It continues to be under enormous pressure in 2010. It may well be the case that the constitutional medicines applied in Lebanon are the best that could be imagined but even so their dangerous neighborhood and internal sectarian divides work against healthy democratic stability.

Even if the patient stumbles along in poor shape without actually expiring, they may be "drug resistant." Rwanda had a Government of National Unity of both Hutus and Tutsis but this failed to stem the spiral down to bloody ethnic genocide precipitated by the assassination of President Habyarimana in 1994. No matter how well applied inclusive democratic institutions are, the inherent fragility of states like Sierra Leone, Afghanistan, and Sri Lanka means that a robust constitution goes only so far in shielding the state from instability and/or violent overthrow.

It is also true that while political institutions can be used as medicines for a nation's maladies, other sociopolitical networks need to be in good working order to facilitate long-term political health. A fully functioning judiciary, a progressive education system, high levels of employment, economic development, and internal security will provide the foundation for a stable polity. At times of sickness appropriate medicines have to be taken, and they may need to be taken for a considerable length of time, but the society also needs to eat well, exercise fully, and avoid stepping in front of the proverbial bus.

DRUG COMPANIES AND INSTITUTIONAL EXPERTS DIRECTLY ADVERTISING TO CONSUMERS

When constitutions are crafted today who is doing the designing, who is advising those designers, and does this all matter? The recognition that there are limits to democracy's effectiveness has not forestalled the stealthy growth of Western states – the drug companies – advertising directly to consumers. Academics and civil servants are increasingly involved in advising on institutional design issues under the auspices of their own national governments, the European Union, the Organization for Security and Cooperation in Europe, the United Nations, and engaged NGOs (mostly) based in the West. To varying degrees advisors tend to recommend what they know and consciously or unconsciously sell their own domestic brand of democracy. This holds true with Americans who often advocate federal and separation of power arrangements, British single-member district (FPTP) election proponents, and Australian preference voting true believers.

This "constitutional colonialism" is typified by political advisors from the international democracy supporting wings of the three main German parties: the

Konrad Adenauer Institute of the conservative CDU, the Friedrich Ebert Stiftung of the social democrat SPD, and the Friedrich Naumann of the liberal FDP (see Phillips 1999). Whether it be Indonesia, South Africa, Kenya, Lebanon, or Burma, advisors from these institutes uniformly recommend German federal länder arrangements and the archetypal German Mixed Member Proportional electoral system which utilizes both majoritarian single-member districts and PR lists. This is not to say that such recommendations are without merit in all cases but rather to highlight the close relationship between what one knows at home and the menu one takes into the field.

Nevertheless, today's advisors work in much restrained parameters compared to their colleagues in the 1940s and 1950s. In those days American and British lawyers and academics went in and imposed new constitutional arrangements at the behest not of the host government but rather of Washington and Whitehall. These institutional colonists wore either black or white hats. The "black hats" were exemplified by senior analysts in the Kennedy administration urging the British government to change the Guyanese electoral system to one of list PR in 1964 (on the eve of Guyana's independence) with the deliberate intention of keeping out of power the left leaning nationalist Cheddi Jagan and his Indo-Guyanese Progressive People's Party, and giving advantage to his rival, the man perceived to be more malleable and west-leaning Forbes Burnham and his Afro-Guyanese People's National Congress. The manipulation worked just as planned and Jagan was shut out of power for thirty years until free elections were reinstituted in 1992.

The "white hats" were personified by the perhaps better intentioned soldier-lawyers of the MacArthur team which drafted a new Japanese constitution in seven days in February 1946. The haphazardness, and occasional serendipity, that constitutional design sometimes demonstrates was illustrated by the role of Beate Sirota Gordon in the process. Sirota had grown up in Tokyo with her Russian émigré parents before moving to the United States to study at Mills College in 1938. After working for Time Magazine and the US government, she was one of the first American civilians to enter Japan in 1945. As one of only sixty Caucasians in the United States who spoke Japanese she was quickly retained on MacArthur's staff in the Government Office. When the call to write a new constitution came Sirota, aged 22, was seconded to the "Civil Rights Committee" and drafted a number of equality clauses protecting the rights of women and children in the new order. Articles 14 and 24 explicitly detailing gender equality in marriage, politics, employment, property rights, divorce, and inheritance were steamrollered through by MacArthur's senior officers and, along with the rest of the Japanese constitution, survive unchanged to this day.[6]

The growth and acceptance of special mechanisms – quotas, reserved seats, legal encouragements to parties – for the representation of women has perhaps

---

[6] See http://www.pinn.net/~sunshine/whm2001/gordon.html

been the greatest development in representative institutions in new democracies over the last decade. Today over fifty countries have a constitutional or electoral quota guaranteeing a minimum number of women in their national legislature – including Afghanistan, Iraq, Rwanda, Djibouti, Sudan, and Pakistan – while over twenty countries have quotas at the subnational level. The diffusion of such "norms" has been promoted by the United Nations (especially the Electoral Assistance Department) and academics such as Pippa Norris of Harvard University.

Then there are cases of outlandish constitutional adoption born when admiration spurs imitation. In a classic "Mouse that Roared" scenario the tiny Pacific island nation of Palau – 12,000 citizens living on over 200 islands in the Caroline chain – were so enamored with the United States that in 1981 they adopted its constitution virtually lock, stock, and barrel. The 6,000 Palauan voters, spread over 178 square miles, are served nationally by a directly elected president, a separately and directly elected vice-president, a Supreme Court, a Senate, a House of Delegates, and sixteen state legislatures who compete for power with sixteen directly elected state governors. If voters have no joy with these institutions they can lobby the municipal and traditional authorities within each province or approach the national sixteen-member Council of Chiefs. If one lives long enough in Palau it is quite an achievement to *avoid* holding elected office.

IS THERE STILL ROOM FOR FRAMERS?

Constitutional engineers often get it wrong and their institutional constructs have unintended consequences. Some critics assert that we can never predict the consequences of institutions accurately; others are mistrustful of Western advice. So why spend so much time worrying about the specifics of design? Why not focus rather on issues of security, economic development, and social upliftment? Are not these the real areas where stability is grown, the underpinnings that make the niceties of liberal democracy possible?

In fact, the question of whether one should concentrate efforts on holistic constitutional design is a redundant one. If a state exists, it has institutions and they are never neutral – they determine how power and resources are distributed and how society is shaped. Institutional design is a Pandora's box which one can only avoid opening if the system is already foolproof and needs left well alone. This is rarely the case – throughout developing world states, and in the vast majority of the developed world, there is no sidestepping the choices. The status quo will benefit one group or another and the decision not to redesign is a choice to compound the sickness of a divided society. It is true that qualms are expressed about foreign involvement in such design processes, and the record of governmental and nongovernmental aid and advice is distinctly mixed, with both unintended negative consequences and intended negative consequences mixing with the occasional good. But as Carothers (1999: 63) notes, democracy has never been crafted from scratch or discovered indigenously with purely indigenous characteristics. Democracy, wherever it is practiced, is a hybrid of local and international practices born of the lessons of political evolution from Europe to the Pacific and everywhere in between.

But all this said, why are we so possessed by electoral democracy? If one has to follow such a murky and prosaic route to get there – and once there few agree on what it should look like – why do we bother so? One motivating force is the belief, increasingly held in academia and to some extent policy making circles, that democracy is the most stable form of government in poor and rich nations – whether they be homogeneous or heterogeneous societies. Adam Przeworski (1991: 13) suggests that democracy is by far the best method for managing and process conflict in any society because at its heart it is defined by "rule open-endedness or organized uncertainty...the less the uncertainty over potential outcomes the lower the incentives for groups to organize institutionally." It is rational for political actors to agree to have their needs addressed through the democratic game when they believe, first, they have a chance to win; second, that even if they lose this time they could still win next time; and third, even if they do lose they will have their basic rights protected, their needs addressed and perhaps retain some influence on the broader governance issues.

But more than that there is something deeper about the link between democracy, choice, and humanity. Ultimately democracy is about individual dignity and collective decency. It is the political expression of human respect. Freedom and choice are two key parts of dignity and while liberal democracy is not a sufficient condition it is an integral underpinning condition. That is why a well-functioning democracy is the best construct for processing preferences and protecting dignity that humankind has yet developed. To paraphrase Churchill: democracy may indeed be the worst form of government invented, but it is better than all the alternatives.

But even if we fail to find a one-size-fits-all constitutional package we can be relatively sure that the component parts matter to democratic stability – and often are the determinants of democratic success or failure. It is probably true to say that while the very best constitutional package cannot save a state from the slings and arrows of socioeconomic misfortune, a badly designed set of institutions will exacerbate, exaggerate, and generally feed creeping fragmentation and instability in a plural society. The mere act of how one actually elects one's government has long been a contentious issue. The Nationalist government in South Africa came to power in 1948 and began the entrenchment of the insidious apartheid system on the basis of 10 percent *less* of the vote than their rivals solely because of the anomalous FPTP electoral system. Chile's presidential election of 1970 gave wide powers to Salvador Allende Gossens on the basis of a third of the popular vote – a popular mandate that proved untenable. The opposition in Lesotho was so outraged that the governing party had won every seat bar one with 60 percent of the vote in 1998 that an attempted coup was launched which left the country in tatters. Few would argue that federalism is a big part of the answer as to why Canada and Spain have survived as nation-states and from Kenya to Estonia voters still debate whether they are Hobbesian Presidentialists or Millian parliamentarists.

3

Diagnosing What Ails a State

This chapter introduces a framework for assessing what lies at the heart of domestic conflict and how to approach the tricky task of choosing democratic institutions for a fragile state. Based on the medical "case histories" of sixty-four countries which have attempted to democratize since 1989 (plus Somalia and Syria as prospective cases – see Table 3.1), I develop guidelines for constitutional design. The first step is to select the sociopolitical-historical factors that need to be considered when diagnosing and crafting a treatment plan. I have divided the characteristics of a state into five areas: demographic context, sociopolitical context, historical context, economic context, and severity of the symptoms of the nation's illness. Within each area between two and five variables are measured to assess baseline health, and in what ways the state is unhealthy. This diagnostic tool allows us to begin to develop a contingent theory of design. Not absolute prescriptions but well-educated suggestions as to which institutional constructs will best help a fledgling democracy given its particular social, economic, political, and historical characteristics.

The term diagnosis comes itself from the Greek word for knowledge "gnonsis" and implies the process of determining the nature of a disease or disorder and distinguishing it from other possible conditions. Unfortunately, the political *diagnosis* of conflict and its relationship to democratic institutions that has been undertaken in recent times has been firmly rooted in evidence drawn from the history of western and developed nations of the nineteenth and twentieth centuries. This is reminiscent of early drug testing which focused on white males and failed to comprehensively understand how new drugs would affect minorities and women. But at the turn of the twenty-first century we now have a solid chunk of empirical evidence bearing on the relationships between multiparty institutions, conflict and democratization, drawn from a burgeoning number of third-wave democracies in Africa, Asia, the Pacific, and Central-Eastern Europe.[1]

If constitutional designers need to be better at diagnosing what ails society what template should they follow – can they learn anything from clinicians? Put another way, how do doctors diagnose an illness and are there parallels with diagnosing what ails a nation? Usually a clinical diagnosis is based on both a

---

[1] As of 2008, Freedom House rates over 140 nation-states as "electoral democracies." See http://www.freedomhouse.org/research

TABLE 3.1 *Stability and Polity VI scores for case study patients (2007)*

Case	Year first (post-1989) election	Stability 2007	Rank	Polity 2007	Rank
Slovenia	1992	1.873013	1	10	1
Czech Rep	1990	1.65211	2	8	14
Slovakia	1990	1.526073	3	10	1
Lithuania	1992	1.465831	4	10	1
Poland	1989	1.383949	5	10	1
Estonia	1990	1.341372	6	6	30
Hungary	1990	1.329528	7	10	1
Latvia	1990	1.26708	8	8	14
Mongolia	1990	1.149742	9	10	1
Croatia	1992	1.039173	10	9	7
Bulgaria	1991	1.014857	11	9	7
Panama	1994	0.886347	12	9	7
Romania	1992	0.866082	13	9	7
Namibia	1989	0.861861	14	6	30
South Africa	1994	0.786321	15	9	7
Ghana	1992	0.754842	16	8	14
Cape Verde	1991	0.706391	17	—	—
Benin	1991	0.612868	18	7	22
Ukraine	1994	0.559907	19	7	22
Mozambique	1994	0.500998	20	6	30
Armenia	1995	0.480307	21	5	42
São Tomé	1991	0.417304	22	—	—
Albania	1991	0.381229	23	9	7
Fiji	1992	0.370836	24	−4	53
El Salvador	1994	0.36639	25	7	22
Zambia	1991	0.309646	26	5	42
Madagascar	1993	0.295563	27	7	22
Mali	1992	0.291118	28	6	30
Guyana	1992	0.290137	29	6	30
Tanzania	1995	0.226506	30	1	47
Lesotho	1993	0.210174	31	8	14
Paraguay	1989	0.210025	32	8	14
Macedonia	1994	0.182361	33	9	7
Georgia	1992	0.100746	34	6	30
Moldova	1994	−0.02269	35	8	14
Rwanda	2003	−0.06971	36	−3	52
Angola	1992	−0.08801	37	−2	50
Malawi	1994	−0.11371	38	6	30
Cambodia	1993	−0.127	39	2	46
Serbia	2000	−0.13904	40	8	14
Bosnia	1996	−0.14978	41	—	—
Sierra Leone	1996	−0.23801	42	7	22
Guinea Bissau	1994	−0.31265	43	6	30
Syria	—	−0.32917	44	—	—
Indonesia	1999	−0.40373	45	8	14
Niger	1993	−0.41787	46	6	30
Congo-B	1992	−0.52395	47	−4	53

TABLE 3.1 *(Continued)*

Case	Year first (Post-1989) election	Stability 2007	Rank	Polity 2007	Rank
Liberia	1997	−0.6146	48	6	30
Kenya	1992	−0.65462	49	7	22
Timor Leste	2001	−0.66049	50	7	22
Burundi	1993	−0.82823	51	6	30
Yemen	1993	−0.89205	52	−2	50
Burma	1990	−0.89733	53	−8	56
Haiti	1990	−0.92865	54	5	42
Nepal	1991	−1.17453	55	6	30
Nigeria	1999	−1.18562	56	4	45
Lebanon	1992	−1.1953	57	7	22
CAR	1993	−1.25933	58	−1	49
Zimbabwe	2008	−1.26248	59	—	—
Ivory Coast	1990	−1.44796	60	0	48
Congo DRC	2006	−1.57191	61	—	—
Afghanistan	2005	−1.59036	62	—	—
Sudan	2009	−1.75984	63	−4	53
Iraq	2005	−1.94729	64	—	—
Somalia		−2.1329	65	—	—
Palestine	1996			—	—

Note: Stability – standardized average of Failed States and World Bank Political Stability Indices 2007.

physical examination *and* a medical history of the patient, which may be confirmed with other procedures (see Sackett et al. 1997). Diagnosis begins with: (*a*) A *clinical methodology*, which shapes how one properly gathers and interprets findings based on a history and examination. In politics one needs to choose the most salient sociopolitical-historical indicators to focus on to aid and contextualize the diagnosis. From these, the doctor can develop an (*b*) *etiology*, or the means to identify causes of the disease. (*c*) *Differential diagnosis* seeks to rank the potential causes of a patient's clinical problem by their likelihood, seriousness, and treatability. (*d*) *Diagnostic tests* are then selected in order to confirm or exclude a diagnosis, based on considering their precision, accuracy, acceptability, and expense. Here, the constitutional engineer might assess the root causes of political instability. Consider what comparative (macro and micro) data needs to be gathered? (*e*) Last, a *prognosis* estimates the patient's likely clinical course over time and anticipates the likely complications of the disease (i.e., the state's trajectory in terms of political stability and ethnic accommodation). From this five-stage process are born strategies of therapy, prevention, and self-improvement. In my metaphor *therapies* are institutional medicines to try and stabilize the politics of the state, *prevention* are institutions which seek to lessen intercommunal hostility, and *self-improvement* mechanisms are institutions which are aimed at consolidating and deepening the democratic values which the post-conflict constitution has introduced.

When applying medical techniques to democratic design, one starting point is to think about broad typologies of sickness relating to different institutional prescriptions. (*a*) The existing institutionalization of electoral and party politics in any given state may range from quite high to very low (e.g., from Kenya to Congo). (*b*) The state itself and its infrastructure may be functioning during a time of crisis (e.g., Burma) or have effectively collapsed (e.g., Afghanistan). (*c*) While hostility and fragility may be high across different cases, actual levels of violence may vary considerably (e.g., the low number of political deaths in ethnically polarized Fiji versus the very high numbers in similar polarized Sri Lanka). (*d*) The degree of ethnic fragmentation varies in the size and number of distinct ethno-cultural groups and their geographic dispersal. (*e*) The cleavages may be based on linguistic, religious, national or geographic identities, or overlapping mixtures of each. (*f*) The core nature of the division may range from disputes over land, economic resources, culture, to religious practice.

With this diagnostic starting point one can begin to make a distinction between the challenges faced by a nation demonstrating, for example, high levels of party institutionalization, state function, and a geographic intermingling of national-religious groups, but where identity groups are violently polarized with the primary fault lines over access to political power (e.g., Northern Ireland). To a case where there is little or no party institutionalization, the state has collapsed, ethnic groups are geographically separated, violence is pervasive, and resource allocation dominates the political discourse (e.g., Afghanistan). Intuitively, prescriptions for appropriate institutions of conflict management in Ireland are unlikely to be the same as those in Afghanistan but a robust diagnostic method moves that answer from an intuition to a finding.

When studying democratic design there is also a tension between case specificity and identifying macro trends. Most political scientists/anthropologists/sociologists are understandably uncomfortable with any mechanism which prescribes institutional remedies for more than a single case at a time. It is said that each fragile state in the developing world is distinctive, if not unique, and a one-size-fits-all approach to constitutional engineering is doomed to fail under the weight of reality of very different historical experiences and cultural practices. The democratic designers must cut the cloth according to the measurements of the body politique. Rousseau (1985) warned that "one must know thoroughly the nation for which one is building; otherwise the final product, however excellent it may be in itself, will prove imperfect when it is acted upon – the more certainly if the nation is already formed, with its tastes, customs, prejudices, and failings too deeply rooted to be stifled by new plantings." How could one disagree with Rousseau!? Thomas Carothers (2004: 181) argues that, "democracy promoters need to focus on the key political patterns of each country in which they intervene, rather than trying to do a little of everything according to a template of idea institutional forms."

But the reality is that there are similar shared experiences and challenges in divergent countries around the world. Furthermore, very few institutional arrangements are unique – they have been tried before somewhere, at some time, and the lessons of how they worked are crucial to understanding how they will work in the future in a new environment. As Carothers (1999: 63) himself notes, democracy has never been crafted from scratch, or discovered indigenously with purely indigenous characteristics. Democracy wherever it is practiced is a hybrid of local and international practices born of the lessons of political evolution from Europe to the Pacific and everywhere in between. One-size-fits-all prescriptions *are* truly meritless but treating every new democratizing case as a blank slate is equally silly. Every patient who has a heart attack is unique but the causes fall under parameters that are known and identifiable, and, to a large extent, treatable with generic interventions and medicines. As Samuels and Wyeth (2006) note "each situation is highly specific and many factors may impact the choice of governance frameworks. However, such efforts essentially face comparable obstacles, and many recent post-conflict constitutions bear remarkable similarities." Those similarities not only allow comparative lessons to be drawn but they make attempts at creating sophisticated theories of design credible and meaningful.

In medicine there has long been a debate over whether a clinical or mechanical method is more efficient in evaluating sickness, guiding diagnoses, and predicting outcomes. The clinical method has always dominated medical practice and relies on specialists contemplating a case, sometimes in association with others, but on the basis of taking a medical history and making a diagnosis often in an impressionistic and nonsystematized way. A mechanical method uses an equation or formula, often based on similar data areas, to deliver a probability of outcome. In essence a clinical doctor will treat a patient with heart problems after reviewing the symptoms of the patient, the data gathered from the patient, what that patient tells her, and on the basis of their expert knowledge of heart disease. The mechanical method would recommend treatment on the basis of a model of hundreds of thousands of former patients with similar symptoms and contextual backgrounds. At its most simplistic the doctor need not assess the individual patient at all. Of course in reality, even if using an algorithm for treatment the patient would need to be evaluated for specific anomalies from the norm.

The surprising thing is that even though clinical methods of diagnosis dominate medical practice, a century's worth of hundreds of empirical evaluations comparing the two methods find that the mechanical method is "almost invariably equal to or superior to the clinical method" (see Grove and Meehl 1996; Hastie and Dawes 2001: ch. 3). These findings are perhaps less shocking when one reads in leading medical textbooks that the first steps of problem solving and diagnosis in the clinical setting occur in a distinctly haphazard way.

Information about the patient is evaluated piecemeal as soon as it is obtained. The gait, clothing, general appearance, handshake, age, and gender register in the problem solver's mind even before a single word is spoken. Then, as you wind your way through the chief complaint and the history of present illness, you should be well on the road to diagnosis. (Cutler 1998: 11)

Could there be a better description of how institutions were designed and imposed in post-Saddam Hussein Iraq in 2003? The occupying administration took a cursory glance at the gait, clothing, and general appearance of Iraq, looked into its eyes and felt a muscular handshake, and decided quickly that all the Iraqis needed was a good dose of Washingtonian democracy. They could not have been further from the truth.

Grove and Meehl find that the mechanical method does not have to be very sophisticated to best the success rate of individuals using expert judgments but they did find that multiple linear regression models did a better job of predicting outcomes than unweighted sums of raw scores. The evidence in favor of diagnosing with algorithms piles up. Not only are fairly unsophisticated models better than individual judgment (Hastie and Dawes 2001: 56) but when the doctors themselves supplied the variables and the weights to the variables they were still beaten by the algorithm they had created in head-to-head comparison. This is because, as Grove and Meehl (1996) note, "the human brain is a relatively inefficient device for noticing, selecting, categorizing, recording, retaining, retrieving, and manipulating information for inferential purposes." Hastie and Dawes (2001: ch. 3) note that algorithms beat "clinical" predictions not just in medicine but in predicting college success, parole violations, and business success and failure. The process of democratic design in post-conflict states has been dominated by failure, ineptness, and a lack of theoretical rigor. Lessons are rarely learnt or transported from case to case and medical histories are misinterpreted, ignored, or in many cases not taken at all. There could be an important role for a contingent theory of democratic design which need not replace proper attention on case specifics, but rather inform designers of the parameters they are working within. As the medical evidence shows, the method does not have to be very good and it will still beat the individual clinical diagnostic approach (or the knee-jerk crisis management school of diplomacy). As Hastie and Dawes (2001: 58) point out, "the practical lesson from all these studies is that in many clinical judgment situations, we should ask the experts what cues to use but let a mechanical model combine the information from those cues to make the judgment."

TAKING A MEDICAL HISTORY TO FACILITATE DIAGNOSIS OF AILING STATES

A clinical trial (or protocol) is a scientific study of how a new medicine or treatment works in a defined group of people. Through such clinical studies, doctors advance knowledge and find new and better ways to prevent, detect, diagnose, control, and treat illnesses. First, a medical history is taken which gives both symptoms and background features which may speak of the overall ailment. To develop a contingent theory of democratic design I base my medical histories of the sixty-four patient countries on a measurement of twenty indicators which fall into five areas: demographic context, sociopolitical context, historical context, economic context, and severity of the symptoms of illness (state instability).[2] I evaluate cases at the time when the medicines (multiparty elections to choose executive and legislative leaders) were first applied, so the data is for the preceding years before the first (post-1989) election. Such case histories can be used for both qualitative and quantitative analysis. In this chapter I begin to track the quantitative relationships between the case history variables and patterns of democracy and stability. In subsequent chapters I root qualitative lessons within the framework of these twenty case history diagnostic indicators.

A medical diagnosis looks for markers – indicators of sickness. We should expect that a variety of illnesses will be present, but the indicators will narrow down the parameters of what is most likely ailing the patient. After first-tier diagnostic tests, other more specific tests will be needed to determine what is the culprit for the sickness, or indeed *culprits*. So what are the best markers to look for when diagnosing the ailing state and deciding what treatments are appropriate? I have chosen variables where both theoretical and empirical evidence confirms that they matter (at least in some places) to democratization and political stability. As noted earlier the diagnostic questions fall into five categories: demographic context, sociopolitical context, historical context, economic context, and severity of the symptoms of the nation's illness.

The scaling of each variable is from low (majoritarian democracy is more likely and/or theoretically appropriate) to high (power-sharing democracy is more likely and/or theoretically appropriate). This is not an exact science and a few of the theoretical hypotheses of how context relates to democratic type are arguable. For example, does higher socioeconomic inequality in a nation lead to more conflict and thus a greater need for inclusion and power sharing, or does higher disparity lead to the need for quick governmental decision making and thus a greater need for exclusion? Lijphart says that the larger the economic differentiation between segments, the more difficult political power sharing will be, but I demur arguing that when political marginalization reinforces economic disparities between groups the need for inclusive power-sharing institutions is magnified. See also variables SP3 and E1 (below) for which a case could be made for scaling in either direction. However, in the vast majority of variables listed below the theoretical scaling of how the context relates to the likelihood of majoritarian

---

[2] Some of the variables are akin to Lijphart's nine favorable conditions for consociationalism. In Lijphart's analysis he looks at conditions that are more likely to give rise to consociationalism; my variables also theorize about the way in which the context leans itself, or not as the case may be, to power sharing or majoritarian government. See Lijphart (1985: 119–26).

or power-sharing institutions is clear cut, and in the cases where it is not obvious, our analysis of the patterns of success and failure will test whether the hypothesis fails or holds.

PATIENT (INDEPENDENT) VARIABLES

Demographic Context

D1. Is There a Majority Segment of the Population?

Theory: If there is a dominant segment with over 50 percent support nationwide, it is more likely that majoritarianism will take hold and that a single community will dominate executive and legislative power. The pressure for minority inclusion in decision making may exist but the level of "interventionist institutions" to reduce the strength of majority rule will have to be higher.

Measurement: A large unified majority segment (very unfavorable = 1), a large but less unified majority segment (unfavorable = 2), slim majority segment or highly fragmented majority segment (neutral = 3), no majority segment but plurality segments of unequal size (favorable = 4), no majority segment but main plurality segments of roughly equal size (very favorable = 5) (Lijphart 1985: 119).

D2. How Ethnically/Communally Fragmented is Society?

Theory: Lijphart (1985: 123) suggests that negotiations among leaders will be facilitated if segments are of roughly equal size and there are not too many elite interests to incorporate. If there are too many segments it will require complicated and bilateral bargaining between elites, which will engender gridlock within legislation and create multiple conflict flashpoints. Ideally there should be a small number of segments with the optimum number being between three and five (Lijphart 1977: 56). However, this may be a nuance that gets lost in the complexity of the real world. While it is certainly true that ethnic homogeneity makes power sharing less relevant and likely, the actual number of plurality segments beyond two may have declining meaning. I would suggest that more segments (of roughly equal size) place even more of a premium on inclusive institutions and there are rarely more than three or four significant national groups anyways. Therefore, my continuum is simply one of homogeneity versus heterogeneity.

Measurement: For the purposes of diagnosis I include a measure of the degree of communal fragmentation and polarization in the nation as a whole. This complements, but does not replicate, the diagnostic data that D1 offers the institutional designer. I use Montalvo and Reynal-Querol's "ethnic polarization" index (2005)[3] which nicely builds the relative sizes of majority and minority groups into existing indices of fragmentation and better captures the decreased polarization that occurs when societies are either very homogeneous or very heterogeneous, or the increased polarization when a large ethnic minority faces an ethnic majority.[4]

D3. How Large is the Population?

Theory: The decision-making process of inclusive power-sharing regimes is simplified if the state has a small population size, because foreign affairs usually takes on less importance and the distribution of resources is easier to manage. A larger population (and larger geographical area) may require single-member districts to adequately represent local interests and enhance accountability.

Measurement: United Nations demographic data from the year closest to the first multiparty elections post 1989 (http://data.un.org).

D4. Are Communal Segments Geographically Concentrated or Integrated?

Theory: A geographical concentration of segments will aid the development of federalism and decentralization, both important aspects of power sharing in a plural society. Cases where groups are more dispersed and integrated may try majoritarian election systems (such as the Alternative Vote) and unitary government.

Measurement: No concentration (geographically interspersed) = 1, low concentration (some geographical focal points but mostly intermixed) = 2, medium concentration (most group members live clustered together in one part of the nation but not all) = 3, high concentration (almost all community members live together in one geographical areas) = 4.[5]

Sociopolitical Context

SP1. Unity in the Face of External Threat

Theory: The existence of *external threats* may help to unify a society around a common nationalism, and thus increase the potential for cooperation among its component segments. Lijphart (1985: 124) maintains that the presence of external

---

[3] Data calculated by author for missing cases based on World Directory of Minorities data.

[4] Insights offered by Horowitz (1985).

[5] Based on World Directory of Minorities and case study evidence. http://www.minorityrights.org/directory

threats (Lebanon, Cyprus) enhances the likelihood of hostile internal groups coming to a power-sharing accommodation.

Measurement: At the time of the first post-1989 multiparty elections: if no significant external threat to national sovereignty and stability = 1, the existence of external threats of a low–moderate level = 2, a high level of external threat = 3.[6]

SP2. Belief in the Nation

Theory: An overarching sense of national loyalty which transcends societal divisions provides a fillip to power sharing. This can be manifested as either a sense of shared national identity and/or a commitment to territorial unity. In some cases (e.g., Georgia) there is little shared nationalism or belief in territorial integrity; while in other cases of historically significant communal conflict there is considerably more common ground on nationhood (e.g., South Africa).

Measurement: No shared national feeling or commitment to territorial integrity (majority of groups would be happy to see the break up of the existing nation-state) = 1; universal national loyalty is low and while a majority of citizens commit to territorial unity, not all do, a significant minority wants secession or closer ties to a state hostile to the majority = 2; national loyalty is not universal but while there are competing conceptions of national identity secessionism is not forefront = 3; despite communal antagonisms people demonstrate a significant shared belief in the nation and a commitment to territorial integrity = 4.

SP3. Multiethnic Cleavages

Theory: Where there is ethnic diversity social cleavages often reinforce and overlap with other cleavages (i.e., most Hindus are poor, or most French speakers are Catholic) but religious or economic differences can cut across ethnic cleavages making the fault lines within society more complex. Cross-cutting cleavages can manifest themselves as multiethnic political parties and/or alliances between ideologically like-minded parties of different groups. The more cross-cutting cleavages, the higher the likelihood that majoritarian government will include representatives of majority and minority communities.

Measurement: Society is homogeneous to a degree that the main political fault lines are noncommunal = 1. There is ethnic diversity, the system is dominated by multiethnic parties, and there are multiple cross-cutting cleavages = 2. There are

---

[6] The Failed States project includes a variable "Intervention of Other States or External Political Actors" for the 2005–8 period. http://www.fundforpeace.org/web/index.php?option=com_content &task=view&id=99&Itemid=140. This data has been averaged and then where appropriate used as a guide for the earlier period of assessment. Obviously in some cases external threat has fluctuated and so the coding is for the period leading up to the first post-1989 elections.

some multiethnic parties and some cross-cutting cleavages but ethnic segmentation is more prevalent = 3. Society is highly segmented, key political parties are homogeneous, and communal cleavages reinforce each other = 4.

SP4. The Focus of the Fight

Theory: There are at least four dimensions which divide communal groups in fledgling democracies: Cultural (ethnic) identity, national identity, territory, and control and allocation of resources. Territorial disputes may be managed by federalism or autonomies, resource allocations are managed by economic power sharing, culture/ethnic inclusion by reserved seats, cultural autonomies. But all types of division require some type of inclusion at the macro level – power sharing, decentralization, etc.; the more the fault lines, the more inclusive mechanisms are needed.

Measurement: A fight over: no salient communal dimensions to conflict = 1, predominantly a single dimension dominates conflict = 2, two dimensions = 3, three or more dimensions = 4.

Economic Context

E1. Overall Income

Theory: Wealthier nations are more likely to sustain democracy, despite the fact that over the last half century transitions to democracy have been made in wealthy and very poor societies (see Przeworski et al. 2000). And once there, wealth reduces the pressure to use democratic institutions as tools of conflict management. Power-sharing institutions address deep-seated anger that comes of being marginalized and discriminated against both politically and economically. If the country is wealthier (and that wealth is spread across the citizenry – see E3) the consequences of antigovernment hostility are more manageable.

Measurement: GDP per capita, PPP (constant 2005 international $) an average of the two years before the first election and the first election year (where data is available).[7]

E2. Overall Development

Theory: In a similar way to the wealth argument, overall development indicates a strengthening middle class, civil society, and foundational stability. The higher the levels of human development, the lower the need for inclusive and stabilizing power-sharing arrangements.

---

[7] http://hdr.undp.org/en/statistics/

Measurement: Human Development Index, from year closest to first multiparty election.[8]

E3. Socioeconomic Inequality

Theory: Lijphart argues that the larger the economic differentiation between segments, the more difficult political power sharing will be and addressing that disparity could require unencumbered majority decision making which would accentuate the need for the exclusion that is integral to majoritarian government. Boix and Acemoglu and Robinson concur arguing that the chances for democratization itself is lower when there are high levels of inequality. Elites have more to lose from change and they have the wealth and power to better resist calls for liberalization (Boix 2003; Acemoglu and Robinson 2006). However, in contrast, higher economic disparity between ethnic groups leads to higher conflict and state fragility and, if there *is* political liberalization, a greater need for inclusion and power sharing. When socioeconomic disparity is high the minority group (which is usually poor) has no business safety net to fall back on if it is politically excluded. Even if the minority is comparatively wealthy (e.g., Chinese in Malaysia, White Africans in Zimbabwe), excluding the minority from the political sphere has proven to retard democratization for all groups.

Measurement: The Gini coefficient for the year closest to the first post-1989 multiparty election.[9]

E4. Dependence on Natural Resources

Theory: A number of scholars have shown that developing world states that have an abundance of natural resources are less likely to democratize. The rents secured from natural resources allow ruling elites to insulate themselves from being responsive to popular demands and entrench their dominance with targeted largesse for supporters (see Karl 1997; Moore 2001). The state is less dependent on tax revenue and as a consequence state infrastructure is undeveloped and repressive internal security forces are emboldened. Civil war is also more likely when natural resources are dominant (see Ross 2004) and mineral resources magnify the geographical scope of the conflict (see Buhaug and Gates 2002).

Measurement: The consequences of natural resource dependency on conflict and democracy are mixed into a plethora of other variables making the specific causal mechanisms difficult to tease out. Thus, when it comes to the relationship

---

[8] http://hdr.undp.org/en/statistics/

[9] http://www.wider.unu.edu/research/Database/en_GB/wiid/

UN Human development report (http://hdrstats.undp.org/indicators/147.html)

Global Peace Index (http://en.wikipedia.org/wiki/Global_Peace_Index). http://earthtrends.wri.org/text/economics-business/variable-353.html

between natural resources and democratic type the hypotheses are inevitably speculative. However, Ross outlines how natural resources accentuate domestic conflict. They can give incentives for separatist rebellion, generally lengthen the conflict, attract foreign intervention, provide a focal point for continuing communal conflict, and encourage repressive states to crack down even more vociferously against insurgents (2004). All these consequences make society more conflictual, ethnically polarized, and fragile. For those reasons we will presume that countries with higher dependency on natural resources are the most likely to benefit from power-sharing institutions. Natural resource dependency is measured by the mineral ores and oil/natural gas (fuel) percentage share of merchandizing exports from the World Bank Development Indicators.[10]

E5. Type of Natural Resource

Theory: As noted above, conflict often revolves around economic interests and who lays claim to the wealth of the nation (see Fearon and Laitin 2003). In E4, I hypothesized about the relationship between a state's dependency and all natural resources, while E5 unpacks the resources themselves to argue that the type of resource will also influence which democratic institutions to use in a fledgling democracy. Natural resources can be legal or illicit, relatively fixed, or susceptible to looting. Economic resources such as agriculture, tourism, and industry are less likely to be looted by elites than drugs (Burma, Afghanistan), diamonds (Sierra Leone, Liberia), or high-end timber (Fiji, Burma). Oil and gas have been different but equally burdensome blessing to some democratizing countries (see Ross 2001, 2006). Elements of majoritarian or power-sharing government lend themselves to the administration of these different types of natural resources.

Measurement: There are significant resources which are illegal and easily lootable (e.g., drugs) which require a more centralized, unitary, executive to enforce state power = 1. There are resources which are legal but lootable (e.g., high-price timber [mahogany, teak] and diamonds and other minerals) which require a lesser degree of central control = 2. Oil reserves are legal commodities but remain a distinct flashpoint. This may warrant decentralization alongside a central government oil-revenue-sharing pact (this may also be true of natural gas) = 3. Resources which are both legal and less vulnerable to looting (e.g., agriculture, fishing) allow for more decentralized government decision making and less intervention from the central state to share out geographically concentrated resources = 4.[11]

---

[10] Ores and metals exports (percentage of merchandise exports), Food exports (percentage of merchandise exports). WDI indicators.

[11] Based on data from the CIA world fact book and other supporting World Bank sources.

Historical Context

H1. The Colonial Legacy

Theory: In the vast majority of developing world states large and influential elements of modern political institutions were "gifted" by colonial regimes. Anglophone nations are more likely to have experience of majoritarian Westminster institutions, former Francophone colonies are more likely to use the two-round system, and Lusophone (and other continental European former colonies) – PR. Former British colonies in the Middle East can be categorized separately as they were "gifted" the Block Vote (Oxbridge University district electoral system) by T. E. Lawrence and his advisors upon their creation in the early part of the twentieth century. I hypothesize that the countries untouched by colonialism or shepherded into the multiparty era by the United Nations (e.g., Namibia, East Timor) are the most likely to opt for consensual, power-sharing institutions. Former Soviet Bloc countries tended to adopt French-style institutions (which had been the pre-Soviet Russian tradition) after their independence post 1989.

 Measurement: Anglophone (Mid-East) super-majoritarian = 1; Anglophone-majoritarian = 2; Francophone/American/Former USSR-Soviet Bloc, semi-majoritarian = 3; Lusophone/German/Dutch/Spanish/Belgian/Italian, proportional = 4; no colonialism/UN mandate, power sharing = 5.[12]

H2. The Nature of the Ancien Regime

Theory: In democratizing states the nature of the previous authoritarian regime has an impact on the infrastructure and institutions that the new multiparty regime inherits. Dictatorships rooted in minority (often ethnic) oligarchies are likely to see pressures for majority rule, regardless of whether the oligarchy is headed by a monarch or a populist demagogue. The heart of such dictatorships is their suppression of the minority and in response the majority will regard majoritarian government as even more just (the ANC in South Africa providing the exception to this rule). Theocracies are also likely to be more centralized and "majoritarian" in their ethos, and the legacy they leave, as are populist/sultanistic dictators. Military regimes justify themselves on the basis of protectors of the nation-state but do not necessarily impose a single ideology of how the state should be structured (beyond that they should be in control). Once they step down their institutions may be less determinant of what comes next. Nevertheless, as H3 argues, a military junta based on a majority communal group, is likely to be resistant to inclusive post-authoritarian arrangements. However, ideological

---

[12] Where colonial power was a hybrid (e.g., Italian and British in Somalia) the scores have been averaged.

dictatorships (communist, Marxist, etc) pay some attention to decentralization even if in reality real power is centralized (e.g., Yugoslavia, USSR), which leaves some institutional legacy of federalism for the new democrats to work with. There is some overlap between these *ancien regime* types but we can offer a simple typology.

Measurement: A minority oligarchy regime = 1, a theocracy or sultanistic (nonideological) dictator = 2, military regime = 3, Leftist ideological authoritarian regimes = 4.

H3. The Military Threat to Democracy

Theory: As a corollary to H2, a state with a history of the military being involved in politics and seizing executive power will weaken the chances for stable democratization generally. In most cases the military is likely to be drawn from the majority group (although not in all cases) so the higher the propensity for military intervention in politics, the higher the likelihood of majoritarianism being supported, and power sharing (which will include minority groups that the army has been hostile too) being rejected by the military.

Measurement: There has been more than one coup d'état in the previous two decades = 1. There has been a single coup d'état within the previous two decades (and/or the current regime is a military junta) = 2. The military accounts for over 5 percent of the labor force and there is limited propensity for military involvement in politics = 3. The military forms a small proportion of the labor force (less than 5%) and there is no precedence of military involvement in politics = 4.[13]

H4. A Culture of Accommodation

Theory: Long-standing traditions of accommodation, which settle conflict by consensus and compromise and are rooted in the culture, will increase the likelihood of a successful power-sharing democracy (Lijphart 1985: 126). Such traditions can be manifested in historical multiethnic pacts and alliances, cultural practices which value compromise and consensus, and laws which include and validate minority communities.

Measurement: This can be approximated with reference to previous experiences of sociopolitical compromise and cultural enmities and predispositions. Low = 1, medium = 2, high = 3. A case may score medium or high in spite of the fact that they are enduring interethnic conflict. Modern times may have seen the withering of a culture of accommodation but this variable assesses whether there are past traditions which can be drawn on.

---

[13] Measure of coup d'états from Banks (decade leading up to first elections) and military as proportion of total labor force from WDI (year of first election).

H5. Type of Transition

Theory: Huntington, Linz, Share, and Mainwaring all note how the nature of the transfer of power/liberalization affects the nature and success of the fledgling democracy that comes after. Huntington (1993) talks of *transformations,* where political liberalization is initiated and led by elites within the authoritarian regime; *replacements,* where a regime resistant to change is overthrown and overwhelmed by the opposition, which then initiates democratization; and *transplacements,* which are the result of a balance of power stand off between government and opposition, producing a negotiated settlement that opens up the political sphere. In addition, Iraq and Afghanistan have exemplified "regime change" promoted by an external superpower. In those cases the process of designing a new constitution was domestically led and to a degree influenced by foreign (American) preferences. However, what was perhaps surprising was the lack of agency the United States played in choosing the main elements of the new "democratic" institutions in Iraq and Afghanistan. They had preferences over certain details, but no consistent or holistic view of the democratic design in toto. This has been the pattern largely followed in historical American promoted regime changes: for example, Chile, Iran, Guatemala, Honduras, Panama, Nicaragua, Grenada, South Vietnam.

Measurement: All else being equal replacements should give rise to fewer pressures for minority inclusion in government = 1, transformations will provide the opportunity for the *ancien regime* to incorporate minority protections in the constitution but such regimes often cling to the hope that they will continue to rule through majoritarian institutions = 2, while the bargaining inherent within transplacements is more likely to lead to power sharing at a variety of levels = 3. Externally driven transformations should follow the government-type preferences of the intervening nation – as long as the invading state takes an interest in crafting what comes next. But as Iraq and Afghanistan demonstrate, at least in the twenty-first century, those preferences are inconsistent and often ill conceived. Because of the lack of a consistent theoretical or empirical argument of how regime overthrow has, or should, influence democratic design, I treat such cases as replacements of the *ancien regime* and thus less likely than transplacements to entrench minority constraints on government (Afghanistan and most other historical cases confirm this, Iraq refutes the theory).

Severity of Symptoms

SS1. Level of Violence as Indicated by Deaths

Theory: A legacy of violence enhances the need for power sharing and inclusion. The new democratic institutions play an important part as elements of the peace process which build confidence among groups. The higher the history of violence, the more likely the state requires inclusive, reassuring institutions that give voice to minorities and former insurgents.

Measurement: UCDP-PRIO armed conflict database – best estimate of battle deaths for a ten-year period preceding first election as a proportion of total population in the year of first election.

SS2. Other Indicators of Conflict – Antigovernment Activity

Theory: Outside of civilian and combatant battlefield deaths we can use a variety of indicators of state instability. Assassinations, strikes, guerrilla warfare, government crises, purges, riots, revolutions, and anti-government demonstrations capture a level of regime fragility beyond the simple death count. I theorize that higher levels of instability indicate more fragility and thus a higher need for inclusive institutions.

Measurement: Banks' weighted conflict measure: assassinations (25), strikes (20), guerrilla warfare (100), government crises (20), purges (20), riots (25), revolutions (150), and anti-government demonstrations (10). The average yearly total for the decade leading up to the first elections.

Democracy and Stability (Dependent Variables)

Ultimately, I am attempting to explain and address the means to improve ***democratic health*** but democracy and political stability are not necessarily synonymous. There is a difference between conflict and violence. Conflict in some form is inevitable, especially in a vibrant competitive state; stability (or peace) is the absence of violence. The correlation between my measure of stability and democracy (in 2007) is 0.58, that is, a relationship but not a determining one. We would expect democracy to bring more stability as it endures over time but this level of relationship supports the thesis that multiparty democracy, at least over its beginning years, brings both stabilizing and destabilizing pressures. This is supported by the way in which democracy becomes more correlated with stability over time in my sample. The correlation between stability and the democracy score at the time of the first election is 0.489. As Table 3.1 demonstrates most countries fall in roughly the same place on the league table of "democracy" in 2007 as they do on the rank ordering of stability. But there are nine countries who are significantly[14] higher up on the stability league table than the democracy table (Czech Republic, Estonia, Namibia, Armenia, Fiji, Zambia, Tanzania, Rwanda, and Angola) and eighteen who as of 2008 were significantly more democratic than they are stable (Ivory Coast, Lebanon, Nigeria, Nepal, Haiti, Burundi, East Timor, Kenya, Liberia, Niger, Indonesia, Guinea-Bissau, Sierra Leone, Serbia, Moldova, Macedonia, Paraguay, and Lesotho).

---

[14] More than ten positions higher.

STABILITY

For my dependent variable of current political stability I considered three indices. (*a*) The Failed States Index (FSI) compiled by the Fund for Peace since 2004.[15] (*b*) Political Stability: Likelihood of Governmental Overthrow compiled by the World Bank since (data since 1996).[16] (*c*) The Global Peace Index compiled by Vision of Humanity for 2008.[17] While The FSI and Political Stability indices had data for all my cases for the 2007–8 period, the GPI missed a quarter of the cases. While my stability measure is the average of the standardized FSI and World Bank scores, the ordering and magnitude was generally confirmed by the GPI scores available.

Sub-indicators

There are a number of sub-indicators of stability which could be utilized to gain purchase on how vibrant democratic society is – most are contained within the overall measure outlined above. However, at various times in subsequent chapters I will pay attention to: (*a*) the trajectory of violence,[18] (*b*) minorities under threat as measured by Minority Rights Group International,[19] (*c*) numbers of internally displaced people,[20] (*d*) corruption as measured by Transparency International (2001–8),[21] and (*e*) socioeconomic inequality between ethnic groups.[22]

DEMOCRACY

I measure democracy with the POLITY data set. Scores were collected for a variety of indicators: the most recent year (2007), the score at the end of the *ancien regime*, the score for the first election year, and the polity score five years out and ten years out. This allows us to capture both the current state of play and trajectories of democratic growth and retreat.[23]

---

[15] http://www.fundforpeace.org/web/index.php?option=com_content&task=view&id=99&Itemid=140

[16] http://info.worldbank.org/governance/wgi/index.asp

[17] http://www.visionofhumanity.org/gpi/home.php

[18] http://www.prio.no/Data/

[19] http://www.minorityrights.org/464/peoples-under-threat/table-1-peoples-most-under-threat–highest-rated-countries-2008.html

[20] http://www.internal-displacement.org/8025708F004CE90B/(httpPages)/22FB1D4E2B196DAA802570BB005E787C?OpenDocument&count=1000

[21] http://www.transparency.org/news_room/in_focus/2008/cpi2008/cpi_2008_table

[22] http://www.fundforpeace.org/web/index.php?option=com_content&task=view&id=99&Itemid=140

[23] http://www.systemicpeace.org/polity/polity4.htm

Sub-indicators of Democracy

There are a number of sub-indicators of democracy which could be utilized to gain purchase on how vibrant democratic society is. In the following chapter I use the disaggregated component parts of POLITY (Executive Recruitment, Executive Constraints, and Political competition) but later in this book I will use at various times: (*a*) the degree of media freedom as indicated by the Freedom House Index of Press Freedom 1994–2007[24] and Pippa Norris' media access scale, (*b*) the public support for democracy as measured by regional barometers and the world values survey, (*c*) the level of voter turnout,[25] (*d*) voter protest and error as measured by spoiled/invalid votes,[26] and (*e*) the occurrence of peaceful alternations of government.

INSTITUTIONAL (INTERVENING) VARIABLES

The core of this book argues that institutional choices can make a difference to outcomes in democratizing nations, whether they have been through destabilizing conflict or not. The four chapters that follow describe how institutions – elections, legislatures, executives, and decentralized governing bodies – mediate between underlying conditions and patterns of success or failure. To prime those discussions I add in institutional variables to our diagnostic background variables to see if on the macro level institutions make a difference to the dependent variable outcomes of stability and democracy. If they do we can then move on to more detailed case discussions of how various institutions mediate between underlying characteristics and the political health of a nation. If they do not then we are left with the disturbing conclusion that a nation's ability to survive peacefully and democratize is solely driven by its socioeconomic-historical traits. Historical inevitability trumps attempts at intervention.

Electoral Systems (i1)

Measuring Electoral Inclusion

The electoral system type is the best measure of party/ideological inclusion in the legislature (and executive, if it is a parliamentary system). Following Norris (2008) for the purposes of the analysis in this chapter, I use a simple three-way classification of electoral systems (Majoritarian, Semi-PR, and Proportional Representation).

---

[24] http://www.freedomhouse.org/template.cfm?page=274
[25] http://www.idea.int/vt/index.cfm
[26] http://www.idea.int/vt/index.cfm

The Inclusion of Regions and Localities (i2)

The types of, and consequences of, decentralization and federalism are dealt with in more detail in chapter 7. For the statistical analysis in this chapter, I use John Gerring and Strom Thacker's scoring of the federal-unitary continuum: 1 = nonfederal (unitary), 2 = semi-federal, 3 = federal, +1 if weak bicameral, +2 if strong bicameral (see Gerring and Thacker 2004). Theory would predict that decentralized and federal states are characteristically consensual while majoritarian governments are unitary.

I have two measures of the nature of the executive. The first assesses realities as well as constitutional provisions, while the second measures how diffused executive power is within the system.

Measuring Executive Inclusion (i3)

The more the constraints placed on the executive, the more hands the executive power lies within and the more formalized power sharing becomes, all increase the consensual ethos of government. For these reasons I use the following scoring system: single-party government = 1, multiparty coalition (minimal winning coalition) or demonstrative ethnic minority inclusion = 2, oversize governing coalition (non constitutionally mandated, i.e., Kenya) = 3, Government of National Unity (constitutionally mandated, i.e., South Africa 1994–9) = 4.

Executive Type (i4)

Similarly presidential systems are more majoritarian than parliamentary systems which in turn are more majoritarian than those rare cases where a multi-person "presidency/executive" exists (i.e., Bosnia Herzegovina). Thus, Presidential = 1, Semi-Presidential = 2, Parliamentary = 3, Multi-person Executive = 4.

SUMMARY

We now have diagnostic indicators for charting a patient history, institutional variables (the medicines) to help us understand how democratic design prescriptions have worked in our cases, and dependent variables of stability and democracy to measure outcomes. In chapter 4, I will analyze the patterns as a whole and in chapters 5 through 8 focus more closely on the consequences of each institutional variable.

4

From Diagnosis to Treatment

A starting point for analysis is to place each country's case on a "need for consensus versus need for majoritarian government" continuum – then compare what our independent variables would predict their government type to be versus what institutions the case uses in actuality (I call this *democratic alignment*). In essence, answering the question: how well are these new constitutions aligning with what theory might prescribe? Based on the twenty background variables outlined earlier, and the aggregate of the institutional variables, we can see that only four of the top fifteen cases with a propensity, or theoretical need, for majoritarian government actually place in the top fifteen for majoritarianism (Lesotho, Yemen, Mali, and Ghana). Six of the fifteen cases most in need of consensus government make the list of the top fifteen consensus governments (Serbia, Iraq, Bosnia, Sudan, South Africa, and Lebanon). However as the graph shows, the more majoritarian a country is in relation to its background need for consensus government (the I cases), the more likely it is to be unstable. Conversely, the more consensual a case is in relation to its background propensity to majoritarianism (the – cases), the higher the chances of stability (Figure 4.1).

The top fifteen cases with the greatest difference between their background propensity for consensus government and their actual majoritarian institutions average 0.21 when it comes to stability and they average 3.5 on the 2007 POLITY democracy aggregate (see table 4.1). The top fifteen cases with the greatest difference between their background propensity for majoritarianism and their actual use of consensual institutions average 0.56 when it comes to stability and they average 6.5 on the 2007 POLITY democracy aggregate. The fifteen best-aligned cases average −0.06 when it comes to stability and they average 8.2 on the 2007 POLITY democracy aggregate.

While useful, this first cut of the data only takes us so far in our understanding of diagnosing state instability and prescribing democratic institutions. First, the "league tables" above assume that each background variable carries equal weight and second that all the variables matter in all cases when it comes to stability and democratic outcomes. The aggregation of the twenty context variables, and indeed the summing of our five institutional variables, washes out the significance of more specific factors from case to case. One way to address the problem of weighting is to see whether a factor analysis reveals clusters of variables. Can we find two or three dimensions among the twenty diagnostic indicators which

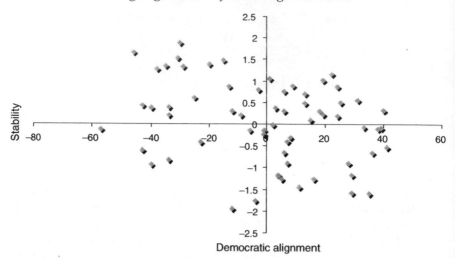

FIGURE 4.1 Democratic alignment versus stability

would allow us to map sickness more easily? Unfortunately a factor analysis revealed at least six clusters and found that the contextual variables were fairly distinct from each other and picking up different traits of the state in question. This confirms the intuition that there are many countries which have characteristics calling for more consensual government on certain dimensions while in other areas they have pressures and requirements for more majoritarian institutions. The lack of conformity in needs or outcomes again reinforces the complexity of a reality of democratic design in post-conflict and fragile developing world nations.

CONTEXTUAL VARIABLES

If we assess each contextual variable's relationship to the dependent outcomes of stability and democracy we find that there is far more correlation between the

TABLE 4.1 *Institutional alignment and stability/democracy*

	Stability	Democracy
Consensus/majority	−0.21 (36th percentile)	3.5 (21st percentile)
Aligned	−0.06 (46th percentile)	8.2 (75th percentile)
Majority/consensus	0.56 (72nd percentile)	6.5 (49th percentile)

diagnostic variables and our measure of stability than between the variables and measures of democracy (regardless of whether we use the POLITY score for 2007 or the change between the POLITY score at the first election year and 2007, or five years out from the first election, or ten years out). A clear statistical correlation between our independent variables and democracy as measured by the POLITY aggregate score simply does not exist. When it comes to stability, no single variable is highly correlated with levels of stability but seven variables have a correlation figure higher than 0.4.

E1. Overall Wealth (Correlation 0.603)

The wealthiest ten countries have an average stability score of 1.38 while the poorest ten have −0.75.

SP4. The Focus of the Fight (−0.0531)

Those nations with no, or one, salient communal dimension of conflict are perhaps unsurprisingly much more stable 0.55 (seventeen cases) than those with three or more communal dimensions to their conflict −0.53 (twenty-seven cases).

E2. Overall Development (0.513)

The ten most developed countries have an average stability score of 1.37 while the ten least developed have −0.22.

H2. The Nature of the Ancien Regime (0.493)

When it comes to the relationship between stability and the former regime the following averages apply: Leftist ideological authoritarian regimes score 0.82 (eighteen cases). All other regimes average 0.5 (forty-four cases) (minority oligarchy regime (−0.16, seven cases), a theocracy or sultanistic (nonideological) dictator (−0.52, twenty-one cases), military regime (−0.26, sixteen cases)).

SP3. Multiethnic Cleavages (0.412)

When society is homogeneous to the degree that the main political fault lines are not communal, the average stability score is 0.54 (sixteen cases). But when society is highly segmented, the key political parties are homogeneous and communal cleavages reinforce each other the average is −0.7 (nine cases).

D4. Are Communal Segments Geographically Concentrated or Integrated? (0.410)

When communal groups are geographically interspersed, the average stability score is 0.45 (sixteen cases), but when there is medium-high concentration the average is −0.47 (twenty-three cases).

SP2. Belief in the Nation (0.400)

Finally, when there is no shared national feeling or commitment to territorial integrity (i.e., a majority of people would be happy to see the break up of the existing nation-state) the stability average is −1.14 (two cases), but when most groups demonstrate a shared belief in the nation and a commitment to territorial integrity the score is 0.03 (twenty-four cases).

This supports the argument that political stability is more likely when (*a*) the state increases in wealth and human development; (*b*) the focal points of conflict are not communally/ethnically based; (*c*) the *ancien regime* was ideologically leftist rather than any other type of dictatorship; (*d*) cross-cutting cleavages are more prevalent; (*e*) communal groups are more geographically integrated; and (*f*) there are overarching feelings of "commitment to the nation" shared among disparate groups.

We are able to show the relationship between stability and the historical severity of the conflict, through cross-tabs. As Table 4.2 illustrates stability is better in 2007 in those countries that did not have political deaths before their attempted transitions to democracy. Stability is in fact worst in those eight cases where between one-tenth of 1 percent and one-half of a percent of the population were killed in the decade leading up to multiparty elections (a raw score which ranges from 1,400 in East Timor to 149,000 in the DR Congo). Average stability scores are somewhat better in the six cases where over one-half of 1 percent of the population were killed. This may be a product of timing. The fact that the case is included in my data set after very high levels of conflict means that a peace settlement has been imposed. Lower levels of violence imply a simmering conflict which has not necessarily been ended by "democratic" elections. When it comes to the degree of executive inclusion the averages show that governments of national unity (GNUs) are associated with higher levels of instability. This says little about the propensity for that institution to help an ailing state, rather it describes the fact that GNUs (or oversize coalition governments) are just more likely to be needed in highly unstable countries.

TABLE 4.2 *Severity of violence and stability*

		Deaths as a percentage of population			
		0	$0 < x < 0.001$	$0.001 < x < 0.005$	< 0.005
		(*n*)	(*n*)	(*n*)	(*n*)
Stability	Single-party government	0.17 (16)	−0.01 (9)	−0.77 (3)	0.14 (3)
	Coalition multiparty	0.84 (14)	−0.27 (7)	−0.78 (3)	0.36 (1)
	Oversize coalition	−1.26 (1)	−0.47 (1)	−0.13 (1)	
	Mandated GNU	0.37 (1)	−0.49 (2)	−1.94 (1)	−67 (2)
	Overall	0.42 (32)	−0.18 (19)	−0.84 (8)	−0.09 (6)

To unpack the relationships more fully we can run OLS multivariate regressions. I took out E2: *Overall Development* because it was overly correlated with income, and SP3: *Multi-Ethnic Cleavages* because of its correlation with SP2: *Belief in the Nation*.

The robust regression[1] in table 4.3 finds that when focused purely on our diagnostic variables the following are statistically significant: As belief in the nation (SP2) and wealth (E1) rise, so does stability. As the *ancien regime* (H2) shifts from being a minority oligarchy to a personalized dictatorship, to a military dictatorship, to a leftist ideological regime, current stability increases. Last, as the dependency on natural resources (E4) decreases stability increases. A model that only included these factors maintains the significance of all these variables.

DO INSTITUTIONS MATTER?

When it comes to stability, the inclusion of the institutional variables (electoral system type, executive inclusion, executive type, and degree of decentralization) helps us explain more of the puzzle (see table 4.4).

As in the previous model, belief in the nation, wealth, and the nature of the *ancien regime* continue to have a statistically significant effect, with income having the greatest impact. In this model the dependence on natural resources moves in significance to the .05 level from the .10 level in the earlier model. When the institutions are added in, we also find that as natural resources become less illicit and vulnerable to looting stability rises at the .10 level. At the institutional

---

[1] Robust regression models are used here in place of traditional OLS models. These models are ideal for correcting for outliers such as those that are present in a data set of this sort.

Designing Democracy in a Dangerous World

TABLE 4.3 *Stability and diagnostic variables*

	Coefficient (standard error)	
Majority segment	0.169	(0.124)
Ethnic fragmentation	0.050	(0.127)
Population	−0.089	(0.118)
Geographical concentration	−0.081	(0.117)
External threat	−0.011	(0.159)
Belief in the nation	0.311	(0.123)**
Focus of the fight	−0.074	(0.161)
Income	0.381	(0.114)***
Inequality	−0.098	(0.127)
Dependence on natural resources	−0.185	(0.098)*
Type of natural resources	−0.147	(0.101)
Colonial legacy	0.034	(0.095)
Ancien regime	0.331	(0.130)**
Military threat	0.169	(0.106)
Culture of accommodation	−0.004	(0.102)
Type of transition	−0.046	(0.125)
Level of violence	−0.403	(0.384)
Antigovernment activity	−0.006	(0.120)
Constant	−0.028	(0.092)
Pseudo r^2	0.66	
F	5.68***	

Note: $n = 62$.
*Significant at $p < 0.10$ (two-tailed).
**Significant at $p < 0.05$ (two-tailed).
***Significant at $p < 0.01$ (two-tailed).

level as the electoral system becomes more proportional, stability increases. A more proportional electoral system seems to have as much effect on stability as belief in the nation and the type of former regime. This mirrors Pippa Norris's finding that proportional representation electoral systems are positively correlated with democracy, when compared to majoritarian systems, and the finding is even stronger when the analysis is limited to plural societies (Norris 2008: 123).

UNPACKING DEMOCRACY

When it comes to democracy – as measured by the aggregate POLITY score – there is very little to tease out from the background diagnostic variables on a quantitative level. The correlations between the independent variables and democracy (measured at the time of the first election, in 2007, the difference between the *ancien regime* score and 2007, and the first election year score and 2007) are all low. OLS regressions show that the variables do a poor job of predicting

TABLE 4.4 *Stability with diagnostic variables and institutions*

	Coefficient (standard error)
Majority segment	0.100 (0.102)
Ethnic fragmentation	0.049 (0.125)
Population	−0.103 (0.120)
Geographical concentration	−0.081 (0.112)
External threat	−0.093 (0.143)
Belief in the nation	0.251 (0.120)**
Focus of the fight	−0.008 (0.150)
Income	0.452 (0.109)***
Inequality	−0.052 (0.124)
Dependence on natural resources	−0.235 (0.095)**
Type of natural resources	−0.186 (0.096)*
Colonial legacy	−0.052 (0.097)
Ancien regime	0.242 (0.116)**
Military threat	0.104 (0.091)
Culture of accommodation	0.060 (0.099)
Type of transition	−0.014 (0.114)
Level of violence	0.106 (0.086)
Antigovernment activity	−0.093 (0.119)
Electoral system	0.229 (0.099)**
Federal-unitary	0.051 (0.094)
Executive inclusion	−0.138 (0.115)
Presidential-parliamentary	−0.135 (0.106)
Constant	0.036 (0.075)
Pseudo r^2	0.71
F	5.70***

Note: $n = 62$.
*Significant at $p < 0.10$ (two-tailed).
**Significant at $p < 0.05$ (two-tailed).
***Significant at $p < 0.01$ (two-tailed).

democracy scores by themselves: only wealth and levels of violence even approach statistical significance. Is our lack of diagnostic power over democracy (as opposed to the good job the variables do on predicting stability) due to the fact that even a robust case history of a fragile state tells us almost nothing about its propensity to be democratic? Or is the aggregate POLITY democracy score too much of a blunt instrument to assess how context and democratic design matters?

Munck and Verkuilen (2002) note that all existing aggregate measures of democracy, when it comes to consistency or robustness, fail in some important respect. Trier and Jackman (2008) point out that this may be an inevitable product of trying to measure the immeasurable, or at the very least "democracy is multifaceted and hence not well characterized by a single indicator." They argue that a better way of qualitatively assessing how context and institutions effect democratization is to unpack the POLITY score into its component parts. The single score used earlier is in fact a composite score of six factors (competitiveness of Executive Recruitment (Xrcomp), Openness of Executive Recruitment (Xropen), Executive constraints/decision rules (Xconst), Regulation of Participation (Parreg), Competitiveness of Participation (Parcomp), and Regulation of Executive Recruitment (Xrreg)). These six sort into three categories – Executive Recruitment (XR), Executive Constraint (XCONST), and Political Participation (PAR); by using these scores separately we can see whether our diagnostic and institutional variables have purchase on specific areas of democratization.

EXECUTIVE RECRUITMENT

By taking the elements of POLITY separately we are able to learn more about which background and institutional variables are influencing different areas of democratic development (see table 4.5). When it comes to how democratic executive recruitment is, we find that as wealth rises, executive recruitment scores also rise, and as the size of the largest communal groups rises to be a dominant majority, executive recruitment scores increase. Surprisingly, as the historical level of instability rises, executive recruitment scores also rise. We also find that as dependence on natural resources decreases, the level of democracy increases, and in a challenge to the thesis that power-sharing regimes are more democratic, as executive inclusion decreases, executive recruitment rises.

EXECUTIVE CONSTRAINTS

When it comes to the extent of constraints on executive power, the variables that matter change to some degree (see table 4.6). Statistically significant variables in the executive constraint model, which were also significant in the executive recruitment model, are a dominant majority group, dependence on natural resources, previous levels of instability, and executive inclusion. All are in the same direction as the previous model on recruitment. New variables that seem to matter to executive constraints, but not recruitment, are: as belief in the nation increases, external constraints increase; as resources become more legal and less vulnerable to looting, external constraints increase; and as the *ancien regime* becomes less oligarchic, external constraints increase. This is the only model where the type of transition has a statistical effect. This aspect of democracy is correlated with replacements, rather than pacted negotiations (transplacements) between the *ancien regime* and opposition. At the institutional level, as the legislative electoral system becomes

TABLE 4.5 *Executive recruitment with diagnostic variables
and institutions*

	Coefficient (standard error)
Majority segment	0.700 (0.168)***
Ethnic fragmentation	−0.237 (0.239)
Population	−0.015 (0.223)
Geographical concentration	0.211 (0.187)
External threat	0.132 (0.259)
Belief in the nation	0.193 (0.184)
Focus of the fight	0.011 (0.230)
Income	0.453 (0.175)**
Inequality	−0.012 (0.203)
Dependence on natural resources	−0.587 (0.152)***
Type of natural resources	0.130 (0.147)
Colonial legacy	−0.149 (0.158)
Ancien regime	0.264 (0.190)
Military threat	0.178 (0.150)
Culture of accommodation	0.093 (0.164)
Type of transition	−0.234 (0.184)
Level of violence	−0.209 (0.129)
Antigovernment activity	0.565 (0.195)***
Electoral system	0.061 (0.159)
Federal-unitary	−0.044 (0.189)
Executive inclusion	−0.870 (0.179)***
Presidential-parliamentary	0.172 (0.179)
Constant	7.121 (0.121)***
Pseudo r^2	0.57
F	4.48***

Note: $n = 56$.
*Significant at $p < 0.10$ (two-tailed).
**Significant at $p < 0.05$ (two-tailed).
***Significant at $p < 0.01$ (two-tailed).

more majoritarian executive constraints improve, and as the executive becomes more parliamentary the extent of democratic constraints on the executive increase.

POLITICAL COMPETITION

The purchase of our diagnostic and institutional variables on the vibrancy of political competition is the most powerful of all the models (see table 4.7). A dominant majority group, natural resource type, higher previous levels of instability, and a

Table 4.6 *Executive constraints with diagnostic variables and institutions*

	Coefficient (standard error)
Majority segment	0.280 (0.137)**
Ethnic fragmentation	0.110 (0.172)
Population	−0.255 (0.161)
Geographical concentration	−0.012 (0.135)
External threat	−0.285 (0.194)
Belief in the nation	0.456 (0.133)***
Focus of the fight	0.253 (0.170)
Income	0.078 (0.128)
Inequality	0.023 (0.150)
Dependence on natural resources	−0.383 (0.110)***
Type of natural resources	0.207 (0.108)*
Colonial legacy	0.159 (0.114)
Ancien regime	0.598 (0.145)***
Military threat	0.187 (0.115)
Culture of accommodation	−0.143 (0.120)
Type of transition	−0.661 (0.141)***
Level of violence	0.300 (0.450)
Antigovernment activity	0.690 (0.156)***
Electoral system	−0.278 (0.121)**
Federal-unitary	0.179 (0.138)
Executive inclusion	−0.425 (0.130)***
Presidential-parliamentary	0.427 (0.131)***
Constant	5.980 (0.105)***
Pseudo r^2	0.57
F	9.56***

Note: $n = 55$.
*Significant at $p < 0.10$ (two-tailed).
**Significant at $p < 0.05$ (two-tailed).
***Significant at $p < 0.01$ (two-tailed).

replacement (rather than pacted) transition are all correlated with higher political competition. New to this model are the following. Political competition scores increase when the geographic concentration of population groups increases, wealth increases, the colonial legacy moves away from being Anglophone, and the culture demonstrates a history of accommodation. Political competition also increases when ethnic fragmentation decreases but the geographical concentration/separation of groups heightens, the level of external threats falls, the military has a history of staying out of politics, and the *ancien regime* becomes more oligarchic.

Further, as the level of violent death during the conflict years decreases, political competition increases (a finding at odds with instability as measured by Banks which does not include battlefield deaths), and that while poverty decreases political competition, economic inequality actually increases it.

TABLE 4.7 *Political competition with diagnostic variables and institutions*

	Coefficient (standard error)
Majority segment	0.306 (0.162)*
Ethnic fragmentation	−0.854 (0.230)***
Population	0.346 (0.215)
Geographical concentration	0.822 (0.181)***
External threat	−0.847 (0.249)***
Belief in the nation	0.198 (0.177)
Focus of the fight	0.011 (0.222)
Income	0.441 (0.169)***
Inequality	0.433 (0.196)**
Dependence on natural resources	−0.148 (0.147)
Type of natural resources	0.397 (0.142)***
Colonial legacy	0.267 (0.153)*
Ancien regime	−0.607 (0.183)***
Military threat	0.626 (0.145)***
Culture of accommodation	0.469 (0.158)***
Type of transition	−0.370 (0.178)**
Level of violence	−0.680 (0.125)***
Antigovernment activity	0.503 (0.189)**
Electoral system	1.191 (0.153)***
Federal-unitary	−0.997 (0.182)***
Executive inclusion	0.104 (0.173)
Presidential-parliamentary	0.515 (0.173)***
Constant	7.24 (0.117)***
Pseudo r^2	0.58
F	12.69***

Note: $n = 56$.
*Significant at $p < 0.10$ (two-tailed).
**Significant at $p < 0.05$ (two-tailed).
***Significant at $p < 0.01$ (two-tailed).

Last, institutional design seems to have most impact on that element of democracy which is about political competition. As electoral systems become more proportional, as states become more unitary and less federal, and executives become more parliamentary, political competition increases.

SUMMARY

Our quantitative models suggest that stability and democracy are driven by somewhat different things, and what might bring stability to a nation-state in the early days of rebuilding from conflict can be at odds with evolving a vibrant democracy.

Designing Democracy in a Dangerous World

TABLE 4.8 *Summary of significant variables*

	Stability	POLITY (democracy)		
		Executive recruitment	Executive constraints	Political competition
Demographic		Majority +	Majority +	Majority +
				Fragmented −
				Concentrated +
Sociopolitical	Nationalism +		Nationalism +	External threat −
Economic	Income +	Income +		Income +
				Inequality +
	Natural res −	Natural res −	Natural res −	Natural res −
	Resource type −		Resource type +	Resource type +
History				Colonialism +
	Ancien reg +		*Ancien reg* +	*Ancien reg* −
				Military +
				Culture +
			Transition −	Transition −
Severity				Violence −
		Antigov +	Antigov +	Antigov +
Institutions	Elect sys +		Elect sys −	Elect sys +
				Federalism −
	Ex inclusion −	Ex inclusion −	Ex inclusion −	Parliamentary +
			Parliamentary +	Parliamentary +

The regression models using stability as the dependent variable imply a framing role for those elements of history that cannot be changed, a contributing effect for those socioeconomic characteristics that are changeable (however glacially that occurs), and last, and most importantly, a significant effect for some of the choices of political institutions in the new dispensation. There is historical molding, but not historical determinism, when it comes to a nation's hopes for political stability. The framing variable that matters and can be considered rigid is the nature of the *ancien regime*. The quantitative analysis also found significant effects of wealth and the state's dependence on natural resources and their type. More wealth, a reduced reliance on natural resources, and fewer illegal and lootable resources all predict increased stability. These are traits which can be changed, but very slowly. However, the statistics also posit a role for the "quick fixes" of democratic design. The choice of electoral system especially affects the chances of stability.

There is overlap between what drives stability and what drives democracy. As Table 4.8 illustrates, having a lower dependence on natural resources enhances the chances for stability and improvements on two of the three dimensions of democracy. Higher national incomes enhance stability, executive recruitment, and political competition (but not the constraints placed on the executive).

A stronger belief in the nation and a more oligarchic *ancien regime* helps stability and executive constraints (but not political competition). Proportional electoral systems seem to improve both stability and political competitiveness in emerging democracies, but not executive constraints. Parliamentary regimes (as opposed to presidential regimes) actually improve executive constraints and political competition (but nothing else), while the military's historical absence from politics helps political competition. Socioeconomic inequality is also correlated with higher political competition. In essence a division between the haves and have-nots may not be particularly healthy for stability but it remains a core element of a vibrant electoral democracy. Last, Anglophone countries have lower levels of democratic political competition. Again, an eerie reflection of colonialism – the British Empire maintained a veneer of stability with a heavy hand of constrained political competition.

Then there are the anomalies. Broadly inclusive governments of national unity, made up of multiple parties and communal interests, actually are correlated with lower POLITY scores when it comes to the executive. Second, our other measure of "severity of the conflict" – Banks' measure of riots, strikes, assassinations, etc – supports the hypothesis that certain types of political instability before democratization leave a positive legacy for the vibrancy of political competition post conflict. Higher levels of antigovernment mobilization before democratization are correlated positively with all three elements of democracy, but if death rates are higher then political competition is actually lower. It is a murky picture but if nothing else it suggests that different types of instability and conflict in a state in crisis have different consequences when that state ultimately seeks to democratize.

The remaining chapters of this book will build upon the quantitative framework offered here, and make the case that a qualitative analysis of the impact of the other institutional choices I have outlined (legislative type, executive type, degree of legislative inclusion, and decentralization) demonstrate that these other elements of democratic design also matter greatly to chances for democracy and stability in fragile, developing world nations.

## 5

Elections and Inclusion: Electoral Systems

This chapter focuses on elections and the systems that they operate under. The history of democratization has demonstrated that competitive elections are always important historical moments – they have ushered in change, rebirth, and renewal. Yet while elections are the bedrock events of any democracy they are also the political institution most open to manipulation. The electoral moment is fraught with fragility. As often as elections have been positive events, they have also precipitated moments of crisis which exacerbated ethnic conflict, political breakdown, and social instability. Key to understanding whether elections are likely to bring progress or instability are questions as to whether the political sphere is ready for competitive elections and how the elections themselves are designed and operated. The electoral system, or how the votes cast are actually translated into seats, has a huge impact not just on inclusion and exclusion but also on the tone of the entire political system. The system will also craft the space for corruption and vote rigging – it will not eliminate the space for malfeasance, but it can limit it. For these reasons, the crafting of appropriate electoral systems is one of the key factors shaping democratization and political conflict.

It has become de rigueur to debunk the emphasis that international aid missions and scholars place on elections as the holy grail of democratic transitions in post-conflict states. In *War, Guns and Votes*, Paul Collier argues that when elections are superficial – corrupt, flawed, and "ethnic" – political violence is heightened and the resulting governance is worse than it would have been if the government had not been chosen through any sort of elections at all. Despots are seemingly "legitimized" through stolen elections and substantive participation never penetrates beyond the existing elites (2009).

Blaming elections for causing political conflict is like saying "the roof leaks... we should live outside to stop getting rained on," no... you should mend the roof. The roof is generally a good thing; it just needs to be built in a way that fits the house. Fortunately, Collier's broader argument is more sophisticated than "all elections in poor places are bad." His analysis is that "elections tend to work better in societies that have larger populations and fewer ethnic divisions. They also tend to work better in polities with checks and balances on the power of government, and in particular where the elections are properly conducted." It is John Stuart Mill's argument that free institutions are next to impossible in a country made up of different nationalities, redone a century later. And while

Collier has the kernels of a point, he fails to build in the crucial variable of institutional design, which, as chapter 4 indicates, contributes to whether elections promote conflict or accommodation.

Clearly, one good election does not a democracy make, nor should foreign assistance and attention atrophy soon after the first votes are counted. The Sudanese scholar Francis Deng (2008: 132) says it well: "democracy is a concept that advocates popular participation in the political, economic, social, and cultural life of the country through ongoing, sustained comprehensive reforms and measures, not just at the election polls." But while accepting that elections without democracy impoverish and often retard progress, elections themselves remain a focal point for elites and lay the foundation for what comes after – good or bad. Elections are the first stage of public involvement in ratifying or crafting that element of a peace process which is about governance. Partly this is symbolic but it is also substantive and the only way popular control can be born. The state asks for consent from the people for its rule. The American declaration of independence notes that "legitimate governments derive their just powers from the consent of the governed" (see Pomper 2008), but there is also a practical element in the sense that elections select the leaders who will then share the spoils. This is especially meaningful if society and voters are ethnically segmented. The election becomes the guiding principle for a just sharing of the resources of the state. It provides a census, not just of parties and ideologies, but of the component parts of society. Elections legitimize some leaders and delegitimize others and without national elections there can be no democratization or any chance of an enduring self-sustaining peace process. As Diamond (2008: 26) notes, "while free and fair elections are only one component of democracy, they are the most indispensible one." O'Donnell also stresses the cathartic moment that elections represent in transitions from authoritarian rule. "This is not because such elections will necessarily lead to wonderful outcomes. It is because these elections…mark a crucial departure from the arbitrariness of authoritarian rule. When some fundamental political freedoms are respected, this means great progress in relation to authoritarian rules and gives us ample reason to defend and promote fair elections" (O'Donnell 2004: 188).

Elections are not only transition points, they are repeatable moments which become critical to democratic development. As Bunce (2008) points out, democratic breakdowns often happen in reaction to national elections, the repetition of elections seems to enhance democratic quality, and aid for elections is the only area of foreign support which is clearly correlated with improved democratic performance. Over time good elections sustain the democratic investment. "People are more likely to express support for democracy when they see it working to provide genuine political competition, including alternation of power, and when it has at least some effect in controlling corruption, limiting abuse of power, and ensuring rule of law" (Diamond 2008:161).

When elections in a democratizing state do not work well the architecture of democracy has no foundation to stand on. In the last decade Afghanistan, Mongolia, and Singapore have exemplified three ways in which failed elections retard democratic progress. In Afghanistan in 2005, contrary to popular opinion, the elections were not won and lost by fraud but rather they failed because the legislative electoral system fragmented parliament and precluded the development of a party system[1] (conversely the 2009 Presidential election failed because of fraud). In Mongolia, elections have become increasingly delegitimized since 1990, but again not because of irregularities but because the system is capricious in the way it handsomely rewards one party and penalizes the other when translating votes into seats (see Fritz 2008; Fish 2001). Singapore is the more stereotypical case where the system is rigged in a myriad of ways to stop the opposition from gaining a voice, let alone a majority (see Fetzer 2008).

ELECTORAL SYSTEM DESIGN

Elections are high-stakes games, and the rules of the game are the election system. Electoral system design is a crucial variable in democratic stability because it is the fault line where the inclusion of political parties and marginalized communities is either assured or defeated. The election system is often the key driver of power sharing or majoritarian government. As Norris shows the "core sequential steps" of consociational theory start with the inclusion of minority and majority groups through election systems that are either proportional or encompass positive action mechanisms. The theory says that this creates incentives for legislative and executive compromise and builds trust between hostile groups. As political stability is strengthened and violent conflict is reduced community members become more invested in supporting the power sharing democracy (see Norris' useful flow chart in *Driving Democracy* (2008: 105)).

This book highlights electoral systems as the most consequential of political institutions when it comes to promoting democratic participation. In chapter 4 we saw that electoral systems were predictors of stability and the executive constraints and political competition elements of democracy (POLITY). The more proportional a system, the more stability and political competition was enhanced, while at the same time proportionality was correlated with weakened executive constraints. Data on the inclusion in legislatures of marginalized

---

[1] See Andrew Reynolds (2006: 104–17).

groups in chapter 6 shows that proportional systems (and list PR in particular) include more representatives of minority groups than majoritarian systems. That inclusion then has an effect on public policy and levels of social tolerance.

These findings confirm, and build upon, Pippa Norris' findings that nations which use PR systems are more successful democracies, when holding other variables constant, and when the analysis is limited to just plural societies the results are even stronger. My analysis goes even further in associating PR with not just democracy but stability as well. But, as noted above, I do add the rider that when the unpacked POLITY scores are used, PR systems appear to weaken the executive constraint dimension.

In the terms of our medical metaphor proportional electoral systems are akin to antibiotics. In the vast majority of cases PR systems are helpful aids in fighting the social ailments of minority exclusion and interethnic hostility. They tend to help stabilize unhealthy states and if used appropriately can bring a different and more constructive tone to political competition. But just like antibiotics PR election systems will not be successful in every case. Sometimes the social ailment is antibiotic resistant, while in other cases the body politic has learnt how to counter the effects over time. Politicians and voters may find new ways of evading the incentives for accommodation and inclusion that proportional systems offer.

HOW AND WHEN DO ELECTORAL SYSTEMS MATTER TO STABILITY?

The impact of the electoral rules of the game is clearly heightened when the state is fragile to begin with. A Presidential candidate can win an election with half a million votes less than his opponent (say, for example, in the United States) with only chads being shed, not blood. But a similar outcome in say Nigeria would undoubtedly lead to significant violence and interethnic conflict. When elections were first envisaged in the post-conflict chaos of both Afghanistan and Iraq international advisers recommended systems of provincially based proportional representation to elect the parliaments of both Afghanistan and Iraq.

Unfortunately, neither country followed through on that advice. Iraq ended up using a national list PR system with disastrous consequences in their transitional Assembly elections of January 2005, while Afghanistan stumbled their way into using the Single Non Transferable Vote (SNTV) for their legislative elections in September of that year.

The national list PR system worked poorly in January 2005 in Iraq because it meant that low Sunni vote turnout resulted in a Constitutional Convention with almost no Sunni representation. In the months that followed interethnic violence spiraled out of control and a provincial list system (in which Sunnis would gain a "fair" share of the seats regardless of voter turnout in their provinces) was introduced for the December 2005 elections – a case of too little too late.

As I describe in more detail in chapter 8, in Afghanistan President Karzai created SNTV. The system resulted in much voter confusion and a highly fragmented parliament. While the experience of SNTV in fledgling democracies is limited, Afghanistan's problems with the system could have been predicted by the experience of Jordan since 1993. There, SNTV was deliberately introduced to maintain legislative fragmentation and disadvantaged the one embryonic party which did exist – the Islamic Front of the Muslim Brotherhood. In Jordan legislative politics revolves around clientelism, elections are effectively a lottery, and the malappointment of underrepresented urban areas (like Amman) versus over-represented rural areas, is compounded. All this delegitimizes the electoral competition further.

On a more positive note Nepal's electoral system for Constituent Assembly (CA) elections in 2008 facilitated steps towards democracy and away from civil war.

The primary goals of the 2008 elections were to move forward the peace process, to establish popular democracy as the governing rubric for conflict resolution, and to draft a permanent constitution acceptable to all significant groups. Thus, to be deemed successful, the 2008 election had to produce an Assembly which maximized inclusion, even if that inclusiveness came at the expense of some degree of parliamentary coherence; gave rise to results that were transparent, legitimate, and reassuring to majorities and minorities; allowed the political elites to be invested in the democratic process; and had agency to govern. Nepal chose a parallel system of both districts and PR lists. While there were problematic areas of the electoral process overall, the system performed very well in the criteria noted above.

In terms of representativeness, the parallel system produced a very high level of inclusion along the dimensions of ideology, geography, ethnicity, caste, and gender. Twenty-five parties and two independent candidates won seats in the CA. The Maoists received the largest seat bonus from the First Past the Post (FPTP) elections, but they still won only 38 percent of the assembly seats, necessitating coalitions to govern. The representation of the historically marginalized mountainous and southern regions was significantly improved over previous parliaments. Further, the assembly is one of the most ethnically inclusive in the world. The PR quota was a significant aid to minority inclusion; in addition previously marginalized groups won FPTP seats even where no quota was applied. Madhesi won 34 percent, Dalits 8 percent, Janajatis 33 percent, and candidates from "backward regions" won 4 percent of seats (Vollen 2008). Women won 191 (33 percent) of the Assembly seats.

TRENDS IN ELECTORAL SYSTEM REFORM

There has been considerable innovation in electoral system design and reform around the globe. Recent changes or proposed reforms in Palestine, Mongolia, Lebanon, Bosnia, Liberia, Jordan, Zimbabwe, Guyana, and Fiji illustrate a variety of criteria that states wish to address through their election systems: (*a*) that the system is perceived to be fair, in that all major interests are represented in parliament; (*b*) that it avoids anomalies in the results which would lead to illegitimacy; (*c*) that there is space for cross-cutting, multiethnic parties; (*d*) that women and minorities are given fair access to representation; (*e*) that internal party democratization is promoted; and (*f*) that the geographic connection between a voter and her representative is maintained in the interests of accountability. But of course there are less noble and less obvious reasons for change. These include regimes which wish to hang on to power through manipulation, decision makers who misunderstand the consequences of reform, and governments who wish to punish other parties or individual MPs. Electoral system change is often a response to public pressure but not always.

I have identified fifty-nine cases of significant election system reform in fifty countries between 1989 and 2009. These are cases of legislative elections moving between families of election systems (i.e., from FPTP to a parallel mixed system, or from a parallel system to a list PR system) and not of changes within systems (i.e., changes to district or parliamentary size, threshold, or between open and closed ballots) or to elections for executive or subnational bodies. If one added in these more detailed reforms (which can be just as consequential) then the scope of electoral system reform over the last two decades would be seen to be much higher.

While there are nuances, the trend in macro electoral system reform is clear (see tables 5.2 and 5.3). Over 38 percent of all the cases recorded moved into the proportional column, while 70 percent of the changes were in a proportional direction (including majoritarian systems that moved to semi-PR). Only three cases (5%) moved in the opposite direction (Liberia, Italy, and Bulgaria). Two cases (3%) changed their electoral system family (from list to MMP) but stayed proportional. Over half of all the cases moved away from plurality-majority systems (FPTP, Two Round System (TRS), Alternative Vote (AV), and the Block vote) while only five (9%) moved towards majority systems. The growth of hybrid/mixed systems is also significant. Twenty-three cases (40% of all changes) moved to using a parallel or mixed member proportional election system for their national legislative elections. Only eleven cases moved away from mixed systems and all but two of those cases were countries with parallel systems which moved to become fully proportional by using lists (Bulgaria moved back to parallel in 2009). Indeed, most of the serious proposals for election reform over the past few years have revolved around making systems less majoritarian and more proportional (e.g., Zimbabwe, Kenya, the United Kingdom, and Canada).

THE CONSEQUENCES TO DEMOCRACY OF
ELECTION SYSTEM CHANGE

If one looks at the change in polity score after electoral system change the overall trends indicate that countries moving from more majoritarianian systems to more proportional systems are associated with democratic improvements, while nations which shift their systems in the opposite direction see a concurrent weakening of democracy. The forty cases in Table 5.1 where nations moved from majoritarian to PR or semi-PR systems averaged an increase of 0.87 on the POLITY scale from the date of change to 2007 (or a subsequent change). The five cases of movement in the other direction demonstrated no improvement. There was also variance in democratic trajectories of states that changed systems but stayed within electoral system families. The four countries which changed systems but stayed majoritarian were, on average, 2.25 lower on the polity scale by 2007. The two moves within the PR family averaged 2.0 lower, while Taiwan and Japan who moved from SNTV to Parallel (both semi-PR systems) improved their polity score by 5.5.

There has been a general and in places dramatic increase in the number of women in parliament around the world (see chapter 6) but in the universe of nations that have changed their election systems the data suggests that becoming more proportional increases the share of women legislators by almost 8 percent. Bolivia and Venezuela who stayed proportional but moved to MMP increased their number of women on average by over 10 percent. There is insufficient data to assess the three cases that became more majoritarian but the cases that shifted systems within the majoritarian family only demonstrated a 0.9 percent increase.

In sum, these rough indicators suggest that becoming more proportional helps with democratic consolidation, becoming more majoritarian is a wash, and moving within systems is usually more negative than positive. These trends are, of course, highly contingent on a plethora of other variables. Sierra Leone did not jump from an anarchic military dictatorship to a more hopeful fledgling democracy because it shifted from first past the post to PR in 1996, but the fact that Sierra Leone endures as a democracy in 2009 may have something to do with the inclusive institutions it has used over the past decade and a half. Similarly Thailand's democracy did not collapse because of its shift from the Block vote to a parallel system in 2001 but the new electoral game did facilitate Thaksin Shinawatra's dominance of Thai politics between 2001 and 2006, which in turn

Designing Democracy in a Dangerous World

TABLE 5.1 *Electoral system changes, 1989–2009*

	Old electoral system	New electoral system	Year of change
Afghanistan	FPTP	SNTV	2005
Albania	TRS	MMP	1992
Albania	MMP	List PR	2008
Algeria	TRS	List PR	1997
Armenia	TRS	PAR	1995
Azerbaijan	PAR	FPTP	2005
Bermuda	BLOCK	FPTP	2002
Bolivia	List PR	MMP	1997
Bulgaria	PAR	List PR	1991
Bulgaria	List PR	PAR	2009
Cambodia	TRS	List PR	1993
Colombia	SNTV	List PR	2006
Congo (DRC)	TRS	List PR	2006
Croatia	PAR	List PR	2000
Estonia	STV	List PR	1992
Fiji	FPTP	AV	1999
Italy	List PR	PAR	1993
Iraq	FPTP	List PR	2005
Japan	SNTV	PAR	1996
Jordan	BLOCK	SNTV	1993
Kazakhstan	TRS	PAR	1999
Kyrgyzstan	TRS	PAR	1995
Kyrgyzstan	PAR	TRS	2005
Kyrgyzstan	TRS	List PR	2007
Latvia	TRS	List PR	1993
Lesotho	FPTP	MMP	2002
Liberia	FPTP	PR	1997
Liberia	PR	FPTP	2005
Lithuania	TRS	PAR	1992
Macedonia	TRS	PAR	1998
Macedonia	PAR	List PR	2001
Moldova	TRS	List PR	1994
Monaco	TRS	PAR	2003
Mongolia	TRS	BLOCK	1992
Mongolia	BLOCK	FPTP	1996
Mongolia	FPTP	BLOCK	2008
Montenegro	PAR	List PR	2006
Montserrat	FPTP	TRS	2001
Nepal	FPTP	PAR	2008
New Zealand	FPTP	MMP	1996
Palestine	BLK	PAR	2006
PNG	FPTP	AV	2002
Philippines	FPTP	PAR	1998
Russia	TRS	PAR	1993
Russia	PAR	LIST PR	2007
Rwanda	FPTP	List PR	2003
Serbia	PAR	List PR	2008
Sierra Leone	FPTP	List PR	1996

TABLE 5.1 *(Continued)*

	Old electoral system	New electoral system	Year of change
South Africa	FPTP	List PR	1994
Sudan	FPTP	PAR	2010
Tajikistan	FPTP	PAR	2000
Taiwan	SNTV	PAR	1992
Thailand	BLOCK	PAR	2001
Timor Leste	NA	PAR	2001
Timor Leste	PAR	List PR	2006
Tunisia	BLOCK	PAR	1994
Ukraine	TRS	PAR	1997
Ukraine	PAR	List PR	2006
Venezuela	List PR	MMP	1993

Note: Fifty country cases, fifty-nine cases of electoral system change.[2]

prompted military overthrow. There are a few exceptions to the general trends: when Russia moved from a parallel system to a list PR system in 2007 it made the country less democratic, not more so, but the reform package within which the electoral system change came was entirely aimed at doing this. Fiji's shift from FPTP to a complicated system of Alternative Vote elections helped precipitate a coup, and thus destroyed democracy. Liberia has become slightly more democratic since its 2005 shift from PR to FPTP but it remains early days.

WHAT DRIVES CHANGE?

There are a variety of driving factors behind significant electoral system reform, but none of them seem to be centered on voters coming together and demanding change. The electorate's perception of electoral system fairness may well be a contributing a factor to reform, and eventually which system is chosen, but there are few cases (outside of New Zealand) where the citizens successfully promote and engineer the change.

In many developing world nations, new election systems are component parts of institutional reforms which are part of a broader peace settlement. This was the case in Nepal, South Africa, and Sierra Leone who each sought to increase

---

[2] I am grateful for the advice given by Matthew Shugart, Ben Reilly, Rob Richie, Nigel Roberts, David Farrell, and Jorgen Elklit while compiling this list. There are somewhat technical disputes among the great and the good of the electoral systems world when it comes to exactly how certain systems should be classified – for example, Italy, Mexico, and Colombia, in particular. In these cases the table follows the personal advice of Shugart and Roberts.

Designing Democracy in a Dangerous World

TABLE 5.2 *Direction of electoral system changes*

Old system	New system				
	Majority	PAR	MMP	List PR	SNTV
Majority	Bermuda	Armenia	Albania[e]	Algeria	Afghanistan
	Fiji	Kazakhstan	Lesotho	Cambodia DR	Jordan
	Mongolia[a]	Kyrgyzstan[b]	New Zealand	Congo	
	Montserrat	Lithuania		Iraq	
	PNG	Macedonia[c]		Kyrgyzstan[p]	
		Monaco		Latvia	
		Palestine		Liberia[f]	
		Philippines		Moldova	
		Russia[d]		Nepal	
		Sudan		Sierra Leone	
		Tajikistan		South Africa	
		Thailand			
		Tunisia			
		Ukraine[l]			
PAR	Azerbaijan			Albania[h]	
	Kyrgyzstan[g]			Bulgaria[n]	
				Croatia	
				Macedonia[i]	
				Montenegro	
				Russia[j]	
				Serbia	
				Timor Leste	
				Ukraine[m]	
List PR	Liberia[k]	Italy	Bolivia		
		Bulgaria[o]	Venezuela		
SNTV		Japan		Colombia	
		Taiwan			
STV				Estonia	

Notes: [a] 1992, 1996, and 2008; [b] 1995; [c] 1998; [d] 1993; [e] 1992; [f] 1997; [g] 2005; [h] 2008; [i] 2001; [j] 2007; [k] 2005; [l] 1997; [m] 2006; [n] 1991; [o] 2009; [p] 2007.

TABLE 5.3 *Patterns of electoral system change*

Old system	New system				
	Majority	PAR	MMP	List PR	SNTV
Majority	7 (12%)	14 (24%)	3 (5%)	12 (21%)	2 (3%)
PAR	2 (3%)			9 (15%)	
List PR	1 (2%)	2 (3%)	2 (3%)		
SNTV		2 (3%)		1 (2%)	
STV				1 (2%)	

minority inclusion by switching to proportionality. Elsewhere the election system had to be simplified purely because of the anarchy of the state and its infrastructure collapse. Single-member districts could not be used in Liberia and DR Congo because of the mass internal displacement of citizens and logistical election administration concerns so nationally based (PR) systems had to be used. Third, there are reforms which are deliberately made by rulers to enhance their power and control over government. Vladimir Putin switched Russia from a mixed parallel system to one of national list PR in 2007 primarily to reduce the power, and existence, of rebellious regional politicians with their own power bases. King Hussein of Jordan transformed the block vote into SNTV in 1993 to curtail the space for an emerging Islamic front party born from the Muslim Brotherhood. In both cases the strategy of suppressing opposition through electoral system manipulation proved to be successful, at least in the short term.

It is striking that many high profile debates over significant electoral system change have focused on adding a list PR element to an existing FPTP systems (see the Jenkins report in the United Kingdom[3], post-2008–9 election debates in Kenya and Zimbabwe, and provincial debates in Canada). Pakistan entertained a mixed system in the 1970s and is doing so again post Musharaf, while some in Jordan see a mixed system as a way to develop new political space to enhance democracy. Palestine is looking to reform the balance of its mixed system, but not the essence, post-2008. Electoral system reform in the United States, the United Kingdom and to some extent in Canada, has focused more on preference voting (AV and STV), although reform at the US congressional level could only ever be a mixed option, even while any reform seems highly unlikely.

THE TENACIOUS FIRST PAST THE POST

With the myriad of problems inherent in both new and old democracies under FPTP is it appropriate that FPTP be chosen for *any* new democracy? As the data above illustrates, over the last two decades only Liberia has switched from PR to FPTP (in 2005), while Azerbaijan moved from a parallel system to FPTP in the same year. There are clear benefits for geographical representation and accountability inherent within single-member districts, especially in agrarian societies, and it is possible that under the *right* conditions FPTP will promote a robust and competitive two-party system, but the overwhelming evidence from a century of FPTP in the developing world suggests that FPTP should always be viewed with great suspicion in fledgling democracies. I would go as far as the blanket statement that it should never be used. As the quantitative evidence in chapter 4 shows,

---

[3] http://www.archive.official-documents.co.uk/document/cm40/4090/4090.htm

majoritarian systems suppress both stability and the political competition in emerging democracies. The specific and most consequential flaws of FPTP are: (a) It exaggerates and perpetuates regionally honed ethnic block voting and makes electoral politics a winner-take-all game of deadly consequences. (b) The system will more-often-than-not throw up vote-seat anomalies which injure the legitimacy of the results. (c) It will exclude from representation the very minority voices that most need to be heard. Even in stable, established democracies FPTP does a poor job of aggregating preferences but in those places the consequences, while significant, are less dire. We can point to FPTP having a significant role in the causes of violence in Kenya, Lesotho, and Mongolia, to name just three cases, while it is highly unusual to see a PR system cited as the cause of violence in any state. Then there are the logistical problems. A high number of internally displaced people not only place greater stress on the state to deliver basic services and humanitarian aid but they make decentralized single-member district election systems much more difficult to operate.

The argument that representation is enhanced and made manifest through small geographically defined districts is important. But as Carey and Hix show that requirement can be just as well addressed through a medium-size district list PR system or indeed a mixed MMP system of both lists and single-member districts.[4]

THE STRANGE LIFE OF THE BLOCK VOTE

If there is one system more poisonous to stability and democratization than FPTP it has to be the Block Vote (or "at large" elections as they are known in the United States).[5] The experience of the Block vote across all nineteen cases that currently use it have been problematic, but Mongolia, Palestine, Lebanon, and Singapore have displayed the most disturbing consequences. Mongolia is a fascinating but understudied case of democratization. Since 1990 the central Asian state has held five administratively successful elections but the ever-changing electoral system has produced anomalous results with polarizing consequences. The former communist party – The Mongolian People's Revolutionary Party (MPRP) which initiated glasnost in the early 1990s – won the first two elections (under a Two Round System in 1990 and the Block Vote in 1992) by dominating almost all of parliament with only a slim majority of the votes. In 1992, the Block Vote allowed them to win

---

[4] http://web.mit.edu/polisci/research/wip/Carey_Hix_Jan_2009.pdf

[5] Matthew Shugart correctly points out that the term "Block Vote" is in fact a poor descriptor for a system which should in fact be called the Multiple Non Transferable Vote (MNTV) but I will use it anyway. See http://fruitsandvotes.com/?p=2976#comment-173639 for Shugart's explanation of why "Block" is really "MNTV."

92 percent of the seats with only 60 percent of the votes cast. In 1996 the system was changed to FPTP but the anomalies *continued*. The opposition Democratic Party (DP) won only a few more votes but three-quarters of parliament. The former communists went back to winning every seat bar four in 2000 (with just over half the votes) and in 2004 the opposition Democrats came back to split parliament virtually down the middle, thirty-eight to thirty-four, with three seats taken by independents. Subsequently a grand coalition of both the former communists and democrats was formed which shared in executive positions and the crafting of legislation, but in January 2006 the ex-communists withdrew from the coalition in the hopes of forming a government with the support of independents. Mass demonstrations against their maneuver began in the streets of Ulaanbaatar.

In 2008 the electoral system was once again changed from FPTP back to the Block Vote and chaos ensued. The MPRP won 60 percent of the seats with the DP going down to 35 percent. The DP argued that the elections were rigged and that they did not accept the results. Protesters attacked the MPRP headquarters in Ulaanbaatar, five were killed, and a state of emergency was declared. While the DP did lose the legislature they regained the Presidency in a close race with the MPRP eleven months later.

Mongolia illustrates two key problems with the Block Vote: first that it is *super* majoritarian, and second that it consistently gives rise to the most extreme vote-seat anomalies. Singapore's system shows that Mongolia is no aberration. Between 1991 and 2006 the People's Action Party won between 61 and 75 percent of the popular vote, but won between 95 and 98 percent of the seats in the national parliament (or every seat bar one or two). The opposition Workers Party won 14 percent in 1997 but only a single seat. These anomalies can still dictate government formation even when the Block Vote is merely the majoritarian side of a mixed parallel system. In Palestine in 2006 the vote race was neck and neck between the incumbent Fatah and the challengers Hamas. Ultimately Hamas won 44.4 percent to Fatah's 41.4 percent. The sixty-six list PR seats were split almost evenly with twenty-nine going to Hamas and twenty-eight going to Fatah (nine to minor parties). But in the block vote elections for the remaining sixty-six seats, Hamas won forty-five and Fatah only seventeen. This gave Hamas seventy-four of the 132 Assembly seats and a comfortable governing majority – all on the basis of 44 percent of the votes. Hamas was able to exploit the flaws of the block vote with a smart candidate nomination strategy (Hamas nominated 0.9 candidates per seat, while Fatah nominated 2.9), and the better discipline of their voters to distribute their votes across Hamas candidates. Hamas were also smart enough to have their candidates put in their nomination papers together so they would appear as a block on the ballot.

The final great flaw of the Block Vote is that it often allows the majority to choose the minority representative, especially when seats are assigned to specific ethnic groups. This has long been the case in Lebanon's confessional electoral system where majority Sunnis can end up choosing the minority Maronite representative, or majority Christians can end up choosing the minority Shia representative from district to district. This is especially the case under a Party Block Vote system where a voter just votes for a slate rather than individual candidates, but because of the high degree of voter discipline in Lebanon the simple block vote resembles the Party Block Vote in this respect.

IS THERE A "BEST SYSTEM"?

It is something of a platitude in electoral systems research that there is "no best system" and indeed the specifics of any successful system are tailored to the distinct needs of a given case. But in fledgling and post-conflict democracies there does seem to be a need to place inclusion, and the political legitimacy it generates, high on the criteria that the system must fulfill. The inclusion of minority voices can be engineered through a variety of mechanisms: full proportionality, reserved seats for marginalized groups, or a proportional element to a mixed system.

Indeed, mixed systems are the dominant trend among states that have reformed their election systems. But as the discussion above illustrates, mixed systems do not always guarantee the same level of stability and inclusion as fully proportional systems. Nepal may be a positive case but clearly the parallel system in Palestine did not generate a stabilizing outcome. The Japanese Diet elections in 2009, that produced a huge majority for the opposition Democratic Party (DPJ), were far less controversial than the 2006 Palestinian Authority elections but the results were just as anomalous. The DPJ and their allies won 308 of the 480 seats (64 percent) but they only won 42 percent of the national popular vote. In the SNTV district side of the elections the DPJ won 221 of 300 seats (74%) with only 47 percent of the vote.

The evidence from Japan and Palestine bodes ill for the Sudan. In that fragile state elections for the national parliament in 2010 will be held under a mixed (parallel) system of FPTP districts and PR party lists. This was the product of the negotiated peace settlement between the Sudan People's Liberation Movement (SPLM) of the South and President Omar al-Bashir's Khartoum National Congress Party (NCP) regime in the North. Two hundred and seventy (60%) of the seats will be single-member districts, with the ten states of the South electing fifty-seven and the fifteen Northern states electing 223. There will be sixty-eight (15%) seats awarded from lists on the basis of party votes in the twenty-five state districts of the country (fifty-three in the North and fifteen in the South). The threshold to be entitled to seats under the PR allocation is 4 percent. Another 112 (25%) seats are reserved for women, awarded on a party list basis (eighty-eight in the North, twenty-four in the South).

TABLE 5.4　*Change in relation to democracy and gender representation*

	Democracy	Women MPs
More proportional	+0.87	7.9 (29)
Less proportional	0	NA
Stayed proportional	−2.0	10.7 (2)
Stayed majoritarian	−2.25	0.9 (3)
Stayed semi-PR[a]	+5.5	4.8 (1)

Notes: (X) number of cases. Democracy = Polity.
[a] Japan and Taiwan both moved from SNTV to parallel systems, for women the data is based only on Japan.
Source: Women MPs from http://www.ipu.org/wmn-e/world-arc.htm. (Data from 1997–2009; data was available for thirty-five of the fifty-eight changes.)

But the reality on the ground makes these seat allocations far less advantageous to the Northerners than it first appears. Nine states within the North are likely to vote overwhelmingly for Northern and Arab parties and candidates (even if not Bashir's NCP), but the other six are almost certain to reject the Northern elites overwhelmingly. The disputed territories of Nuba Mountains, Abyei, and the Blue Nile are geographically within the North but are likely to vote en masse with the South, if, of course, there is anything approaching a free election. The three large states that make up the Darfur region are, to say the least, unlikely to vote in large numbers for the government of Khartoum (but again this assumes the people of Darfur will be able to vote at all). Last, the Beja people living in the northeastern state of the Red Sea are the sleeping "Darfur." The paramilitary Beja Congress and Rashaida Free Lions have been skirmishing with the Khartoum government for years and feel just as marginalized from power as the Darfurians ever did.

President Bashir's NCP is not only unlikely to do well outside of the nine core states that he controls, but a variety of Arab and Islamic groups may strongly challenge him in his heartland. Bashir has never been tested in a free election and again, if there is any space for free choice, parties and voters may fragment. The NCP has a history of fracturing between moderates and hard-liners. A splinter group, the Popular Congress Party of Hassan al-Turabi, could do very well in popular elections. The Umma party of al-Mahdi also has little love for the existing Khartoum regime and has formed a common cause with Southerners in the past (and more recently with the rebel Darfur Justice and Equality Movement [JEM]). Bashir's NCP may well use its considerable carrots and sticks to build alliances with potential competitors in the North, but the success of such a project is far from assured.

In dramatic contrast, the forceful strategy of the SPLM over forty years has delivered them a dominant role throughout the South, because Nuer leaders like Riek Machar (Vice President of the South) and Shilluk leaders like Pagan Amum (General Secretary of the SPLM) have allied with the majority Dinka ethnic group. The SPLM is the only major player in town for the time being. While the National Assembly seats of the North will be shared among a multitude of players, the SPLM is likely to wipe out all electoral opposition in the South. They will win the FPTP seats and the women's seats and no doubt do well in the disputed territories, large parts of Darfur, and in the Southern Sudanese enclaves of Khartoum.

The electoral system actually reinforces this one-party dominance because there are not enough PR seats in the system to ensure proportionality in the South. Each southern state will have either one- or two-party list seats and thus any group wishing to challenge the SPLM will need more than a third of the state-wide votes to win a seat – a very high bar considering there is no serious opposition to the SPLM in the South.[6] However, in the North some states will have many PR seats – Khartoum (9), Southern Darfur (7), Gezira (6) – and in these districts minority parties will be able to steal seats away from the government.

All this is little more than educated guesswork, but it suggests that if elections approximate anything close to a free vote, the SPLM, along with its allies, could be the largest party in the new National Assembly of Sudan, perhaps with as much as 45 percent of the legislature. Not only would they be able to seize independence for the South, they could take control over the entirety of the state. But what would that predict for stability in the Sudan as a whole? Would the Southerners administer the North? One cannot imagine a scenario more likely to lead to renewed bloodshed. Of course, there will be national presidential elections at the same time, which may be tougher for any SPLM candidate to win. Even with support from the Beja, Southern Darfurians, and those in the disputed territories, the votes of the South may not be enough to challenge the Arab majority. The Comprehensive Peace Agreement of 2005 does ensure that a national President from the South must have a Northerner as their Vice President. But even if a Northern candidate does ride a tide of Arab unity to the Presidency, they may be facing a legislature controlled by the other side.[7]

The election system to be used in Sudan in 2010 is not finely tuned enough to respond to the tensions that elections will undoubtedly bring to that nation. But the elections are merely one cog in a wheel of many institutional arrangements that need to work together to stop conflicts being processed by the bullet rather than the ballot. Nevertheless, it has been proven beyond a doubt than authoritarian rule does not lead to stability in Sudan. The roof may still be leaky, but at least now there is a roof to mend.

---

[6] In June 2009 the former SPLM-nominated Sudanese Foreign Minister, Lam Akol, set up a rival SPLM-DC party but there is scant evidence to show any nascent electoral strength for the new party.

[7] In actuality the election proved to be very far from a free vote, opposition parties boycotted, and predictions of Bashir's electoral downfall were confounded.

If systems such as FPTP, SNTV, and the block vote are all beyond the pale and mixed systems are variable in their ability to deliver legitimate and inclusive outcomes, then we are left with the family of proportional systems when it comes to embryonic democratizing states. The Single Transferable Vote may be much beloved by academics but its preference vote, complex count, and anti-party elite ethos makes it almost impossible to sell to most politicians. That leaves us with either the mixed, but fully proportional, Mixed Member Proportional (MMP) system of New Zealand, Lesotho, and Germany (among others) or varieties of list PR. MMP has its advocates and powerful advantages but may not in actuality be any better at maintaining geographic accountability than small district list PR.

In their article "The Electoral Sweet Spot," John Carey and Simon Hix study 610 elections in eighty-one "democracies" between 1945 and 2006 to analyze the relationship between the electoral system and proportionality, coalition formation, government spending, human development, minority inclusion, and party system coherence. They find that there *is* an electoral "sweet spot" of list PR systems with a medium of approximately six members per district when it comes to maximizing the quality of governance and representation. Such smaller magnitude list systems are virtually as proportional and inclusive as the large district systems but much better at delivering public goods and forming stable governing coalitions (see Carey and Hix 2010). In *Voting for a New South Africa* (1991), I proposed a system of 300 MPs elected in thirty-seven multimember constituencies ranging from five to twelve members in size (with a mean of eight) alongside 100 additional national PR seats which would be awarded as "top-ups" to parties to guarantee overall proportionality. As Carey and Hix suggest the top-up seats may not have ultimately been needed, but the system would have corrected the disturbing lack of geographical accountability that has existed since large-district closed-list PR was introduced to South Africa in 1994.

6

Legislatures and Inclusion:
Marginalized Groups

This chapter builds on my core argument that inclusion is an integral part of stabilizing a fragile polity. Here the focus is on legislative inclusion, the descriptive representation of society within parliament. To get at this issue, I look at the representation of diversity through four lenses: gender, ethnicity, age, and sexual orientation. The gender dimension has received significant scholarly attention over the last quarter century but among the other three areas there has been almost no data measurement or scholarly analysis. I seek to answer four interrelated questions: (*a*) What are the varying levels of comparative representation in national legislatures for the four focus groups identified? (*b*) What explains those divergent levels of representation? (*c*) What is the value of the inclusion of marginalized groups in elective office? (*d*) What are the consequences of minority inclusion, and exclusion, when it comes to the adoption of policies that directly impact each group?

Over the last quarter century, the inclusion of women and ethnic minorities in national parliaments has increasingly been seen as an indicator of the strength of democracy in established democracies and as a *sine qua non* of democratization in the developing world. Much has been written about the growing numbers and influence of women MPs in the parliaments of the world (see Reynolds 1999; Baldez 2003; Wolbrecht, Beckwith, and Baldez 2008). In June 2008, the Inter Parliamentary Union (IPU) identified 6,834 female members of national lower houses (18.4% of the total).[1] Such *descriptive* (sometimes called "passive" or "symbolic") representation does not necessarily imply that the group votes together or that individual representatives see themselves as primarily "women MPs" or "minority MPs." But without some visible inclusion of the faces and voices of the historically marginalized it is likely that the interests of such groups are not at the forefront of decision-maker minds. A literature is also beginning to emerge on the existence and influence of ethnic minority MPs in national legislatures. The largest survey to date of minority MP presence (elected through both reserved seats and open seats) covered fifty nations and identified over a thousand MPs with an ethnic minority background (see Reynolds 2006). However,

---

[1] http://www.ipu.org/wmn-e/world.htm

two communities of interest that have not been analyzed to date are lesbian, gay, bisexual, and transgendered (LGBT) peoples and movements, and the political representation of younger adults (defined here as under thirty years of age). I include those as my third and fourth focus communities in this chapter.

For each community I seek to explain the factors which determine various levels of representation, and gauge the consequences of inclusion on policies which disproportionally affect the community of interest. Are levels of representation determined by the same factors across all four groups and what level of inclusion ensures that a marginalized group begins to effect national policy in a positive way? That is, are large numbers of women needed in parliament to effect "women friendly" laws while a very small number of openly gay legislators can make a significant impact on public policy? Do ethnic minority MPs ensure the protection and enhancement of marginalized minority groups while MPs under the age of thirty have little impact on "youth friendly" policy? Or conversely, are the issues around exclusion and representation consistent across marginalized groups, regardless of the identity which binds the group together?

THE IMPORTANCE OF REPRESENTATIVE INCLUSION

There remains a debate over whether descriptive representation leads to substantive (or active) representation, in which the interests of a given group are protected and enhanced by the presence of their own community in elected office. "Difference" theorists such as Phillips (1993) and Young (1989) believe that engineering a highly inclusive legislature, made up of all the significant majority and minority groups in society, is key to good governance and democratic stability. Young goes further arguing that groups should have veto power over policies which directly affect them (Young 1989). Similarly, Walzer (1994) and Cohen and Rogers (1992) argue that the state should enable such inclusive representation by actively promoting marginalized groups. But Dryzek (1996) offers a strong cautionary note. Arguing that democratization is more than just inclusion – it is about increasing the scope of issues brought under popular control and increasing the "authenticity" of that control – he notes than simple inclusion in elective office need not necessarily lead to improvements in the other two areas.

Indeed, Dryzek argues that if the interests of the group are not directly linked to the existing state imperative (powers of the state) then descriptive representation will only lead to symbolic rewards which are inadequate substitutes for more tangible benefits. Rather than be hoodwinked by tokenistic representation, the minority group should remain in the "oppositional sphere of civil society" from which almost all pressures for greater democracy emerge. Goodin (2008: 235) falls somewhere in between Phillips and Dryzek in arguing that attempting to include all the communal diversity of a nation in a legislative body becomes impossible and dangerous. Rather one should aim for "partial presence" where "merely being reminded if the sheer fact of diversity can have salutary effects on the behavior of such representatives."

The key to understanding these contending approaches is to recognize that disputes over the *best* type of representation are less about constituting parliamentary assemblies as end goals in themselves than they are about representation as an instrumental tool to advance, in a normative sense, a particular type of society, as Pitkin (1969: 20) points out:

> What position a particular theorist adopts on this range depends very much on how he sees and understands all of the substantive political issues involved: the nature of interest, welfare, or wants; the capacities of the representative and represented; the relationship between a nation and its subdivisions; the role of political parties and elections; and the very nature of political questions. It depends, in short, on what one might call his *metapolitics*.

Can descriptive representation lead to substantive representation when the numbers of minority legislators are very small? A fuller answer to that question requires an in-depth analysis of the case histories of individual MPs. But, as Pitkin (1967) notes, the mere presence of marginalized community representatives in a legislature is a significant, if still symbolic, sign of tolerance. Guinier (1992: 292) asserts that in the United States, "black legislative visibility . . . is an important measure of electoral fairness. This is especially true when black Americans largely vote together and often will vote for a black candidate if one is on the ballot. Indeed, there is anecdotal evidence that familiarity breeds tolerance (see Smith and Haider-Markel 2002). The presence of minority members in a legislature aids in breaking down intolerance and in building alliances that cut across pre-existing cleavages within society. Openly gay MPs sometimes act as advocates for "gay issues," but they almost always must build alliances with heterosexual sympathizers. The same is true of women and ethnic minority caucuses. Rarely have any of our four focus communities been numerous enough to flex their political muscles as voting block with leverage, but even a handful of minority politicians can be legislative entrepreneurs, who help set agendas and educate their colleagues on issues. Indeed, the mere existence of minority faces in government acts as a spur to other members of that group to become involved in matters of civic responsibility. If people believe they have no ability to initiate change through the democratic process, feelings of their alienation may push them to initiate acts that attack the system. The sight of role models, who look like them, in positions of power, is more likely to invest them with a sense of democratic opportunity.

There is evidence to suggest that the representation of marginalized groups is correlated with policy which benefits the marginalized group. Summarizing the study of women in political office, Reingold (2008: 128) says that a "clear, empirical link" has been established "between women's descriptive and substantive representation." The links may sometimes be murky, but, by and large, women in office are more likely to take liberal positions, more likely to support feminist proposals, and more likely to take the lead on women's issues. Thus, their presence leads to a greater likelihood of "women friendly" policies being adopted (Saltzstein 1986; Crowley 2004; Reingold 2008). Similarly, in the realm of ethnic politics, there is evidence that the election of black and Hispanic state legislators in the United States produces policy outcomes which benefit the communities represented (Eisinger 1982; Saltzstein 1989; Bratton 2002; Bratton and Haynie 1999).

However, for a marginalized community to have an impact must it reach a certain level of representation to be effective? Critical mass theory posits that the number and proportion of minority group legislators has to reach a certain level before significant policy impacts are felt. Grey (2002) and Saint-Germain (1989) placed that threshold at 15 percent. But Bratton (2005) and Crowley (2004) find that even a small number of "token" women in US State Legislatures make a significant difference to public policy issues that primarily effect women. Indeed, Bratton (2005: 121) argues that "women serving in legislatures with little gender balance are actually *more* successful relative to men than their counterparts in more equitable settings." This implies that the very nature of a small "token" legislative insurgency enhances the influence of the group seeking policy change.

If even a tiny number of politicians from marginalized groups do indeed make a difference to public policy then what is the mechanism at work? As noted earlier, minority MPs can act as advocates, educators, and physical embodiments of a community shut out of public life. When the gay legislator becomes a person with a name, human talents and foibles, aging parents and young children, sport team obsessions, and opinions about the latest TV show, it becomes more troublesome for many of their parliamentary colleagues to overtly discriminate against them through legislation. Harvey Milk extrapolated on the importance of openly gay candidates running, and winning office, in his "Hope" speech of 1978.

> Like every other group, we must be judged by our leaders and by those who are themselves gay, those who are visible. For invisible, we remain in limbo – a myth, a person with no parents, no brothers, no sisters, no friends who are straight, no important positions in employment. A tenth of a nation supposedly composed of stereotypes and would be seducers of children…a gay person in office can set a tone, can command respect not only from the larger community, but from the young people in our own community who need both examples and hope.[2]

---

[2] As quoted in Shilts (1982: 362).

Countering stereotypes is particularly important for any marginalized group, no more so than gays and lesbians; but women, ethnic minorities, and the young also have to challenge the assumptions of power of men, dominant ethnicities, and the not-so-young any more.

However, the nature of political mobilization and appropriate remedies to address such exclusion for each of the communities can be quite different. As Htun (2004) notes, women are usually dispersed across territory and cut across partisan divisions, while ethnic groups can be geographically concentrated and are more likely to vote as a block for a political party. For Htun this affects both potential remedies and the ultimate goal of group representation. Women are more likely to seek (and achieve) representation through quotas and list proportional representation systems but "realign themselves as a category" once they have power, and the group identity "tends to weaken and dissipate." In contrast ethnic minorities seek group rights which are "reinforcing rather than self-cancelling" and lobby for reserved seats to have their "particularism recognized and legitimized" (2004: 451).

Are LGBT communities like women, ethnic groups, or neither? They are geographically and ethnically dispersed like women but they do tend to vote for parties that are sympathetic to their "group" needs. LGBT representatives may cut across partisan politics in many countries but once a significant number are elected they are likely to still promote policies that are, to some degree, based on their sexual orientation identity. Young voters are more like women in that they are geographically dispersed, and while they may favor one or more political parties, they still vote across partisan lines.

SUMMARY OF OVERALL REPRESENTATION
OF MARGINALIZED GROUPS

As noted earlier, as of 2008 there were 6,834 female members of national lower houses (18.4% of the total) based on the Inter Parliamentary Union's survey of 189 national parliaments (see Appendix 6.F). In a survey I conducted of ethnic minority representation in fifty nation-states in 2007, I found out of 115 distinct minority groups fifty-four were "over-represented" in their national legislatures while fifty-nine groups were under-represented (two were exactly on the nose when proportion of population was compared to proportion of parliamentary seats held). In these fifty countries there were 1,510 MPs, or 13.6 percent of the total (see Reynolds 2007). As of December 2008 there were sixty-six openly gay Members of Parliament (MPs) found in eighteen national legislatures. This represents an average of 0.0015 percent per legislature (based on 187 national legislatures) and an average of 2.4 percent in the eighteen legislatures that do have open LGBT members.

TABLE 6.1 *Descriptive representation summary (national legislatures)*

	No. of MPs	MPs (%)	No. of Cases
Women	6,834	18.4	189
Ethnic minorities[a]	1,510	13.6	50
LGBT	66	0.0015	189
Young adults	506	5.2	72

[a] 2007, other data for 2008.

Finally, in the seventy-two legislatures that I have data for the age of legislators, there are 506 MPs under the age of thirty (usually 18–29) which represents 5.2 percent of the total (see Table 6.1).

ETHNIC MINORITIES AND REPRESENTATIVE INCLUSION

When the first democratic National Assembly convened in Cape Town, South Africa, in 1994 it was the living embodiment of Archbishop Desmond Tutu's dream of a rainbow nation. A parliament which was not merely elected by all but included all. Blacks sat with whites on the government's benches, colored MPs joined with Afrikaners in opposition. But beyond that the Assembly of 1994 contained Zulus, Xhosas, Twanas, Sothos, Ndebele, Venda, Pedi, along with Indian South Africans, Anglo-Whites, and Afrikaans-speaking Cape Coloureds, and Afrikaans speakers of Dutch and French Huguenot descent. The descendants of Mohandas Gandhi, Henrik Verwoerd, and Govan Mbeki sat together – side by side on the benches of the African National Congress. The theory of power-sharing governance rests heavily on the belief that without adequate descriptive (even over-representation) marginalized minorities may destabilize the polity (see Lijphart 1977; Reynolds 1999).

South Africa's ethos of political inclusion has waned over the last sixteen years but the over-representation of minority groups still remains the norm. While the inclusion of minorities is less dramatic in most other parts of the world there is not a nation-state, rich or poor, democratic or not, where minority groups do not press for their voices to be heard at the highest levels of decision making. Most countries seek to create at least a small space for minorities in their national parliaments: there are Christians and Samaritans in the Palestinian Authority, Maoris in the New Zealand house, nomadic Kuchi in the Afghan Wolesi Jirga, white African MPs in Zambia and Zimbabwe, German-speaking MPs in Poland, and Roma members of the Romania parliament. Whether these representatives are enough, have influence on government policy, or are even *representative* of the minority groups they come from are debatable questions, but when minority communities have no representatives in national legislatures we can be pretty sure that those minority groups are not being heard in the policy dialogue, their rights are being trampled, and their importance to electoral competition is slim. In fragile and divided societies, ensuring that a significant number of minority MPs are elected is a necessary, if not sufficient, condition of short-term conflict prevention and longer term conflict management. There is not a single case of peaceful democratization where the minority community was excluded from representation.

Perhaps of most importance, the inclusion of both majorities and minorities within national parliaments can reduce group alienation and violence in those divided societies where politics is often viewed as a win or lose game. Many peace settlements have revolved around inclusive electoral systems or reserved seats for communal groups as part of broader power-sharing constructs. There is a debate about how best to include minority MPs. Should systems be designed so that minorities can be elected through "usual channels" or are special affirmative action measures needed like quotas or special appointments? Furthermore, is it better when minority MPs represent "minority parties" that are rooted in an ethnic community, or should they be integrated into the "mainstream" parties which may be ideologically driven or dominated by majority communal groups?

Ethnic Minority MPs: the Numbers

As Appendix 6.A illustrates, just under half, or twenty-three, of the nation-states surveyed over-represent their minorities when seat share is compared to population share, while the remaining twenty-seven cases, on average, under-represent minority groups. The league table is based on 115 distinct minority groups in the fifty countries. A few minority groups have MPs in legislatures in numbers well above what their population share would suggest. Most notable are Zanzibaris in Tanzania, Whites in South Africa, Maronites in Lebanon, Croats in Bosnia, Walloons in Belgium, Sunnis in Iraq (December 2005 legislative election), and Herero in Namibia. Sometimes minorities achieve significant representation because their members vote in higher numbers than other groups but more often the "over-representation" is a product of special mechanisms (such as reserved seats or geographical malapportionment). In contrast, Russian speakers in Latvia and Estonia, Serbs in Montenegro, Albanians in Macedonia, Bosniaks in Bosnia, Arabs in Israel, and Catalans in Spain are all significantly under-represented.

The top of the league table is something of a surprise. No single type of country consistently over-represents minority populations. The top ten most "inclusive" legislatures in the world are found in Africa, Europe, Oceania, North America, and the Middle East. Some are peaceful, wealthy, Western democracies, while others are poor, democratically weak, and wrestling with ethnic divisions which still turn violent. The strands that unite the countries which over-represent their minority communities are four-fold: first, there are post-conflict democracies where minority inclusion was a core plank of the power-sharing settlement which brought about an end to civil war and the beginnings of multiparty democracy; for example, South Africa, Lebanon, Bosnia Herzegovina. Second, there are nation-states that entrenched power-sharing democracy over a century ago and while the pressures for minority inclusion may have ebbed over time the norm of inclusion has remained strong, for example, Belgium. Third, there are cases which do well on the inclusion of minorities in their parliaments because significant elements of society and party politics are sensitive to minority issues and value minority candidates, for example, the Netherlands, Canada, and New Zealand. Last, there are countries where the very geographical concentration of a minority group allows such groups to gain significant representation in their national legislatures, for example, Tanzania.

Interestingly the three top cases are all Sub-Saharan African cases: South Africa, Tanzania, and Namibia. Why should these new and sometimes troubled states produce parliaments which are so inclusive of their many minorities? The South African parliament is the most ethnically representative of any democratic legislature in the world. For the reasons discussed below, the promotion of multi-ethnic parties and the deliberate "over-representation" of minorities was the watchword of the first decade of democracy in South Africa. The same has been true in Namibia where the liberation movement, the South West Africa People's Organisation (SWAPO) while being rooted in the Ovambo majority, sought to present itself as a catch-all party similar to the ANC or Congress Party of India. In the current Namibian National Assembly ten distinct ethnic groups are represented and the majority Ovambo group (representing 60% of the population) only has 50 percent of the seats. It is true that the Congress of Democrats (COD), Democratic Turnhalle Alliance of Namibia (DTA), United Democratic Front (UDF), National Unity Democratic Organisation (NUDO), Monitor Action Group (MAG), and Republican Party (RP) opposition parties have non-Ovambo (bar one) MPs, but SWAPO has six Kavango, five Nama, four Caprivian, four Herero, three white, two Damara, two Baster, a colored and San representatives. Tanzania's high spot is a result of the over-representation of the island of Zanzibar in their national assembly.

South Africa is an interesting case study of the positive good of including minorities in governance over and above their population size. Post-apartheid South Africa has consistently done well on indicators of minority representation as a result of two pressures toward accommodation. First, the post-apartheid peace-settlement of 1994 (and permanent constitution of 1996) rested upon a universally accepted principal of multiethnic inclusion in the new politics of the nation. A principal beyond that of mere equality, which emphasized the very opposite of the former apartheid laws, that is, in the new South Africa, government would deliberately reach out to minorities to visibly demonstrate their full role in governance. Second, it quickly became apparent that to be successful any

Xhosa party had to reach out to non-Xhosas, a Zulu party would atrophy if Zulu nationalism remained its *raison-d'être*, and White parties could only gain leverage if they became multiethnic vehicles. Thus, the African National Congress under Nelson Mandela deliberately placed Zulus, Whites, Coloureds, and Indians high up on their lists of candidates between 1994 and 2009. This diversity goes beyond the simple black–white divide. As a "catch-all" national movement, the ANC seeks to exist in a universe beyond the Xhosa community which has historically dominated its leadership. It strives to attract the votes of Sothos, Tswanas, Vendas, Pedis, Ndebele, along with Zulus in KwaZulu, Coloureds in the Cape, and English and Afrikaans-speaking Whites throughout the country. These appeals are often based on policy promises but just as much on having senior "ethnic" politicians high up on the party lists. The same has been true for the opposition, the white dominated Democratic Alliance place non-white leaders in visible positions, and was even true for the now defunct National Party who in their failure to attract sufficient non-white leaders and voters were ultimately subsumed into the ANC in the most remarkable power-shift between too long opposed movements in the history of modern politics. While the level of minority over-representation declined under Thabo Mbeki and Jacob Zuma, it still exists as of 2009. Nevertheless, consolidating democracy and stability will rest upon continuing this ethos of minority inclusion and respect.

The deliberate reaching out to smaller minority groups and institutions designed to ensure the widest inclusion possible were particularly key in 1994 when South Africa made its first tentative steps to a multiparty electoral democracy. Two very small parties gained representation in the first National Assembly (the Freedom Front and Pan-Africanist Congress of Azania) facilitating conflict resolution by democratic rather than violent means. Although the Afrikaner Freedom Front only won nine (or 2%) of the seats the importance of their inclusion in democratic structures was disproportionate to their numbers. General Constand Viljoen's Freedom Front represented a volatile Afrikaner constituency that could easily have fallen into the hands of white supremacist demagogues such as Eugene Terre'blanche had its representatives been shut out of the political process. As it was Viljoen, as former head of the South African Army, became chair of the National Assembly's Defence Select Committee and the paramilitary Afrikaner resistance faded away.

Representing a very different place and time, the inclusion of minority politicians in Canada over the last decade demonstrates a second positive example of how majority politics can provide a space to hear and reassure minority communities. Electoral system specialists would expect the first-past-the-post (FPTP) system of elections in Canada to provide a high hurdle to the election of non-white, non-majority MPs, but Canadian parties and voters have managed to circumvent the majoritarianism of their Anglo election system to produce a parliament which includes, and over-represents, Francophone, Asian, and Canadians of African extraction. Inuits are under-represented in the House of Commons but they have some access to self-governance through the semi-autonomous province of Nunavut.

The inclusion of French-Canadian politicians in large numbers is perhaps unsurprising considering the powerful leverage Quebec has long had over national Canadian politics but much smaller minorities are also heard in parliament. As of 2008 there were twenty-one MPs from minority backgrounds in addition to the French-speaking MPs – ten of South Asian extraction, five Chinese, four African or Afro-Caribbean, one Middle Eastern, and one Canadian Inuit. Importantly, these minority MPs are not clustered in "ethnic" political parties. Twelve are in the opposition Liberal Party, six in the governing Conservative party, two in the Bloc Quebecois, and one in the New Democratic Party. The spread of minority MPs across parties is mirrored in the Netherlands where the fifteen MPs of African, Turkish, Moroccan, Iranian, or Afro-Caribbean background are split between Christian Democratic Appeal (CDA) (four), Green Left GL (four), Labour Party (PvDA) (three), Peoples Party for Freedom and Democracy (VVD) (two), List Pym Fortuyn (LPF) (one), and Democrats 66 (D66) (one). While the Netherlands does demonstrate the progress that can be made when parties and voters promote multiethnicity, the country also illustrates the reality that even in the most progressive polities issues of minority rights and respect can still be problematic and vulnerable to anti-immigration elements of society.

The bottom of the league table is also a jumble of very different countries. Half of the bottom ten are Central European/Baltic states that democratized in the early 1990s and in those cases the underrepresentation is focused on Russian, Albanian, or Serb minority communities. Nevertheless, only in Montenegro is the Serbian community assessed by MRG International as being significantly "under threat." Outside of Central Europe, the most under-represented minorities are found in Israel, Brazil, and Spain. All ten cases represent very different levels of human development, wealth, and democracy.

One of the most important cases that scores poorly on the indicator of minority inclusion in parliament is Afghanistan. On one level there was a high degree of diversity in the first post-Talbian Afghan Wolesi Jirga elected in 2005: there were fifty-three Tajiks, thirty Hazaras, twenty Uzbeks, and twenty-eight others, representing minority communities outside of the largest ethnic group, the Pashtuns. There were significant "minority" leaders in parliament and government. Yunus Qanooni (a Tajik) is Speaker of the Wolesi Jirga, Mohammed Mohaqeq (a Hazara) received the most votes of any candidates in Kabul, and Rashid Dostom (an Uzbek) was made Chief of Staff of the Afghan National Army. Ten seats are reserved in the Assembly for the nomadic Kuchi population. President Karzai's cabinet is also diverse and minority MPs can be found within both on the pro-government and opposition benches, but as Appendix 6.A shows each of the four main minority groups is under-represented in the legislature, while the largest group, Pashtuns, is over-represented. This became a sensitive political issue as Tajiks from the

Northern Alliance and Uzbeks from the North feel increasingly marginalized by what they term the "Pashtun mafia" which surrounds President Karzai.

Explaining Ethnic Minority Representation?

What explains minority inclusion in legislative politics: electoral systems, development, or level of democracy? There are often calls for special reserved seats to ensure and encourage minority access to elected office but while such mechanisms can help, the data suggest that such seats only have a limited role in promoting minority representation. Half of the countries that reserve seats for minorities end up over-representing them, while the other half under-represent. Just over half the countries that do not have reserved seats under-represent their minorities but the other half manage to over-represent despite having any special mechanisms.

When it comes to electoral systems we can discern patterns in the data but the results are again surprising in certain respects. The five countries that use the Block Vote and Mixed-Member Proportional (MMP) systems do best at including minority faces but Lebanon and New Zealand drive those high figures. Interestingly FPTP systems, long criticized for providing hurdles to minority representation, do better than list proportional systems. But again the average scores can be misleading as seven of the top ten states in the league table use List PR election systems (see table 6.2).

Does Ethnic Minority Representation Impact Policy and Minority Rights?

As noted earlier, the inclusion of some minority MPs within a national legislature is only the first step toward minority protection. One could imagine a situation where a few token minority MPs were elected (or appointed) but minority rights remained severely curtailed. So is there a relationship between the number

TABLE 6.2 *Minority representation and electoral system*

	FPTP	List PR	MMP	PAR	TRS	STV	AV	BV	SNTV
Average	−0.2	−1.8	0.3	−2.3	−0.7	−0.3	−1.3	1.4	−7.9
# cases	11	26	3	1	2	1	3	2	1

Notes: These scores are based on the Least Squares Index used to aggregate minority under/over-representation, invented by Michael Gallagher of Trinity College Dublin to measure electoral system disproportionality. In principle it treats one group with 15 percent of the population but no seats as a *more* disproportional outcome than fifteen groups each winning 1 percent less of the seats than their population share would suggest. Thus the measure gives a more accurate impression of minority inclusion. See Appendix 6.A for details.

of minorities in parliament and the level of security enjoyed by minority groups? Are minorities more at risk when they are under-represented and does their presence in parliament reduce the discrimination and threats they face? There is only a limited relationship between minority MPs and the degree of threat minority groups live under. Most of the top twenty cases are either not ranked at all in the Minority Rights Group's *People's Under Threat* (PUT) index, or are ranked lowly among the 130 cases assessed by MRG International. However, Bosnia (#20 in the PUT index), Sri Lanka (#22), and Iraq (#2) all make it into the minority representation top twenty illustrating the fact that sometimes minorities can gain significant political representation and still be marginalized from real decision making influence and live under significant challenges to their security.

Conversely, three of the bottom five countries in the league table are not considered to have minorities under immediate or serious threat: Spain (#109), Latvia (#110), and Estonia (#113). The implication is that while Russian speakers are excluded from the political sphere in the Baltic states, they do not suffer the level of discrimination and insecurity in other aspects of their lives that many other minorities do. The low Spanish score may relate to the fact that Catalans, and the Basque region, in Spain have a semi-autonomous regional assembly which possesses significant self-governing powers. The under-representation of Catalans in the Spanish Lower House is not an indicator of marginalization, rather a product of minority rights being taken care of outside of the national political scene. The same case could be made to justify the under-representation of Sami in Norway (there is a Sami parliament) and Inuits in Canada (the new province of Nunavut has some autonomous powers).

LESBIAN, GAY, BISEXUAL, AND TRANSGENDERED (LGBT) REPRESENTATIVE INCLUSION

There is evidence from state legislative politics in the United States that even tiny numbers of openly gay legislators can have a positive impact on legislation. Using data from the late 1990s, Haider-Markel, Joslyn, and Kniss (2000) found that the presence of openly gay legislators has a positive impact on the adoption of domestic partner benefits. In a more extensive study based on data from 1992–2002, Haider-Markel (2007) finds that descriptive representation was associated with the passage of a variety of LGBT-related bills. This effect persists above and beyond those of ideology, interest group strength, and public opinion. Furthermore, higher numbers of LGBT legislators increase the likelihood of laws that ban discrimination of the basis of sexual orientation. The study also found however, that the presence of LGBTs in public office heightened a legislative backlash against gay rights. Overall though the presence of openly gay legislators produced a positive net result for the LGBT community (Haider-Markel 2007). Moreover, even unsuccessful campaigns for office may assist in creating a more positive environment for the passage of progressive law. Wald, Button, and Rienzo (1996) find that antidiscrimination policies were more likely in cities where open LGBT politicians had run for office but lost.

Appendix 6.B identifies sixty-six openly LGBT current members of national assemblies/lower houses drawn from eighteen countries at the end of 2008. The largest number is fourteen in the British House of Commons, and the largest percentage is 5.3 percent in the Dutch parliament.[3] Forty-nine MPs identify themselves as gay men, fourteen as lesbians, two as bisexual, and one as transexual. The majority of LGBT MPs are found in the established democracies of Western Europe, North America, or Australasia (sixty of the sixty-six), but there are two Africans, two Latin Americans, one in the Middle East, and one in Asia. The current crop of sixty-six is undoubtedly the largest collection of openly gay MPs in history, although there were significant individual cases of openly gay MPs in earlier times. Those nations who have had gay MPs before, although they currently have none in their national assemblies, include Hungary, France, Belgium, Portugal, and India. In Spain, Jeronimo Saavedra Acevedo served in the lower house from 1977 to 1996, then moved to the Senate (until 2003), coming out as gay in 2000.

The growth in openly gay legislators has been significant if not dramatic. In 1998, there were fewer than twenty openly LGBT MPs around the world. Today there are over sixty. At the executive level Jóhanna Sigurðardóttir became Prime Minister of Iceland on February 1, 2009, while Per-Kristian Foss had briefly been acting Prime Minister of Norway in 2002. At the subnational level, the growth in LGBT elected officials has been more impressive. The American-based Gay and Lesbian Victory Fund identifies 764 appointed and elected officials worldwide (August 2008), at all levels of government. The vast majority are at the local level.[4] In the United States, there were approximately twenty out-of-the-closet gays and lesbians in elected office in 1987, fifty-two in 1991, 146 in 1998, and 180 in 2000 (Smith and Haider-Markel 2002: 185–6). By 2003, the Fund noted that 218 of the roughly 511,000 Americans in elective office were openly LBGT – less than 0.05 percent. Three served in Congress, forty-seven in state legislatures, and the rest in local government. As of August 2008, the total number of LGBT officeholders in the United States had tripled to 602, including seventy-nine state legislators and twenty-eight mayors.

[3] The Netherlands is the single case in the data set based on 2006, rather than 2008, data.
[4] http://www.glli.org/out_officials

Explaining Differing Levels of LGBT Candidate Success

A variety of factors could explain the differing levels of representation of openly gay candidates for high office. On the institutional level, one might consider political party ideology and the type of electoral system. Left parties are more likely to have ideologies rooted in the protection and promotion of marginalized communities, while socially liberal parties are more likely to be tolerant of different sexual orientations. Studies have also found significant links between electoral system variation and the chances of minority and female success and thus the system used should also affect a marginalized and geographically diverse community like LGBTs.

Sociocultural variables such as (*a*) the level of social acceptance of homosexuality and (*b*) the religious orientation of the state could also have an impact. The higher the acceptance of sexual diversity among the electorate, the more likely it is that openly gay MPs will be selected and elected. While mainstream religions fall on a continuum which is mostly negative in their attitudes toward homosexuality, some religions are more overtly discriminatory than others. Finally, one might hypothesize that the level of (*c*) democracy and (*d*) human development also could influence the hurdles placed in front of openly gay political candidates. Established democracies are more likely to be based on a civil rights foundation and higher levels of LGBT activism, and social acceptance are correlated with higher levels of human development.

Institutional Explanations

As predicted the majority of openly gay MPs are members of left or post-materialist parties (thirty-four of sixty-six or 51%) but a surprisingly large number (fifteen of sixty-six or 23%) are from ethno-nationalist or conservative parties. This seems to indicate that the total number of gay MPs remains small enough that successful candidates often are remarkable individuals who overcome barriers in a variety of political movements. Certainly, left or socially liberal parties are more likely to have ideologies sympathetic to gay inclusion; but voter hostility to gay equality (and party leadership reticence) still precludes mainstream parties from putting up substantive numbers of openly gay candidates. However, as the total number of gay MPs grows we would expect a higher proportion of them to come from left or liberal parties across the world.

Political history suggests that electoral systems matter greatly to the chances of openly gay candidates being elected. Harvey Milk attempted twice to win election to the San Francisco Board of Supervisors in the 1970s but under the "at large" (Block Vote) system used he was unable to attract enough city wide votes to be successful. However, in 1977, when the election system was altered to one of single-member districts, he won election from a district centered on The Castro and Haight-Ashbury neighborhoods. List proportional representation systems

TABLE 6.3 *Electoral systems and openly gay MPs (2008)*

	FPTP	List PR	MMP	PAR	TRS	STV	AV	BLK	SNTV
# MPs	23	29	14	0	0	0	0	0	0
# cases	42	72	10	19	20	2	3	12	3
Average %	0.1	0.2	0.6	0	0	0	0	0	0

are the most inclusive of women and minority candidates, and they tend to give political parties a means of bypassing some of the prejudices of the electorate, by putting minority candidates on their lists. These candidate lists are either closed (thus unalterable by the voters) or open to some degree, but often difficult for the electorate to reorder. It is true that when ethnic groups are heavily concentrated they are able to win seats in single-member district systems, but FPTP systems give an incentive for parties to run lowest common denominator candidates, very often a straight male from the dominant ethnic group. Thus women and gay candidates have a particularly difficult time winning FPTP seats unless there are some special mechanisms (e.g., reserved quota seats or affirmative action districting). I expect it to be more likely that LGBT members are elected from list proportional representation systems, than majoritarian systems.

The hypothesis is born out, but not entirely. As Table 6.3 indicates, twenty-nine of the sixty-six gay MPs were elected using List PR, while twenty-three were elected in single-member districts. If one includes all PR systems – List, MMP, and STV – the PR dominance is more obvious: forty-three of sixty-six MPs (or 65%) but two of the MMP MPs were elected from the single-member district side of their systems. The relative success of gay MPs in New Zealand, Germany, Italy, and Mexico means that MMP systems have the highest proportion of gay MPs, with approximately 1 percent (twelve elected from the lists, two from the districts). When all 184 country cases with direct elections are considered, FPTP parliaments have an average of 0.1 gay MPs while List PR parliaments are at 0.2.

We might expect that the seats won by openly gay MPs are more likely to be "safe" party seats and perhaps in liberal areas. However, the analysis is complicated somewhat by the fact that only eleven of the twenty-five single-member district MPs were out when first elected (see Appendix 6.D). When not out, the average time between being elected and coming out is 4.2 years. There is evidence to suggest that the majority of gay MPs are elected from relatively safe seats: if one takes marginal seats to be those held with less than a 5 percent majority, only three of the twenty-five are held with such slim margins. The average percentage margin of victory for "not out" candidates is 18 percent, for "out" it is 15 percent. Interestingly, all fourteen MPs who came out after being elected were subsequently re-elected.[5] Finally, there is a roughly even split between constituency

---

[5] Simon Hughes and Gregory Barker in the United Kingdom and Rob Oliphant in Canada have yet to stand for re-election since coming out.

type, with thirteen of the twenty-five MPs elected from urban districts and twelve from rural or suburban ones.

Public Attitudes Toward Homosexuality

Between 1999 and 2003, the fourth wave of the World Values Survey (WVS) asked respondents whether homosexuality was "justifiable" on a ten-point scale with one being "never justifiable" and ten being "always justifiable" (see Appendix 6.C). Indeed, gay MPs are found mostly in countries where a majority of people fall on the "justifiable" end of the scale (the highest being 7.8 in the Netherlands). But Mexico (WVS = 3.7), Brazil (3.2), and South Africa (2.9) have gay MPs, even with most voters categorizing homosexuality as unjustifiable. New Zealand (4.7), Italy (4.8), the United States (4.8), and Israel (4.9) are close to the center. However, having open LGBT MPs is clearly not inevitable, even in a progressive polity. Switzerland (6.1), Spain (5.8), Luxembourg (5.8), and Belgium (5.2) all fall on the "homosexuality is justifiable" end of the scale, but currently have no openly gay MPs (although Belgium and Switzerland are among those nations which have had a gay MP in the past).

Democracy and Openly Gay MPs

All the countries with gay MPs are "free" democracies, apart from Nepal (which may improve its democracy rating substantially if their Constituent Assembly can produce a new constitution). Most cases are long-established democracies; the exceptions are South Africa, Mexico, and Brazil, where democratic regimes are too young to be considered consolidated. While liberal democracies do dominate many full democracies do not have, or have never had, openly gay MPs. Most striking are the cases of Spain and Andorra, which have high scores on the progressive LGBT law scale (below) but no openly gay MPs in their national parliaments.

Gay MPs and Progressive LGBT Legislation

To delve into the relationship between the presence of gay legislators and progressive gay law I have collected data relating to six key legal areas. (*a*) Are same-sex acts between consenting adults legal? (*b*) Are same sex couples allowed to marry or form civil unions? (*c*) Can same sex couples and gay individuals adopt children? (*d*) Are there national/federal laws against discrimination on the grounds of sexual orientation? (*e*) Is homophobia a distinct category of hate crime law? (*f*) Does the state ban gay people from military service? (see Appendix 6.C for a summary score of these five measures).

In bivariate terms, there is a correlation between gay MPs' presence and progressive law (.44). The eighteen countries with gay MPs average 2.6 on the progressive law scale, while the fifty-eight nations with no gay MPs average 0.5 – a significant difference. But does a nation implement progressive laws when the parliament includes a handful of dynamic and persuasive openly gay MPs, or are we more likely to see openly gay MPs in a polity that has already demonstrated its commitment to equality through progressive laws? Laws initially promoted and passed by straight legislators.

Table 6.4 includes data on same sex marriage and partnership laws, whether there were gay MPs in the legislatures that adopted the laws, and the length of time between the first gay MP and the law being passed. Of the six countries with same sex marriage on the books all (bar Spain) had openly gay MPs in their chambers at the time the law was passed. Those five first elected a gay MP between seven and twenty years previously (an average of fourteen years between the first open gay MP, either elected or to come out, and the passage of a gay marriage law). When it comes to lesser civil union or registered partnership laws, five of the fifteen cases had openly gay MPs when their laws were passed (an average of five years between the first openly gay MP and the law). Conversely, the presence, or not, of open LGBT cabinet ministers does not correlate with the likelihood of marriage/partnership law.

These patterns are confirmed by the universe of countries with open LGBT MPs (eighteen) and without (fifty-eight). Ten of eighteen nations with openly gay MPs have passed same sex marriage/partnership laws (59%) while only eleven of fifty-eight countries without gay MPs (19%) have such laws. As Table 6.4 notes, the countries with the most progressive LGBT rights have had some level of gay representation for the longest time, and continue to do so today. The variation across the seventy-eight cases in my data set has remained remarkably constant. Only five of the seventy-eight cases had a gay MP in the legislature before 2008 but no longer in 2008, and of those five only Belgium passed a same-sex marriage law when they had a single gay MP (in 2003), and no longer do so today.

The OLS regression[6] in Table 6.5 considers the relationship between the number of open LGBT MPs in 2008 and the progressiveness of law in 2008.[7] This model, suggests a statistically significant relationship (negative because lower scores on the democracy indicator are given to more democratic regimes) between the degree of democracy and progressive laws. The results show that democracy

---

[6] With eight dependent variable categories, methodologists recommend using OLS in such a case and not an ordered logit analysis.

[7] While the model is cross national for 2008, and does not include the numbers of gay MPs over time, there is reason to believe that the 2008 MP levels are a good proxy for the time period since 1989 when gay rights laws were first adopted in a few countries. The overall numbers where much lower a decade ago but the patterns of presence and scale were very similar to 2008. The evidence outlined here on the correlation between the presence of gay MPs and the adoption of marriage or civil union laws backs up this intuition.

TABLE 6.4 *Same-sex relationship laws*

	Marriage year	Gay MPs in parliament?	First gay MP elected/out	Gay cabinet minister?	Govt. ideology
Norway	2008 (9)	Yes	1979 (29)	(2001–5)	LEFT
South Africa	2006	Yes	1994 (12)	No	LEFT
Canada	2005	Yes	1988 (17)	Yes	CENT
Spain	2005	No	—	No	LEFT
Belgium	2003	Yes	1996 (7)	No	LEFT
Netherlands	2000 (1)	Yes	1981 (19)	No	LEFT
	Civil Union/RP Year				
Hungary	2008 (9)	No	—	Yes	LEFT
Uruguay	2007 (8)	No	—	No	LEFT
Czech Rep	2006	No	—	No	LEFT
Andorra	2005	No	—	No	CENT
Switzerland	2005 (7)	Yes	1999 (6)	No	CENT
Luxembourg	2004	No	—	No	RIGHT
Slovenia	2005 (6)	No	—	No	CENT
New Zealand	2004 (5)	Yes	1993 (11)	Yes	LEFT
United Kingdom	2004	Yes	1984 (20)	No	LEFT
Finland	2002	No	2004	No	LEFT
Germany	2001	Yes	1985 (16)	No	LEFT
France	1999	Yes	1991 (8)	No	LEFT
Iceland	1996	Yes	1978 (18)	(1987–94)	RIGHT
Sweden	1995	No	1991 (4)	No	LEFT
Denmark	1989	No	1977 (12)	No	RIGHT

Notes: Year 2008(9) year passed (year enacted).
Jeronimo Saavedra Acevedo was a Spanish MP from 1977 to 1996 but did not come out until 2000. Andre Labarrere was a member of the French National Assembly 1967–8 and 1973–2001 and came out in 1998.
(X) Average time between first gay MP elected (or out) and marriage law is fourteen years. For civil unions the average time is five years.
"Government Ideology" at time of marriage/civil union/registered partnership legislation.
Sources: http://www.iglhrc.org/files/iglhrc/reports/990604-antidis.pdf, http://www.ilga.org/map/LGBTI_rights.jpg, http://en.wikipedia.org/wiki/Same-sex_marriage, http://en.wikipedia.org/wiki/LGBT_adoption, www.legislationline.org, http://www.stonewall.org.uk/information_bank, Kollman (2007), and Fish (2005).

matters but among democracies government ideology also has an impact. Left or liberal or post-materialist parties are more likely to enact progressive legislation as they campaign on ideologies which are rooted in social equality, support of the marginalized or individual rights. As Table 6.4 illustrated, a country is more likely to have some type of marriage or partnership recognition if the government is Left, with or without openly gay MPs, while marriage seems to require both Left-leaning governments and openly gay MPs in parliament.

In addition, public opinion is significantly linked with progressive laws. The public acceptance of gay people is also a strong predictor of progressive law. At first blush this finding is unsurprising. But it does indicate that politicians and governments have been responding to public opinion, and it suggests that, if the

TABLE 6.5 *Multivariate analysis, progressive laws*

Dependent variable: progressive laws	Coefficient (standard error)	Variable mean	Variable standard deviation
% gay MPs	0.26* (0.14)	0.38	1.08
Homosexuality justifiable?	0.24* (0.13)	3.35	1.85
Democracy	−0.22** (0.11)	2.58	1.91
Human development	1.41 (1.51)	0.83	0.13
European Union	0.27 (0.33)	0.30	0.46
Left government	0.76** (0.31)	0.41	0.49
Center government	0.38 (0.32)	0.17	0.38
Religion	0.38 (0.32)	0.26	0.44
Constant	−1.03 (1.26)		
N	69		
Model R^2	0.69		

Note: Homosexuality Justifiable: *World Values Survey*. Wave 4 (surveys conducted between 1999 and 2003).
*$p < 0.10$; **$p < 0.05$.
Source: http://www.worldvaluessurvey.org. Question V202: Please tell me for each of the following actions whether you think it can always be justified, never be justified, or something in between, using this card. "Homosexuality." Answered on a 1 to 10 scale with 1 being "never justifiable" and 10 being "always justifiable."
Democracy: Freedom House (2008) F = Free, PF = Partly Free, NF = Not Free.
Source: http://www.freedomhouse.org/template.cfm?page=410&year=2008
Government type: Left, Center, Right
Religion: Protestant/Buddhist/Hindu versus Eastern Orthodox/Catholic/Muslim.
Human development: UN Human Development Index 2005.
Source: http://hdr.undp.org/en/media/hdr_20072008_en_complete.pdf

general public becomes more supportive of sexual orientation equality, then governments may respond with broader laws accepting gay marriage, adoption, and legal protections. The correlation between gay-friendly law and the World Values Survey "is homosexuality justifiable" question is a high .74. The outliers are Hungary and South Africa (both with progressive laws out of alignment with their population's negative attitudes to homosexuality) and the Philippines, Greece, and Switzerland (whose moderately high acceptance of homosexuality is not reflected in progressive gay rights law).

Crucially, this model suggests that, even once public opinion, government ideology, and the degree of democracy are taken into account, the presence of openly gay legislators plays a not insignificant role in explaining policy outcomes. Human development, or religious type, on the other hand are not significantly linked with legal progressiveness.

YOUNG ADULTS AND REPRESENTATIVE INCLUSION

On average MPs who are under thirty years of age are one out of every twenty elected representatives, but in the seventy-two countries for which data is available the population share of 21–30 year olds is approximately 15 percent and citizens under 30 are often over half the population. As Appendix 6.E illustrates, the highest number of young MPs in parliament is often found in new and inchoate democracies in the developing world, and something of a rarity in established developing world democracies. Of the top ten cases for proportion of under thirty-year-old MPs only Norway and Denmark represent the world of consolidated democracies while four of the top ten are nondemocracies (Oman, Niger, Singapore, and Syria) where the legislatures are largely meaningless. The average share that young adults have in the parliaments of twenty-six established democracies is 2.6 percent, half of that of all seventy-two cases included in the data set (5.2%). Illustrative are the cases of the United Kingdom (with only three MPs under thirty years of age) and the United States, Australia, and Luxembourg (with none). However, this does not take into account the wide variations in population shares of people in their twenties (ranging from 9.9% in Japan to 25% in Sudan). For that reason the deficit league table is more illustrative of the comparative data (see Appendix 6.E). Here we find only four countries have more young MPs than their population share would suggest (Cape Verde, Oman, Antigua and Barbuda, and Estonia). The average deficit for the twenty-four established democracies in the data set is –9.22 versus –11.6 for all seventy-two cases.

TABLE 6.6 *Electoral systems and young adult MPs (<30) (2008)*

	FPTP	List PR	MMP	PAR	TRS	STV	AV	BLK	SNTV
# MPs	74	281	31	37	38	1	0	44	—
# cases	14	37	3	7	6	1	1	3	—
Average %	7.1	4.7	2.2	3.0	4.7	1.4	0	9.0	—
Deficit %	–12.0	–10.0	–13.6	–14.4	–16.2	–13.9	–13.2	–10.5	na

Notes: Average = 21–30 MP share of legislature.
Deficit = 21–30 MP share of legislature/21–30% of population.

TABLE 6.7 *Predictors of youth unemployment*

	Coefficient (standard error)	
% Youth in parliament	−0.065	(0.353)
GDP	−0.00007	(0.0001)
% GDP agricultural	0.377	(0.140)***
Polity score, 2007	−1.079	(0.374)***
Constant	−54.700	(4.175)***
r^2	0.34	
F	8.56***	

Note: $n = 71$.
*Significant at $p < 0.10$ (two-tailed).
**Significant at $p < 0.05$ (two-tailed).
***Significant at $p < 0.01$ (two-tailed).

When it comes to electoral systems the highest number of young MPs are elected from PR systems but on average FPTP and Block Vote systems do better at producing younger MPs (although with the Block Vote this is only based on three nondemocratic cases – Singapore, Syria, and Laos) (see table 6.6).

Younger MPs and Public Policy

To what extent does the presence of younger MPs in a legislature improve the social state for young adults? It is not immediately clear what the best proxy for a society friendly to young adults would be. Education policy and funding has many more dimensions and constituencies to consider than just the users, and maternal health care, while it primarily effects women under the age of 40, again is effected by much more than its beneficiaries. In a 2008 report the International Labor Organization warned that unemployed young people made up 44 percent of the world's unemployed despite being only 25 percent of the population.[8] High rates of youth unemployment have not merely deleterious economic consequences but create a hopelessness and helplessness which can morph into anti-system violence and criminality. To assess the impact of youth MPs on youth status I have taken the proportion of a nation's unemployment rate that is under thirty as my dependent variable.

Table 6.7 takes youth unemployment as its dependent variable and tests whether the presence of younger MPs improves unemployment levels. The regression also poses the questions: do more democratic countries do a better job at insulating the young from disproportionately being effected by unemployment? Do more agrarian societies have more access for young people to be gainfully employed? To what extent does the general state of the economy (captured by GDP per

---

[8] Global Employment Trends for Youth. ILO. Geneva. http://www.ilo.org/public/english/employment/strat/download/gety08.pdf

capita) effect youth unemployment? (see O'Higgins 2007). The regression shows that the percentage of youth MPs is not a predictor of unemployment but the degree to which the economy is dominated by agriculture and the level of democracy is significant. A one unit increase in the agricultural GDP leads to a .37 increase in youth unemployment. A one unit increase in the polity score decreases youth unemployment by 1.

WOMEN AND REPRESENTATIVE INCLUSION

In 1998 there were 4,209 women MPs in 180 national parliaments representing 12.5 percent of the total. A decade on, that number had risen to 6,834 in 189 parliaments representing 18.4 percent of the total. In previous work I found that for 1998 data the percentage of women in legislatures was determined by a patchwork of institutional and cultural variables (Reynolds 1999). Most significant were the level of female socioeconomic empowerment (as measured by the United Nation's Gender Related Development Index (GRDI)) and the electoral strength of left-wing parties. Also significant predictors were the number of years women had the right to stand for office, the number of multiparty elections, the effective number of political parties (fewer parties leading to more women elected). When Catholicism was taken as a baseline, Eastern Orthodox and Muslim nations had significantly fewer women in parliament. Last, in the late 1990s the electoral system had an important effect on the number of women who made it into high office. All electoral systems suppressed the number of women when compared to List PR, however, only FPTP and the Block Vote were statistically significant. Interestingly, democracy was not correlated with the number of female MPs.

I have rerun the models with similar independent variables for the 2008 data. In certain respects the determinants have changed. While democracy was not significant in 1998, in 2008 countries with higher democracy (POLITY) scores actually had fewer women MPs. This is indicative of the trend for new democracies to introduce quotas regardless of their democratic strength, and for old democracies to be resistant to affirmative action mechanisms to promote women in politics. Indeed, as Table 6.8 shows in 2008 having any form of quota system increases the number of women MPs by 8.7 percent (all else being equal). In 1998 the Gender Related Development Index and the number of elections were significant but they ceased to be so in 2008, but overall GDP was significant (higher GDP more women MPs) in 2008. When it comes to religion, Catholic countries continue to be correlated with more women MPs than Muslim nations but ten years on Protestant nations now predict more female MPs than Catholic nations (an opposite finding to 1998). The electoral system predictors remained consistent,

TABLE 6.8 *Predictors of women MPs (2008)*

	Coefficient (standard error)
Polity score	−0.41 (0.16)**
GDP	0.0003 (0.0001)***
GRDI	−4.70 (6.61)
Number of elections	−0.07 (0.17)
Quota system	8.66 (1.71)***
Religion	
Protestant	7.14 (2.31)***
Eastern Orthodox	−3.99 (2.92)
Islam	−4.02 (2.20)*
Other	1.36 (2.41)
Government	
Center	−4.56 (2.62)*
Right	−6.36 (1.77)***
Other	−8.24 (2.35)***
Electoral system	
Block Vote	−7.22 (3.46)**
Two round	−5.28 (2.63)**
Alternative vote	12.72 (5.36)**
FPTP	−7.91 (2.27)***
SNTV	−15.98 (8.59)*
Parallel	−0.76 (2.59)
SDV	−9.88 (8.71)
MMP	−2.70 (2.88)
Constant	25.97 (4.61)***
r^2	0.51
F	6.48***

Notes: $n = 144$.
*Significant at $p < 0.10$ (two-tailed).
**Significant at $p < 0.05$ (two-tailed).
***Significant at $p < 0.01$ (two-tailed).

and in many cases more significant. As noted, in 1998 only FPTP and the Block Vote were statistically correlated with suppressing the number of women MPs when compared to List PR, but in 2008 those two systems were joined by the Francophone Two Round System, the Alternative Vote, and the Single Non-Transferable Vote in reducing female representation. Table 6.9 confirms the finding that legislatures elected by list PR have more women than any other system (PR systems as a family have almost double the number of women MPs as plurality-majority systems do) and when compared to the number of women in a nation the PR "democratic deficit" is significantly lower than both majoritarian and semi-PR systems.

By far the greatest increase in women's representation has been made in the Arab world, for while the overall numbers are lower than any other region the progress has been great. Africa experienced the second highest growth rate,

TABLE 6.9 *Electoral systems and women's legislative representation (lower house, 2008)*

	FPTP	List PR	MMP	PAR	TRS	STV	AV	BLK	SNTV
No. of cases	42	72	10	19	20	2	3	12	3
Average %	12.0	21.8	20.7	17.3	14.7	11.0	9.4	11.2	12.6
Deficit %	−37.2	−29.4	−30	−33.6	−35.2	−38.9	−37.9	−33.6	−36.5

while the Asia-Pacific regions gains were smaller than the global average. The diffusion of quotas and new gender power relations suggests that different parts of the world are converging on a proportion of women in parliaments which is between one-third and one-half of the proportion of women in the population as a whole (see table 6.10).

Female Representation and Public Policy

To what extent are women parliamentarians linked to "better representation" and improved policy outcomes? The few studies that have been undertaken on the relationship between descriptive representation and substantive policy outcomes for women are somewhat mixed in their findings. This is mostly due to the complexity of trying to tease out statistical relationships between the number of women and "women friendly" policies when there are so many other variables at work. Indeed, Childs and Krook point out that there are at least three other mechanisms at work beyond merely women MPs promoting public policy. First, women representatives can mold male MPs' behavior in positive ways; second, they can create a male backlash against their advocacy; and third, a small "insurgent" caucus of women MPs may be more effective than a larger group (2009: 129).

Lindgren, Inkinen, and Widmalm argue that "a more equal representation of women increases opinion congruence between masses and elites." In a study of 5,000 elite-mass dyads in Indian villages they find that "women are not only better equipped than men to politically represent women but also that they are better at representing men" (2009: 31). In an earlier study of village councils in India (West Bengal and Rajasthan) Chattopadhyay and Duflo (2004) find that women leaders invested in the infrastructures that were deemed most important to their gender. In West Bengal women complained most about drinking water and roads and in women led councils the investment in roads and water was higher than in councils where men where the heads. In Rajasthan women were more concerned by drinking water than by roads and again female council heads reflected this difference. Looking at a variety of cases, Phillips (1995), Reingold (2006), and Swers (2001) support the contention that women MPs help generate positive public policy outcomes for women as a group, but others (Dahlberg

TABLE 6.10 *Women's legislative representation by region (1998 and 2008)*

	Africa	Asia	Arab	Pacific	Americas	Europe	Total
1998	11.4	14.1	3.5	9.9	15.4	15.0	13.0
2009	18.1	18.0	9.7	13.0	21.7	21.3	18.5
% Increase	59	28	177	31	41	42	42

TABLE 6.11 *Predictors of the gender-related development index (2008)*

	Coefficient (standard error)
Polity score	0.006 (0.002)**
GDP	0.00001 (0.000001)***
Women MPs	0.0002 (0.001)
Religion	
Protestant	0.0009 (0.036)
Eastern Orthodox	0.14 (0.04)***
Islam	0.03 (0.03)
Other	0.03 (0.04)
Electoral system	
Block Vote	−0.004 (0.05)
Two round	−0.001 (0.04)
Alternative vote	0.03 (0.08)
FPTP	−0.08 (0.04)**
SNTV	0.14 (0.13)
Parallel	−0.007 (0.04)
STV	−0.04 (0.13)
MMP	0.05 (0.04)
Constant	0.59 (0.04)***
r^2	0.56
F	11.12***

Note: $n = 145$.
*Significant at $p < 0.10$ (two-tailed).
**Significant at $p < 0.05$ (two-tailed).
***Significant at $p < 0.01$ (two-tailed).

and Mork 2006) argue that the descriptive representation of women (in Sweden) does not necessarily lead to improved outcomes.

If one seeks to explain the empowerment of women in 2008 (as measured by the United Nation's Gender Related Development Index) there is not a predictive role for the number of female MPs (see table 6.11). This may be a product of the trend of new democracies (with lower baseline GRDIs) to adopt quotas for women in parliament, and for it to be too early for those women to have a significant impact of broadly conceived gender roles in society. The GRDI is predicted by the level of democracy (as measured by POLITY) and a nation's gross domestic product. Surprisingly, Eastern Orthodox nations have higher GRDIs than Protestant countries, but perhaps less surprising is the fact that FPTP systems are significantly correlated with a lower GRDI score (all else being equal).

But clearly, the impact of women MPs as psychological mold breakers is significant above and beyond their immediate impact on public policy provisions which enhance the rights and roles of women. Countless individual and group cases have demonstrated the role of women as role models spearheading waves of new politics in established and developing democracies. In Afghanistan individual women like Malalai Joya have been the loudest voices against the machismo of warlordism, while, as a caucus, the sixty-eight female Afghan MPs have had a significant role in reframing a debate which previously was entirely male dominated (see Wordsworth 2007). In Iraq the quota for women produced a significant block of parliamentarians but they were driven by sectional differences, nevertheless many of these legislators have been influential advocates for gender equality in the legal code (see Al-Ali and Pratt 2008).

EXPLAINING LEVELS OF DESCRIPTIVE INCLUSION

Are the levels of legislative inclusion of our four focus groups explained by similar institutional and cultural factors? When it comes to the electoral system used Table 6.12 shows that, when it comes to absolute numbers, the family of proportional systems does substantially better at facilitating women and LGBT parliamentarians than majoritarian systems and semi-PR systems. But majoritarian systems are associated with slightly higher numbers of young MPs and representatives of ethnic minorities. (The three semi-PR cases are dominated by the outlier cases of high ethnic inclusion in Afghanistan and Nepal). The more detailed electoral system break down in Table 6.13 reveals that List PR systems produce more women, ethnic minorities, and LGBT MPs but FPTP systems do better for young adult representation. The Block Vote does well for ethnic inclusion in the reserved communal seat case of Lebanon and it also does well in young adult representation (based on three cases).

A more useful measure is the "representation deficit" score shown in Tables 6.14 and 6.15. This is the proportion of the group in the legislature minus the proportion

TABLE 6.12 *Electoral systems and descriptive representation (%) (2008)*

	Plurality-Majority	Semi-PR	PR	No. of cases
Women	12.4	16.6	21.4	184
Ethnic	18.5	45.0	17.2	50
LGBT	0.05	0	0.25	184
Young	6.1	3.0	4.7	72

TABLE 6.13 *Electoral systems and descriptive representation (%) (2008)*

	FPTP	List PR	MMP	PAR	TRS	STV	AV	BLK	SNTV
Women	12.0 (42)	21.8 (72)	20.7 (10)	17.3 (19)	14.7 (20)	11.0 (2)	9.4 (3)	11.2 (12)	12.6 (3)
Ethnic	14.3 (11)	18.9 (26)	8.4 (3)	44.9 (1)	0.9 (2)	0.0 (1)	13.9 (3)	96.1 (2)	45.3 (1)
LGBT	0.1 (42)	0.2 (72)	0.6 (10)	0.0 (19)	0.0 (20)	0.0 (2)	0.0 (3)	0.0 (12)	0.0 (3)
Young	7.7 (14)	4.7 (37)	2.2 (3)	3.0 (7)	4.7 (6)	1.4 (1)	0.0 (1)	9.0 (3)	—

Note: (x) number of cases.

TABLE 6.14 *Electoral systems and descriptive representation by representation deficit (2008)*

	FPTP	List PR	MMP	PAR	TRS	STV	AV	BLK	SNTV
Women	−37.2	−29.4	−30.0	−33.6	−35.2	−38.9	−37.9	−33.6	−36.5
Ethnic	−0.2	−1.8	0.3	−2.3	−0.7	−0.3	−1.3	1.4	−7.9
LGBT	−4.9	−4.8	−4.4	−5	−5	−5	−5	−5	−5
Young	−12.0	−10.0	−13.6	−14.4	−16.2	−13.9	−13.2	−10.5	Na

Notes: Difference between parliamentary share of group and population share. For the multiple ethnic groups the LSQ Index of Disproportionality is used. For the LGBT population a constant 5 percent population figure is used merely for illustration purposes and to make the signs of the data consistent across focus categories. Lower scores represent higher inclusion.

of that group in the population. As the numbers of ethnic minority, women and 21–30 year olds varies from case to case this figure gives a much truer indication of the shortfall in descriptive representation. Data on the LGBT population is not available globally so I have used a standard 5 percent rate purely to illustrate the LGBT deficit in the same terms as the other three categories. As we can see in Table 6.14 the broad findings from the raw data hold, with some slight nuances. PR systems are still better at electing women and LGBT MPs, while majoritarian systems still are associated with a more inclusive levels of ethnic minority MPs, but when we look at population proportions we find that PR systems improve in the representation of the young. That means that while PR countries have fewer 21–30-year-old members as a raw number the countries using PR generally have fewer twenty-somethings in their population as a whole. Conversely, while there are actually more ethnic minority MPs on average in List PR systems than FPTP systems, the fact that there are more ethnic minority groups in PR countries means that when we look at the democratic deficit the FPTP systems do a better job of ethnic inclusion than List systems.

In sum, when one leaves out cases of reserved communal seats (for women or ethnic minorities) one finds that, outside of young MPs, List PR systems are the most inclusive of marginalized population groups.

In OLS regression models other variables which help determine levels of descriptive representation across the marginalized groups are less consistent. Higher incomes (as measured by GDP per capita) do correlate with more women and young adults in parliament and majority Protestant countries have more

TABLE 6.15 *Electoral systems and descriptive representation by representation deficit (2008)*

	P-M	Semi-PR	PR
Women	−36.2	−34.6	−29.7
Ethnic	−0.1	−2.2	−2.8
LGBT	−4.9	−5.0	−4.8
Young	−12.5	−14.4	−10.2

Notes: Difference between parliamentary share of group and population share. For the multiple ethnic groups the LSQ Index of Disproportionality is used. For the LGBT population a constant 5 percent population figure is used merely for illustration purposes and to make the signs of the data consistent across focus categories. Lower scores represent higher inclusion.

TABLE 6.16 *Determinants of inclusion*

	Increases	Decreases
Women	Quota	Democracy
	Income	Islam
	Protestantism	
	List PR	
	Left government	
LGBT	Social tolerance (WVS)	
	Protestantism	
Young	Income	

Notes: Not enough cases to run a model for ethnic minority representation and policy impact. (WVS) World Values Survey, see above.

women and openly gay MPs when compared to Catholic nations. Social values of tolerance are particularly influential when it comes to gay MPs while a left government enhances the likelihood of women being elected. Quotas clearly increase female and ethnic minority representation and no doubt would do the same for youth and LGBT communities if they were introduced. Last, and perhaps most interestingly, democracy is not correlated with increasing the representation of any of the marginalized groups considered here, although higher polity scores are linked with lower numbers of women in 2008 (see table 6.16).

EXPLAINING IMPACT

Does the presence of members of these marginalized groups in legislatures improve the legal and/or social position of the group, as measured through legislation, public policy, and social status? As summarized in this chapter the

TABLE 6.17 *Descriptive inclusion and public policy*

	Improves	Worsens
Women (GRDI)	Democracy	First past the post
	Income	
	Eastern Orthodox	
LGBT (law)	LGBT MPs	
	Democracy	
	Left government	
	Social tolerance	
Young (employment)	Democracy	% agricultural

Note: Not enough cases to run a model for ethnic minority representation and policy impact.

mechanics of influence are more complex than the simply algorithm, more minority MPs = better minority policy. Qualitative evidence dealing with agenda setting, role modeling, and breaking down prejudices suggests that female, gay, ethnic, and young MPs have a significant influence on improving the status of their descriptive group. But in, admittedly simplistic regressions, only gay MPs have a clear statistical relationship with policies that affect their community. As Table 6.17 illustrates, higher democracy scores improve outcomes for all three groups that we have data for. The gender-related development index improves when income is higher and Eastern Orthodox religion is present (against a Catholic baseline). LGBT law is enhanced by a left government and higher levels of social acceptance of homosexuality, along with the already mentioned variables of gay MPs and democracy. FPTP election systems actually predict a lower position for women in society and youth unemployment is worse when the economy is more dominated by agriculture.

CONCLUSIONS: MINORITY INFLUENCE IN PARLIAMENTS BEYOND INCLUSION

In sum, this chapter has demonstrated that institutions (i.e., electoral systems) are important in promoting minority inclusion and the resulting descriptive representation matters. But the ways in which descriptive representation matters vary across the groups concerned. Much of the progress on issues of women, ethnic minority, and young adult inclusion and representation has occurred not in the established democracies of Europe and North America but in new electoral regimes in Africa, the Mid East, and the South Pacific. Further, even when minorities do gain representation in national parliaments they are often discriminated against, face threats to their integrity, and are marginalized from real power. The actual method and scope of minority inclusion needs to be crafted to fit the needs of the given country. Some states may do better with reserved seats or autonomous self-governing assemblies while others will require incentives for minority MPs to be involved in "mainstream" parties and have a guarantee of both legislative and executive representation. The key is to ensure both visibility and voice to have minorities in parliament and enable them to impact policies which affect not only their communal affairs but the well being of society as a whole.

APPENDIX 6.A *Minority members in national legislatures (2007)*

Rank	Country	Minority	Seat %	Minority population %	Under/over	LSQ score	No. of elections
1	South Africa[b]	White	29.3	14.0	(15.3)	11.3	2
		Colored	8.9	8.0	(0.9)		2
		Indian	6.9	2.4	(4.5)		2
2	Tanzania	Zanzibaris	18.6	2.8	(15.8)	11.2	1
3	Namibia	White	9.0	5.0	(4.0)	6.1	1
		Kavango	6.4	8.0	(−1.6)		
		Damara	7.7	6.6	(1.1)		
		Herero	12.8	6.0	(6.8)		
		Nama	6.4	4.0	(2.4)		
		Colored	3.8	3.0	(0.8)		
		Caprivian	5.1	3.0	(2.1)		
		San	1.3	2.0	(−0.7)		
		Baster	3.8	2.0	(1.8)		
		Tswana	0.0	0.6	(−0.6)		
4	Bosnia-H	Bosniak	33.3	43.7	(−10.4)	8.7	1
		Croat	33.3	17.3	(16.0)		
		Serb	33.3	31.4	(1.9)		
5	Belgium[a]	Francophones	40.3	32.0	(8.3)	5.9	4
6	Fr. Polynesia	Whites	15.8	10.1	(5.7)	4.2	1
		Chinese	5.3	3.7	(1.6)		
7	Lebanon	Shias	21.1	32.0	(−10.9)	4.0	1
		Sunnis	21.1	18.0	(3.1)		
		Maronites	26.6	16.0	(10.6)		
		Druze	4.7	7.0	(−2.3)		
		Greek Orthodox	10.9	5.0	(5.9)		
		Greek Catholics	6.2	5.0	(1.2)		
		Armenians	3.9	3.0	(0.9)		
		Alawis	1.6	3.0	(−1.4)		

(Cont.)

APPENDIX 6.A *(Continued)*

Rank	Country	Minority	Seat %	Minority population %	Under/over	LSQ score	No. of elections
8	Canada	Francophones[a]	24.5	20.9	(3.6)	3.0	3
		Asian	5.2	1.5	(3.7)		
		Black	1.3	1.2	(0.1)		
		Inuit	0.6	3.5	(−2.9)		
9	Iraq	Kurds	23.4	22.0	(1.4)	2.9	1
		Sunni	23.4	17.0	(6.4)		
		Turkmen	0.4	4.0	(−3.6)		
		Christian	0.4	4.0	(−3.6)		
10	Netherlands	AF/ME/Turk	6.7	4.0	(2.7)	2.4	1
		Caribbean	3.3	1.3	(2.0)		
11	New Zealand	Maori	16.0	12.3	(3.7)	2.4	1
		Pacific Islander	3.0	5.0	(−2.0)		
		Asian	2.0	0.5	(1.5)		
12	Switzerland	Francophones	24.0	21.0	(3.0)	2.2	1
		Italophones	4.0	4.3	(−0.3)		
		Romansh	1.5	0.6	(0.9)		
13	Sri Lanka	Tamils	16.9	18.0	(−1.1)	2.0	1
		Muslims	10.7	7.6	(3.1)		
14	Slovenia[a]	Hungarians	1.1	0.4	(0.7)	1.6	4
		Italians	2.3	0.1	(2.2)		
15	Finland[a]	Swedes	7.7	5.8	(1.9)	1.3	4
16	Kiribati	Banabans	2.4	0.6	(1.8)	1.3	3
17	Slovakia[a]	Hungarians	12.4	10.8	(1.6)	1.1	5
		Russian	0.7	1.0	(−0.3)		
18	Sweden	Med/Middle East	1.8	1.9	(−0.1)	0.8	5
		Black	1.2	0.1	(1.1)		
		Latino	0.6	0.1	(0.5)		
		Sami	0.3	0.2	(0.1)		

(Cont.)

19	Zambia	White	0.7	0.1	(0.6)	0.6	1
		Asian	0.7	0.1	(0.6)		
20	Malawi	Asian	1.0	0.1	(0.9)	0.6	1
21	Albania	Greeks	3.6	3.1	(0.5)	0.3	1
22	Zimbabwe	White	0.7	0.5	(0.2)	0.1	1
23	Denmark	Muslim	1.1	1.3	(−0.2)	0.1	1
		Inuit	1.1	0.9	(0.2)		
		Faroese	1.1	0.9	(0.2)		
24	Papua New Guinea	Bougainvilleans	3.7	4.0	(−0.3)	−0.2	1
25	Ireland	Non-Whites	0.0	0.5	(−0.5)	−0.3	1
26	Australia[a]	Aborigines	0.0	1.4	(−1.4)	−1.0	5
27	Norway	Asian	0.6	2.0	(−1.4)	−1.0	1
28	Romania[a]	Hungarians	7.5	7.1	(0.4)	−1.0	3
		Roma	0.3	1.8	(−1.5)	3	
29	Mongolia	Kazaks	4.2	5.9	(−1.7)	−1.2	2
30	Poland	Germans	0.4	2.4	(−2.0)	−1.4	1
31	Pakistan	Non-Muslims	2.9	5.0	(−2.1)	−1.5	1
32	United Kingdom	Afro-Caribbean	0.6	0.9	(−0.3)	−1.6	3
33	Germany	Asian	0.7	2.9	(−2.2)		3
		North African/Middle East	0.6	3.0	(−2.4)	−1.7	1
34	Bulgaria[a]	Turks	6.9	9.4	(−2.5)	−1.8	4
35	Azerbaijan	Lezgins	0.8	4.0	(−3.2)	−2.3	1
36	France	North Africa	0.2	2.5	(−2.3)	−2.7	1
		Overseas territories	0.7	3.8	(−3.1)		
37	Fiji	Indo-Fijian	38.0	42.0	(−4.0)	−2.8	1
38	United States[a]	African Americans	8.4	12.1	(−3.7)	−4.2	7
		Latino	4.3	8.9	(−4.6)		7
		Native Americans	0.1	0.8	(−0.7)		7

APPENDIX 6.A *(Continued)*

Rank	Country	Minority	Seat %	Minority population %	Under/over	LSQ score	No. of elections
39	India[a]	Muslims	5.3	11.4	(−6.1)	−4.4	4
		Dalits	14.5	15.8	(−1.3)		
		Adivasis	7.5	7.5	(0.0)		
40	Lithuania[a]	Poles	3.1	7.0	(−3.9)	−5.1	3
		Russians	2.4	8.5	(−6.1)		3
41	Trinidad and Tobago	Afro	41.7	37.0	(4.7)	−5.3	1
42	Brazil	Mixed	11.1	20.0	(−8.9)		
		Chinese	3.0	2.0	(1.0)		
		Afro	3.9	13.2	(−9.3)	−6.6	1
43	Israel	Arabs	7.5	17.5	(−10.0)	−7.1	4
		Druze	1.0	1.5	(−0.5)		4
44	Croatia	Serbs	2.4	12.2	(−9.8)	−7.5	1
		Czech	0.8	0.7	(0.1)		
		Hungarian	0.8	0.5	(0.3)		
		Italian	0.8	0.4	(0.4)		
		Others	1.6	5.7	(−4.1)		
45	Afghanistan	Hazara	12.0	16.0	(−4.0)	−7.9	1
		Tajik	21.3	30.0	(−8.7)		
		Uzbek	8.0	13.0	(−5.0)		
		Kuchi	4.0	7.0	(−3.0)		
46	Macedonia	Albanians	10.8	23.0	(−12.2)	−8.9	1
		Turks	1.7	4.0	(−2.3)		
		Roma	0.8	2.3	(−1.5)		
		Serbs	0.8	2.0	(−1.2)		
47	Spain	Catalan	5.1	16.0	(−10.9)	−9.6	1

		Galician	0.6	7.9	(−7.3)		
		Basque	2.3	2.0	(0.3)		
		Canary Islands	0.9	4.6	(−3.7)		
48	Latvia[a]	Russians	9.3	33.1	(−23.8)	−16.8	4
49	Montenegro	Albanians	2.6	5.0	(−2.4)	−17.2	1
		Serbians	7.8	32.0	(−24.2)		
50	Estonia[a]	Russophones	4.7	30.3	(−25.6)	−18.1	4

Notes: Minority percentage: *World Directory of Minorities*. MRG International. 1997.

Seat percentages are from the most recent election unless noted.

Data is for the lower house in bicameral parliaments.

[a] 1990–2003 average data from David Lublin, American University.

[b] South Africa 1994 and 1999.

Sources: Data collected by the author Marusca Perazzi from MRG International anc partners of MRG International. Very grateful to Catherine Kannam, Susan Glover, Wendy Wolford, Altin Iranjani, Bernt Aardal, Krzysztof Jasiewicz, Michael Gallagher, Burt Monroe, John Carey, Nenad Stojanovic, Juan Díez-Nicolás, and the Center for Peace, Legal Advice and Psychosocial Assistance, Vukovar, Croatia.

See also Stojanovic, Nenad (2006 forthcoming) and David Lublin.

Notes: LSQ index.

The Least Squares Index used to aggregate minority under/over representation in this table was invented by Michael Gallagher of Trinity College Dublin to measure electoral system disproportionality. In principle it treats one group with 15 percent of the population but no seats as a *more* disproportional outcome than fifteen groups each winning 1 percent less of the seats than their population share would suggest. Thus the measure gives a more accurate impression of minority inclusion.

The adaptation of Gallagher's LSQ index used in this table is that positive and negatives of each disproportionality have remained in the equation.

APPENDIX 6.B *Openly LGBT members of national legislatures (December 2008)*

	Number	Leg size	% gay	Name(s)	Party	First open gay elected/notes
United Kingdom	14	646	2.2	Clive Betts (G)	Labour	Tom Driberg (1942–74)
				David Borrow (G)	Labour	
				Ben Bradshaw (G)	Labour	Angela Eagle, first UK lesbian MP
				Nick Brown (G)	Labour	
				Chris Bryant (G)	Labour	Chris Smith (1984), first MP to announce HIV positive status (2005)
				Angela Eagle (L)	Labour	Bradshaw, first MP to have civil union
				Gordon Marsden (G)	Labour	
				Nick Herbert (G)	Cons	
				Alan Duncan (G)	Cons	
				Gregory Baker (G)	Cons	
				Stephen Williams (G)	LibDem	
				Simon Hughes (B)	LibDem	
				Mark Oaten (G)	LibDem	
				Adam Price (G)	Plaid Cymru	
Netherlands	8	150	5.3	Boris van der Ham (G)	D66	Peter Lankhorst – 1981–2002
				Vim van der Camp (G)	CDA	
				Ger Koopmans (G)	CDA	Evelien Eshuis – 1982–6
				Clemens Cornielje (G)	VVD	
				Boris Dittrich (G)	D66 (2006)	Gerritje (Gerda) Verburg CDA 1999–2007
				Gerda Verburg (L)	CDA (2007)	
				Joop Wijn (G)	CDA (2007)	
				Peter Rehwinkel (G)	PvdA (2007)	
Norway	6	169	3.5	Anette Trettebergstuen (L)	Labour	Wenche Lowzow – 1977–85 (came out 1979, re-elected 1981)
				Andre Dahl (G)	Cons	
				Bent Hoie (G)	Cons	
				Andre Kvakkestad (G)	Progress	
				Siri Hall Arnoy (L)	Socialist	
				Per Kristian Foss (G)	Cons	

Country				Names	Party	Notes
Canada	6	301	2.0	Real Ménard (G)	BQ	Svend Robinson 1988
				Libby Davies (L)	NDP	
				Scott Brison (G)	Liberal	
				Bill Siksay (G)	NDP	
				Mario Silva (G)	Liberal	
				Rob Oliphant (G)	Liberal	
Sweden	6	349	1.7	Tobias Billström (G)	Left	Kent Carlsson 1991
				Andreas Carlgren (G)	Centre Party	Andreas Carlgren, first gay cabinet
				Elisebeht Markström (L)	Social Dem.	minister 2006
				Martin Andreasson (G)	Liberal	
				Ulf Holm (G)	Greens	
				Borje Vestlund (G)	Social Dem.	
New Zealand	6	120	5.0	Tim Barnett (G)	Labour	Georgina Bayer, world's first
				Chris Carter (G)	Labour	transsexual MP 200
				Chris Finlayson (G)	National	
				Maryan Street (L)	Labour	Marilyn Waring 1984. Chris Carter
				Charles Chauvel (G)	Labour	1993
				Louisa Wall (L)	Labour	
United States	3	435	0.7	Barney Frank (G)	Dem	Steve Gunderson (1980–96)
				Tammy Baldwin (L)	Dem	Gerry Studds (out in 1983)
				Jared Polis (G)	Dem	
Italy	4	630	0.6	Daniele Capezzone (B)	Ital. Radicals	Luxuria, first transgender in a Euro.
				Franco Gillini (G)	Communists	Parliament and second trans MP
				Titti de Simone (L)	Social Dem	worldwide 2006
				Vladimir Lxuria (T)	Communist	
Germany	3	669	0.5	Volker Beck (G)	Greens	Herbert Rusche 1985
				Birgitt Bender (L)	Green	Sabine Junger 1998–2002
				Guido Westerwelle (G)	FDP	

(Cont.)

APPENDIX 6.B *(Continued)*

	Number	Leg size	% gay	Name(s)	Party	First open gay elected/notes
South Africa	2	400	0.5	Ian Ollis (G)	DA	1994
				Mike Waters (G)	DA	2009
Iceland	1	63	1.6	Jóhanna Sigurðardóttir	Social Dem	Sigurðardóttir 1978
Brazil	1	513	0.2	Clodovil Hernandez (G)	Christian Labour Party	Hernandez 2006
Denmark	1	179	0.6	Louise Frevert (L)	DF	Yvonne Herløv Andersen 1977 (out 1998) Torben Lund (out in 1998)
Finland	1	200	0.5	Oras Tynkkynen (G)	Greens	Tynkkynen 2004
Israel	1	120	0.8	Uri Even (G)	Meretz	Even 2002
Mexico	1	500	0.2	David Sanchez Camacho (G)	PRD	Patricia Jimenez 1997
Austria	1	183	0.6	Ulrike Lunacek (L)	Greens	Ulrike Lunacek 1999
Nepal	1	601	0.2	Sunil Babu Pant (G)	CPN-U	Pant 2008 CA
Total	66					

Note: Data gathered between 2002 and 2008. Totals are as of August 2008 unless otherwise noted.

APPENDIX 6.C *Gay MP variables*

Country	Gay MP %	WVS (2003)	Marriage (2003)	Marriage (2006)	Adoption (2003)	Adoption (2006)	WVS/ Marriage	Democ.	HDI (2005)	Elect. sys	Govt type	Relig.	Law score
Netherlands	5.3	7.8	80	82	64	69	7.8	1	0.953	L.PR	LEFT		5
New Zealand	5.0	4.7	—	—	—	—	4.7	1	0.943	MMP	LEFT		2
Norway	3.5	5.7	66	—	37	—	5.7	1	0.968	L.PR	LEFT		4
United Kingdom	2.2	5.1	47	46	35	33	5.1	1	0.946	FPTP	LEFT		4
Sweden	1.7	7.7	70	71	42	51	7.7	1	0.956	L.PR	LEFT		3
Iceland	1.6	7.2	—	—	—	—	7.2	1	0.968	L.PR	RIGHT		3
Canada	2.0	5.5	—	—	—	—	5.5	1	0.961	FPTP	CENT		5
Israel	0.8	4.9	47	—	25	—	4.9	1.5	0.932	L.PR	RIGHT		1.5
Italy	0.6	4.8	47	31	25	24	4.8	1	0.941	MMP	RIGHT		1
Denmark	0.6	6.5	82	69	54	44	6.5	1	0.949	L.PR	RIGHT		3.5
Austria	0.6	5.2	48	49	33	44	5.2	1	0.948	L.PR	LEFT		1
South Africa	0.5	2.9	—	—	—	—	2.9	2	0.674	L.PR	LEFT		4
Germany	0.5	5.3	65	52	57	42	5.3	1	0.935	MMP	LEFT		2.5
Finland	0.5	5.2	56	45	30	24	5.2	1	0.952	L.PR	LEFT		2
United States	0.4	4.8	—	—	—	—	4.8	1	0.951	FPTP	RIGHT		1.5
Brazil	0.2	3.2	—	—	—	—	3.2	2	0.800	L.PR	LEFT		1.5
Mexico	0.2	3.7	—	—	—	—	3.7	2.5	0.829	MMP	RIGHT		0.5
Nepal	0.2	—	—	—	—	—	—	4.5	0.534	PAR	LEFT		0
France	0	5.2	58	48	39	35	5.2	1	0.952	TRS	LEFT		3
Belgium	0	5.2	67	62	47	43	5.2	1	0.946	L.PR	LEFT		5
Hungary	0	1.4	37	18	34	13	1.4	1	0.874	L.PR	LEFT		2.5
India	0	3.0	—	—	—	—	3.0	2.5	0.619	FPTP	CENT		−1
Spain	0	5.8	68	56	57	43	5.8	1	0.949	L.PR	LEFT		5
Ireland	0	4.2	46	41	34	30	4.2	1	0.959	STV	CENT		1.5

(Cont.)

APPENDIX 6.C *(Continued)*

Country	Gay MP %	WVS Marriage (2003)	Marriage (2006)	Adoption (2003)	Adoption (2006)	WVS/ Marriage	Democ.	HDI (2005)	Elect. sys	Govt type	Relig.	Law score
Philippines	0	3.9	—	—	—	—	3.9	3.5	0.771	L.PR	RIGHT		−1
Australia	0	4.9	—	—	—	—	4.9	1	0.962	AV	LEFT		2
Switzerland	0	6.1	65	—	47	—	6.1	1	0.955	L.PR	CENT		1
Mozambique	0	—	—	—	—	—	—	3	0.384	L.PR	LEFT		0
Russia	0	2.1	—	—	—	—	2.1	5.5	0.802	PAR	RIGHT		0.5
Andorra	0	—	—	—	—	—	—	1	—	L.PR	RIGHT		3
Czech Republic	0	5.5	50	52	35	24	5.5	1	0.891	L.PR	LEFT		2
Luxembourg	0	—	71	58	49	39	5.8	1	0.944	L.PR	RIGHT		2
Slovenia	0	4.6	40	31	30	17	4.6	1	0.917	L.PR	CENT		2
Uruguay	0	4.0	—	—	—	—	4.0	1	0.852	L.PR	LEFT		2
Argentina	0	4.3	—	—	—	—	4.3	2	0.869	L.PR	CENT		1.5
Portugal	0	3.4	43	29	25	19	3.4	1	0.897	L.PR	LEFT		1
Malaysia	0	—	—	—	—	—	—	4	0.811	FPTP	RIGHT		−2
Greece	0	4.9	16	15	11	11	4.9	1.5	0.926	L.PR	RIGHT		0
Singapore	0	2.4	—	—	—	—	2.4	4.5	0.922	BLK	RIGHT		−2
South Korea	0	—	—	—	—	—	—	1.5	0.921	PAR	RIGHT		−1
Venezuela	0	2.4	—	—	—	—	2.4	4	0.792	MMP	LEFT		0
Estonia	0	3.0	35	21	27	14	3.0	1	0.860	L.PR	CENT		1
Slovakia	0	4.9	30	19	17	12	4.9	1	0.863	L.PR	LEFT		1
Malta	0	2.5	23	18	10	7	2.5	1	0.878	STV	CENT		1
Poland	0	2.8	19	17	10	7	2.8	1	0.870	L.PR	RIGHT		1
Lithuania	0	1.9	26	17	13	12	1.9	1	0.862	L.PR	CENT		1
Bulgaria	0	2.6	20	15	14	12	2.6	1.5	0.824	L.PR	LEFT		1
Cyprus	0	—	9	14	6	10	1.4	1	0.903	L.PR	LEFT		1

	0	19	12	11	8							
Latvia	0	—	—	—	—	1.9	1.9	1.5	0.855	L.PR	RIGHT	1
Chile	0	—	—	—	—	4.0	4.0	1	0.867	L.PR	LEFT	0
Japan	0	—	—	—	—	4.4	4.4	1.5	0.953	PAR	RIGHT	1
Zimbabwe	0	—	—	—	—	1.1	1.1	6.5	0.513	FPTP	RIGHT	−1
Albania	0	—	—	—	—	1.5	1.5	3.0	0.801	MMP	RIGHT	0
Algeria	0	—	—	—	—	1.2	1.2	5.5	0.733	L.PR	LEFT	−1
Bangladesh	0	—	—	—	—	1.0	1.0	4.5	0.547	FPTP	RIGHT	−1
Bosnia & He.	0	—	—	—	—	2.0	2.0	3.5	0.803	L.PR	CENT	1
Belarus	0	—	—	—	—	2.9	2.9	6.5	0.804	TRS	RIGHT	0
China	0	—	—	—	—	1.1	1.1	6.5	0.777	—	LEFT	−1
Croatia	0	—	—	—	—	2.7	2.7	2.0	0.850	L.PR	RIGHT	1
Indonesia	0	—	—	—	—	1.1	1.1	2.5	0.728	L.PR	CENT	0
Iran	0	—	—	—	—	1.2	1.2	6.0	0.759	TRS	RIGHT	−1
Jordan	0	—	—	—	—	1.0	1.0	4.5	0.773	SNTV	RIGHT	0
Kyrgyzstan	0	—	—	—	—	1.8	1.8	4.5	0.696	TRS	RIGHT	0
Moldova	0	—	—	—	—	2.3	2.3	3.5	0.708	L.PR	RIGHT	0
Nigeria	0	—	—	—	—	1.5	1.5	4.0	0.470	FPTP	RIGHT	−1
Pakistan	0	—	—	—	—	1.0	1.0	5.5	0.551	FPTP	RIGHT	−1
Peru	0	—	—	—	—	2.6	2.6	2.5	0.773	L.PR	LEFT	1
Saudi Arabia	0	—	—	—	—	1.4	1.4	6.5	0.812	—	RIGHT	−2
Vietnam	0	—	—	—	—	1.6	1.6	6.0	0.733	TRS	LEFT	0
Turkey	0	—	—	—	—	1.5	1.5	3.0	0.775	L.PR	RIGHT	0
Uganda	0	—	—	—	—	1.3	1.3	4.5	0.505	FPTP	RIGHT	−1
Ukraine	0	—	—	—	—	2.3	2.3	2.5	0.788	PAR	CENT	0
Macedonia	0	—	—	—	—	1.9	1.9	3.0	0.801	L.PR	RIGHT	1
Egypt	0	—	—	—	—	1.0	1.0	5.5	0.708	TRS	RIGHT	−2
Tanzania	0	—	—	—	—	1.1	1.1	3.5	0.467	FPTP	LEFT	−1
Serbia	0	—	—	—	—	1.7	1.7	2.5	0.803	L.PR	CENT	1

(Cont.)

APPENDIX 6.C (*Continued*)

Notes: Gay MPs (%): December 2008 data gathered by author (see Table 6.1)

WVS—World Values Survey. Wave 4 (surveys conducted between 1999 and 2003).

Source: http://www.worldvaluessurvey.org. Question V202: Please tell me for each of the following actions whether you think it can always be justified, never be justified, or something in between, using this card. "Homosexuality." Answered on a 1 to 10 scale with 1 being "never justifiable" and 10 being "always justifiable." Marriage (2003): Percentage of respondents agreeing to the proposition. "The authorization of homosexual marriages throughout Europe?"

Source: European Omnibus Survey. Gallup. "Homosexual marriage, child adoption by homosexual couples: is the public ready?" 2003.

Marriage (2006): Percentage of respondents answering "Yes" to the question, "Do you agree with Homosexual marriages being allowed throughout Europe?"

Source: Eurobarometer (2006). http://www.angus-reid.com/polls/view/eight_eu_countries_back_same_sex_marriage/

Adoption (2003): Percentage of respondents agreeing to the proposition. "The authorization of child adoption by homosexual couples throughout Europe?"

Source: European Omnibus Survey. Gallup. "Homosexual marriage, child adoption by homosexual couples: is the public ready?" 2003.

Adoption (2006): Percentage of respondents answering "Yes" to the question, "Do you agree with authorizing the adoption of children for homosexual couples throughout Europe?"

Source: Eurobarometer (2006). http://www.angus-reid.com/polls/view/eight_eu_countries_back_same_sex_marriage/

WVS/Marriage: For the two cases where the WVS data is missing (Luxembourg, Cyprus) Marriage 2006 is used as a proxy.

Democracy Score. Freedom House (2008), F = Free, PF = Partly Free, NF = Not Free. http://www.freedomhouse.org/template.cfm?page=410&year=2008

HDI score: Human Development Index 2005. http://hdr.undp.org/en/media/hdr_20072008_en_complete.pdf

Elect.Sys: FPTP (First Part the Post), L.PR (List Proportional Representation), MMP (Mixed-Member Proportional), PAR (Parallel System), BLK (Block Vote), AV (Alternative Vote), TRS (Two Round System), STV (Single Transferable Vote).

Gay law:

Legal: Legal 0, illegal -1.

Marriage: Same sex marriage 2, not legal 0

Civil Unions/registered partnerships: Provisions for civil unions/partnerships 1, none 0

Adoption: Same sex couples and gay individuals able to adopt 1, partial rights 0.5.

Anti-discrimination: National anti-discrimination laws included sexual orientation 1, none 0

Hate Crimes: National hate crime laws include sexual orientation 1, none 0

Military ban: Gays banned from military service -1, no ban 0.

Sources: http://www.iglhrc.org/files/iglhrc/reports/990604-antidis.pdf,

http://www.ilga.org/map/LGBTI_rights.jpg, http://en.wikipedia.org/wiki/Same-sex_marriage,

http://en.wikipedia.org/wiki/LGBT_adoption. www.legislationline.org.

http://www.stonewall.org.uk/information_bank.

Government type: When marriage or partnership law was passed, or, if no law, government as of 2008.

Religion: Majority/largest religious affiliation (CIA Factbook).

APPENDIX 6.D *Gay MPs elected from single-member districts*

	Out/not out when first elected	Party	District	First elected	Majority first elected (%)
United Kingdom					
Clive Betts	Not out (2003)	Labour	Sheffield Attercliffe	1992	31
David Borrow	Not out (1998)	Labour	South Ribble	1997	9
Ben Bradshaw	Out	Labour	Exeter	1997	19
Nick Brown	Not out (1998)	Labour	Newcastle East	1983	18
Chris Bryant	Out	Labour	Rhondda	2001	47
Angela Eagle	Not out (1997)	Labour	Wallasey	1992	7
Nick Herbert	Out	Cons	Arundel & S. Down	2005	23
Simon Hughes	Not out (2006)	LibDem	Southwark & Berm.	1983	32
Gordon Marsden	Not out (1998)	Labour	Blackpool South	1997	23
Mark Oaten	Not out (2006)	LibDem	Winchester	1997	0
Adam Price	Out	Plaid Cymru	Carmarthen East	2001	7
Alan Duncan	Not out (2002)	Cons	Rutland and Melton	1992	40
Stephen Williams	Out	LibDem	Bristol West	2005	9
Gregory Barker	Not out (2007)	Cons	Bexhill and Battle	2001	23
Canada					
Real Menard	Not out (1994)	BQ	Hochelaga	1993	36
Libby Davies	Not Out (2001)	NDP	Vancouver East	1997	5
Scott Brison	Not out (2002)	Liberal	Kings-Hants	1997	6
Bill Siksay	Out	NDP	Burnaby-Douglas	2004	2
Mario Silva	Not out (2004)	Liberal	Davenport	2004	17
Rob Oliphant	Out	Liberal	Don Valley West	2008	5
New Zealand					
Tim Barnett	Out	Labour	Christchurch Central	1996	2
Chris Carter	Out	Labour	Te Atatu	1993	10
United States					
Barney Frank	Not out (1987)	Democrat	Mass 4th	1982	20
Tammy Baldwin	Out	Democratb	Wisconsin 2nd	1998	6
Jared Polis	Out	Democrat	Colorado 2nd	2008	28

APPENDIX 6.E *National MPs under the age of 30*

	Percentage of legislature (21–30)	Percentage of Population (21–30)	Percentage of legislature – percentage of Population
Cape Verde	40.28	21.8	18.48
Oman	30.95	20.6	10.35
Antigua and Barbuda	26.32	20.0	6.32
Estonia	14.85	13.9	0.95
Denmark	11.73	12.3	−0.57
Norway	11.83	13.1	−1.27
Singapore	12.77	14.3	−1.50
Niger	15.04	17.9	−2.86
Trinidad and Tobago	14.63	18.0	−3.40
Belgium	8.00	12.0	−4.00
Russian Federation	7.69	14.4	−6.70
Netherlands	4.67	11.7	−7.03
Turkey	9.84	17.6	−7.80
Portugal	3.04	11.1	−8.10
Croatia	3.92	12.1	−8.18
Hungary	3.89	12.5	−8.61
Sweden	2.87	11.8	−8.90
Austria	3.23	12.5	−9.27
Syrian Arab Republic	11.60	20.9	−9.30
Switzerland	3.00	12.6	−9.60
Greece	1.00	10.6	−9.60
Japan	0.21	9.9	−9.69
Samoa	8.16	18.0	−9.80
Poland	4.13	14.0	−9.90
Germany	1.47	11.6	−10.13
Andorra	3.57	13.8	−10.27
Latvia	4.00	14.3	−10.30
Spain	3.43	13.8	−10.40
Canada	2.62	13.3	−10.68
Bulgaria	1.25	12.0	−10.75
Italy	1.11	11.9	−10.79
Finland	1.50	12.3	−10.80
Iceland	3.17	14.5	−11.33
Micronesia	7.14	18.6	−11.46
Thailand	3.33	14.8	−11.50
Slovakia	2.67	14.2	−11.50
Cyprus	3.57	15.1	−11.53
Luxembourg	0.00	11.7	−11.70
France	0.35	12.2	−11.85
San Marino	0.00	12.0	−12.00
Mali	8.16	20.4	−12.24
United Kingdom	0.46	13.1	−12.60
Australia	0.00	13.2	−13.20
Suriname	3.92	17.4	−13.50
Belarus	0.91	14.7	−13.79
United States	0.00	13.9	−13.90
Malta	1.45	15.4	−13.95
Israel	0.83	15.4	−14.57

APPENDIX 6.E *(Continued)*

	Percentage of legislature (21–30)	Percentage of Population (21–30)	Percentage of legislature − percentage of Population
Uganda	5.42	20.0	−14.60
Burundi	5.93	20.9	−14.87
Congo	4.38	20.1	−15.72
Argentina	0.39	16.8	−16.41
Moldova	1.98	18.6	−16.60
Dominica	3.23	20.0	−16.77
Seychelles	2.94	20.0	−17.10
India	0.67	17.3	−17.12
Solomon Islands	2.00	20.3	−18.30
Armenia	0.76	19.2	−18.46
Tajikistan	4.76	23.3	−18.50
Uzbekistan	3.33	22.0	−18.70
Indonesia	0.73	17.6	−18.87
Mozambique	4.40	20.3	−18.93
Morocco	0.62	19.7	−19.08
Azerbaijan	1.63	20.8	−19.17
Algeria	0.26	20.5	−19.24
Haiti	1.02	20.9	−19.88
Swaziland	0.00	20.0	−20.00
Namibia	3.85	24.0	−20.15
Laos	2.61	23.2	−20.59
Car	0.00	21.2	−21.20
Zimbabwe	0.00	24.2	−24.20
Sudan	0.00	25.0	−25.00

APPENDIX 6.F *Women in legislatures 2008*

Country	Women MPs (%)
Rwanda	56.3
Sweden	47
Cuba	43.2
Finland	41.5
Netherlands	41.3
Argentina	40
Denmark	38
Angola	37.3
Costa Rica	36.8
Spain	36.3
Norway	36.1
Belgium	35.3
Mozambique	34.8
New Zealand	33.6
Iceland	33.3
Nepal	33.2
South Africa	33

(Cont.)

Designing Democracy in a Dangerous World

Country	Women MPs (%)
Germany	32.2
Belarus	31.8
Macedonia	31.7
Uganda	30.7
Burundi	30.5
Tanzania	30.4
Guyana	30
Peru	29.2
Timor Leste	29.2
Switzerland	28.5
Portugal	28.3
Afghanistan	27.7
Austria	27.3
Namibia	26.9
Trinidad and Tobago	26.8
Australia	26.7
Vietnam	25.8
Kyrgyzstan	25.6
Iraq	25.5
Suriname	25.5
Laos	25.2
Andorra	25
Ecuador	25
Lesotho	25
Monaco	25
Singapore	24.5
Liechtenstein	24
Seychelles	23.5
Honduras	23.4
Luxembourg	23.3
Mexico	23.2
Tunisia	22.8
Pakistan	22.5
United Arab Emirates	22.5
Canada	22.1
Mauritania	22.1
Eritrea	22
Senegal	22
Ethiopia	21.9
Moldova	21.8
Bulgaria	21.7
Serbia	21.6
China	21.3
Italy	21.3
Croatia	20.9
Estonia	20.8
Philippines	20.5
Poland	20.2
North Korea	20.1

APPENDIX 6.F *(Continued)*

Country	Women MPs (%)
Latvia	20
Dominican Republic	19.7
United Kingdom	19.5
Guinea	19.3
Slovakia	19.3
Dominica	18.8
Venezuela	18.6
Nicaragua	18.5
France	18.2
Saint Vincent and the Grenadines	18.2
Cape Verde	18.1
Sudan	18.1
Lithuania	17.7
Tajikistan	17.5
Uzbekistan	17.5
United States of America	17.4
Mauritius	17.1
Bolivia	16.9
El Salvador	16.7
Gabon	16.7
Panama	16.7
Cambodia	16.3
Turkmenistan	16
Kazakhstan	15.9
Czech Republic	15.5
Burkina Faso	15.3
Zambia	15.2
Zimbabwe	15.2
Bangladesh	15
Chile	15
San Marino	15
Greece	14.7
Cyprus	14.3
Israel	14.2
Russian Federation	14
Cameroon	13.9
Djibouti	13.8
Swaziland	13.8
Republic of Korea	13.7
Grenada	13.3
Ireland	13.3
Jamaica	13.3
Slovenia	13.3
Sierra Leone	13.2
Malawi	13
Liberia	12.5
Paraguay	12.5
Niger	12.4
Syria	12.4

(Cont.)

APPENDIX 6.F *(Continued)*

Country	Women MPs (%)
Bahamas	12.2
Uruguay	12.1
Guatemala	12
Maldives	12
Bosnia and Herzegovina	11.9
Thailand	11.7
Indonesia	11.6
Azerbaijan	11.4
Romania	11.4
Botswana	11.1
Hungary	11.1
Montenegro	11.1
Saint Lucia	11.1
Togo	11.1
Ghana	10.9
Benin	10.8
Malaysia	10.8
Antigua and Barbuda	10.5
Central African Republic	10.5
Morocco	10.5
Mali	10.2
Barbados	10
Kenya	9.8
Gambia (The)	9.4
Japan	9.4
India	9.1
Turkey	9.1
Brazil	9
Côte d' Ivoire	8.9
Malta	8.7
Bhutan	8.5
Armenia	8.4
Colombia	8.4
Congo	8.4
Samoa	8.2
Somalia	8.2
Ukraine	8.2
Madagascar	7.9
Algeria	7.7
Libyan Arab Jamahiriya	7.7
Congo	7.3
Sao Tome and Principe	7.3
Albania	7.1
Fiji	7
Nigeria	7
Saint Kitts and Nevis	6.7
Jordan	6.4
Equatorial Guinea	6
Georgia	6

APPENDIX 6.F (*Continued*)

Country	Women MPs (%)
Sri Lanka	5.8
Chad	5.2
Lebanon	4.7
Kiribati	4.3
Mongolia	4.2
Haiti	4.1
Vanuatu	3.8
Kuwait	3.1
Tonga	3.1
Comoros	3
Marshall Islands	3
Iran	2.8
Bahrain	2.5
Egypt	1.8
Papua New Guinea	0.9
Yemen	0.3
Belize	0
Guinea-Bissau	0
Micronesia	0
Nauru	0
Oman	0
Palau	0
Qatar	0
Saudi Arabia	0
Solomon Islands	0
Tuvalu	0

## 7

Governments and Inclusion: Sharing Power

This chapter deals with how power and influence is apportioned within the political system beyond elections – in the executive, between the center and periphery, in the machinery of the state, and in the sharing of wealth. Throughout modern history, forms of power sharing have been promoted as attractive options for any society fraught with cultural division and conflict. The theory being that institutionalized power sharing promotes an ethos of inclusion – bringing minority voices into the conversation and restraining majorities from monopolizing power.

Such arrangements at the very highest levels of governance seek to address the destabilizing paralysis of governing driven by fear, unfairness, and inefficiency. The fear is that one group will dominate and oppress others through the institutions of the government. Power-sharing institutions seek to challenge the unfairness of a significant section of society being shut out of decisions which effect them. Last, the theory goes that power-sharing structures provide the foundation for a more efficient form of policy making, which includes the talents and skills of a broad cross section of society and puts into place policies which can be sustained for the long run because they have the support of a majority of leaders. In contrast, in majoritarian systems governments can switch back and forth every few years providing little consistency in economic or social planning.

Nevertheless, two elements must be in place for any power-sharing arrangement to have any chance at success – a State and a will. That is, the government must have some ability to enforce its laws, tax its citizens, and distribute its resources, and there must be sufficient will among the leaders and their followers to make a go of the new inclusive government structures.

The goal of inclusion in the form of power sharing is to provide guarantees and reassurances to weaker groups that they will not be exploited or marginalized in the existing, or new, political order. Power sharing provides such groups with incentives to work within the system rather than following an anti-system or violent path. Well-crafted structures reduce the danger that one group becomes dominant and threatens the security of others. The most formal and rigid power-sharing structures are often used in highly divided societies. In elections neither party may be able to claim an outright victory and a peace-deal is brokered, which promises that all parties to the conflict will be included in government and will have access to power and resources.

At their best, power-sharing structures promote broad-based governing inclusive coalitions that guarantee influence to legitimate representatives of minority groups and ensure that minority interests are protected. Indeed, power sharing is often the only mechanism that will ensure some form of peace agreement between various groups in a bitter post-conflict environment. In this context, the political arrangements are best recognized as a short-term way of dividing power between the dominant forces emerging from the conflict to ensure some form of cohabitation between the groups. A longer term goal is also to breed understanding and compromise through familiarity. Power sharing will at the very least force elites to work together and one hopes that once elites share the space of their foes they will become more empathetic and conciliatory. Such elite accommodation might then trickle down to the masses, although it may not. How power sharing actually operates in both principle and practice varies considerably from case to case. There may be formal rules and regulations entrenched in the constitution, which compel communal groups to share political power and resources, or there may be more informal norms of behavior where majorities are conditioned to reach out to minorities in the act of governing.

The theory of minority incorporation and majority constraint resonates with any student of ethnic conflict, and indeed there is evidence to suggest that appropriately designed power-sharing institutions can suppress conflict and build stability. Norris (2008) defines power sharing around proportional election systems, decentralized power structures, parliamentary systems, and an independent and pluralistic media. Although Norris (2008: 214) does not explicitly address executive power sharing, she finds that "power sharing arrangements increase the probability of democratic governance's succeeding, even after controlling for factors such as economic development, ethnic heterogeneity, and colonial background."

Even before deciding how power is shared, the questions of who counts as a "group," and which groups should be included, have to be addressed. Are the puzzle pieces that define the society ethnic groups, or are they ideological blocks? Should every group be in the government and legislature, or only the larger groups, or indeed only the groups that might turn to violence if left out?

Regardless of how power sharing is structured, at its core it offers an alternative to simple majoritarian government where minority groups are often permanently excluded from power. The precise way in which power sharing is crafted depends on the needs and history of the given society. One nation may do best with very structured political rules, which include each and every communal group within the nation's borders, while another country may be better served by flexible arrangements which leave room for new alliances and identities.

In some post-conflict cases a winner-take-all majority rule system has been implemented but many other nations have opted for varieties of power sharing. On occasion, the largest parties in the parliament have been required to share seats in the cabinet (South Africa 1994–9); religious groups have been guaranteed executive positions (Lebanon); minorities have an effective veto over legislation that affects them (Northern Ireland); or power is shared between groups in the capital *and* through a confederal system (Sudan). Political power can be shared in a number of ways – on the basis of electoral support, on the basis of the recognition of communal blocks, or on the basis of regional elites. Even when power sharing is not required by the law, fragile governments have sought to informally include former combatants in unity administrations (Sierra Leone and Afghanistan being good examples).

HOW TO SHARE POWER

Power can be shared by a few groups or many, for all time or as a temporary arrangement to get a nation through a particularly trying period of conflict. And power can be shared in at least four different realms. (*a*) The *sharing of government* where policy decisions are made by not merely the majority but by minorities as well. The representative institutions are truly that – *representative* – they reflect the social diversity of the population, sometimes over-representing minority communities to make certain that their voices are heard. (*b*) The *sharing of jobs* can be just as important as the sharing of government. When the groups that administer or enforce the law, that is, the civil service, military, police, and judiciary are monopolized by a single group, the resentment born of exclusion can poison the smooth running of the society. (*c*) Equally crucial is the *sharing of wealth*. Many breakdowns in multiethnic states can be traced to a fight over real or perceived injustices over sharing the wealth of the nation. A group may have oil, precious minerals, or other commodities in its territory but receives little of the profits. Or one group may try and force another group off their land to lay claim to the riches. Agreed wealth-sharing provisions are key to hopes for stability in most divided societies, not least in Iraq and Sudan. (*d*) *Shared Respect for Different Values*. In addition to the previously noted ways of giving minorities a voice in decision making, power-sharing structures can include institutions which promote an ethos of toleration of difference. There may be legal bodies which protect minority rights, or institutions of reconciliation to build bridges between communities, or government funding for minority school systems and cultural activities.

PARTY/GROUP INCLUSION IN THE EXECUTIVE

Classic "Westminster" winner-take-all democracy allows a party with 51 percent of the legislature to take all the power of the executive, but in power-sharing executives minority parties take positions, usually in proportion to their vote share or population size. This can be very formal, as in Sudan where 28 percent of the ministerial positions in the Khartoum-based government are reserved for the Southern People's Liberation Movement (of the South), or in the executive of the government of Northern Ireland where each party receives cabinet positions in proportion to their legislative strength and portfolios are chosen in turn in order of party size. In 2008, the Democratic Unionists held five seats (including the First Minister), Sinn Fein four (including the Deputy First Minister), the Ulster Unionists two, and the Social Democratic and Labour Party one. The transitional government of Somalia operates on the explicit sharing of government power on what is called the 4.5 formula. The largest four clans are included equally, while the remaining smaller clans receive a half share in total.

Executive power sharing can also be formal but temporary. In South Africa between 1994 and 1999, any party with over 5 percent of the seats of the national assembly was entitled to take up a proportionate share of the cabinet positions. The National Party won 20 percent of the vote and seven positions, the Inkatha Freedom Party 10 percent and three portfolios, while the majority African National Congress won 62 percent and the remaining twenty ministerial positions. In addition, any party winning over 20 percent was awarded with a Deputy Presidency role under-studying Nelson Mandela. Thus, Thabo Mbeki (ANC) and F.W. de Klerk (NP) became Deputy Presidents. But this formal requirement for executive power sharing lapsed in 1999, and since then any non-ANC members of the cabinet have served at the invitation and pleasure of the ANC President.

However, more often than not the "grand coalition" is informal. Executive power sharing can be the result of a peace accord to stem political-ethnic violence. The formal inclusion of warring parties in a joint government may be temporary but the deal can entrench some significant innovations in democratic institutions. The National Accord and Reconciliation Act of March 2008 in Kenya created a prime minister with the authority to coordinate government functions. The Prime Minister is the leader of the largest party or coalition in parliament. In 2008, the Prime Minister was Raila Odinga, the losing presidential candidate, but if President Kibaki's party had won more seats in the legislature then they would have taken the PM position. However, the accord did put into place two Deputy Prime Ministers (one from each of the two largest parties) and called for the cabinet to proportionally reflect the main parties' parliamentary strength.

In Iraq after the fall of Saddam Hussein, cabinet posts were shared out between the dominant groups. In that state, it is difficult to imagine any government that would not include representatives from the three main ethnic blocs. The President, whose position is a largely ceremonial position, is a Kurd, the Prime Minister a Shia, and the two Deputy Presidents are Sunni and Shia. However, there was, and still is, no constitutional mandate for this and in 2010 it was unclear whether the balance would remain. In 2007, the Defense Minister was a Sunni, as were eight of his cabinet colleagues (while there were twenty-two Shia Ministers, eight Kurds, and one Christian). There is not a formal supermajority or Government of

National Unity requirement in the constitution, but the parliamentary proportional representation system makes coalitions inevitable. The sharing of executive posts is unsurprising in a nation so fragile. Kenya and Zimbabwe illustrate the pitfalls of "informal" band-aid power sharing at the executive level. Both cases demonstrate the dangers of such quick fix forms of piecemeal power sharing: (*a*) bloated cabinets, (*b*) a shallow elite commitment to the new institutions, and either (*c*) magnified elite cartels, or their mirror, (*d*) stultifying gridlock in policy making. Kenya since 2008 has demonstrated at least three of these problems. To fill the space required for supporters of both President Kibaki and Prime Minister Odinga, the Kenyan cabinet bloated to forty ministers and over forty Deputy Ministers, sucking much-needed resources from the government and creating multiple focal points for graft. Early on, Odinga's Orange Movement accused the President of ignoring ODM ministers, and in April 2009 Odinga's ministers began a boycott of cabinet meetings. The interim power sharing has apparently done little to address the divides that flared up around the 2007 elections when 1,500 people were killed in ethnically defined election result-prompted violence. As of 2009, there were rumors and reports of ethnic mobilization and polarization in advance of the scheduled 2012 elections.

In Zimbabwe, the arrangement brokered in 2009, which brought in the opposition leader Morgan Tsvangarai as Prime Minister along with sixteen other MDC cabinet ministers (three from a breakaway faction), in almost every respect has been an unmitigated failure. It may have brought a modicum of reduced state repression and economic improvement, but in governance the power-sharing turned out to be simply another subterfuge in a long line of Mugabe maneuverings. The governing ZANU-PF party signaled its true intent on the day of swearing in of the new cabinet by arresting Roy Bennett, the MDC's Deputy Minister of Agriculture nominee. The lack of vibrant "sharing" was even more apparent in Zimbabwe than Kenya and by October 2009 Tsvangarai's MDC was boycotting meetings arguing that it was their right to disengage from a dishonest and unreliable partner.

Theoretically and empirically, it is clear that a temporary executive power-sharing deal, which marries together the top two warring leaders is a poor substitute for a well-crafted permanent settlement that is embedded in either the constitution or basic law. Permanence is born of a much higher investment from all sides in the new political institutions. They may not like how they came to the place that brought them power sharing, but the leaders have become convinced that such majority constraining institutions are inevitable. However, informal and temporary arrangements as found in Kenya, Zimbabwe, and Madagascar are inherently built on foundations of sand. They are not believed in, and rarely abided by.

Alongside a grand coalition in the cabinet, other important executive and legislative positions can be shared along communal lines. In Lebanon, the President must be a Maronite Christian, the Prime Minister a Sunni Muslim and the powerful Speaker of the House a Shia. Or the very presidential office itself can be passed back and forth between the main communities. The seven members of the Federal

Council in Switzerland (an executive that includes representatives of the Radical, Socialist, Catholic, and Peasant parties, and thus German, French, and on occasion Italian-speaking Swiss) rotate the Presidency of the nation for a year at a time until all seven Council members have had a turn. Some Nigerians have proposed such a system for their country, rotating the head of state between the Yoruba, Ibo, and Hausa-Falani communities. The Liberal and Conservative parties in Colombia alternated their Presidency for sixteen years between 1958 and 1974.

Last, even when minority groups/parties are in the executive, it may be important to limit the majorities' dominance within that small body. A consensus (or sufficient consensus) ethos of decision making served the first South African cabinet well with only three decisions requiring a formal vote (1994–6). Similarly in Northern Ireland, the Executive Committee takes decisions by consensus wherever possible, but if a vote is forced it may still need the cross community support percentages as outlined earlier.

DESCRIPTIVE INCLUSION IN THE EXECUTIVE (CABINET DIVERSITY)

The data in chapter 6 suggested that the descriptive inclusion of minorities and marginalized groups in legislatures has a significant and positive impact on stability and democratization in many states. Is the same true of descriptive inclusion in executives, as defined by government ministers? I approach this question through the same four lenses: ethnic diversity, gender, sexual orientation, and age.

ETHNICITY

Cross-country data for minority representation in executive cabinets has never been systematically collected, firstly because of the difficulties in categorizing who counts as an ethnic minority in a nation state and secondly because of the lack of information about the background of politicians in those countries where identity is a sensitive subject. Table 7.1 shows the degree of ethnic diversity for twenty national cabinets as of January 2010. While the case pool is limited, the data is illustrative. Nine of the cases are established democracies, nine can be found in my list of sixty-four "patient" cases that have attempted to democratize since 1989 (see Table 3.1), while Brazil and Sri Lanka complete the list. As I did in chapter 6 for ethnic diversity in legislatures, I have compared the minority

TABLE 7.1 *Ethnic diversity in cabinets*

Case	Cabinet size	No. of minority	Minority (%)	LSQ ID
Bosnia	13	13	100	7.8
United States	23	10	43	7.3
Germany	16	1	6	3.7
Malawi	21	1	5	3.3
Sudan	25	9	36	2.1
United Kingdom	32	2	6	1.5
Zimbabwe	38	1	3	1.5
Zambia	29	0	0	−0.1
Ireland	15	0	0	−0.3
Netherlands	28	1	4	−0.9
France	20	1	5	−2.0
New Zealand	28	4	15	−2.6
Iraq	43	17	39	−3.8
Lebanon	30	30	100	−4.5
Sri Lanka	50	10	20	−5.5
Canada	38	7	18	−5.6
South Africa	30	5	17	−6.1
Brazil	30	1	3	−7.0
Israel	28	1	4	−9.9
Fiji	11	2	18	−16.9

Source: Data from 2009.

proportion of the cabinet to the minority proportion of the population and then applied Michael Gallagher's Least Squares measure of disproportionality to give a single score measure of the cabinet's inclusiveness.

As Table 7.1 shows, the highest degree of minority inclusion is demonstrated in the most plural, conflictual, and democratically fragile states. Lebanon and Bosnia's cabinets are entirely "minorities" while Iraq and Sudan currently go out of their way to include the most influential minority communities. President Obama's US cabinet also demonstrates a high degree of descriptive inclusion – although this is driven by the "over-representation" of African-Americans and Asians, while Latinos remain disproportionally under-represented. At the bottom of the table is Fiji where there are only two Indian cabinet ministers from a community that is approximately 42 percent of the population.

WOMEN

In 1998, there were 302 female cabinet ministers around the world representing 8.7 percent of the total. Ten years on that number had more than doubled to 634 representing 15.9 percent of the world (data for 1998 included 3,486 ministers in

TABLE 7.2 *Women cabinet ministers 1998 and 2008*

	Africa	Asia	Central and Eastern Europe	Middle East	North America & Caribbean	Oceania	South and Central America	West Europe	*Total*	*Established democracy*
#1998	84	26	31	5	36	7	33	80	*302*	*108*
% 1998	7.8	5.9	5.3	2.1	14.7	3.9	10.5	20.0	*8.7*	*17.1*
#2008	222	48	63	21	53	26	94	107	*634*	*171*
% 2008	17.7	8.2	12.2	6.0	18.8	11.9	23.4	28.6	*15.9*	*25.7*
% increase	127.0	28.0	130.2	186.1	27.9	205.1	122.8	43.0	*82.8*	*50.3*

Note: December 1998 – 180 cases; January 2008 – 190 cases.
Sources: Reynolds (1999) and compiled by author from IPU data for 2008.

180 nation states while data for 2008 is based on 3,983 cabinet members in 190 states). The most impressive gains for women in executive positions occurred in Oceania and the Middle East where numbers tripled, albeit from very low baselines. The number of women in African, Central/Eastern European, and Latin American cabinets more than doubled, while Western Europe maintains the highest levels of women ministers with 29 percent. The smallest advances were seen in Asia and North America/Caribbean, with Asian nations now having only a slighter higher proportion of women leaders as the Middle East nations. The gain for established democracies over the decade was 50 percent while for all other nations it was 139 percent (Table 7.2).

When it comes to the type of portfolios held, women continue to be relegated most often to the "softer" social ministries. However, even in this respect there has been progress since 1998. In 1998, only 6 percent (19) of the "big four" ministries (Foreign Affairs, Finance, Home Affairs, and Defense) were held by women but by 2008 that number had almost doubled to 11 percent (indeed ninety-nine women hold a related "big four" portfolio if not top job). In 1998, the soft five ministries was where one would find the most women (Women, Children, Culture, Sport, and Tourism) – 34 percent. But by 2008 that proportion had declined to 23 percent (Table 7.3).

The link between female cabinet ministers and a nation's gender progressiveness is a murky one. There is no correlation between the simple cabinet percentage and the UN Gender Related Development Index or the World Economic Forum's Global Gender Gap Index.[1] This is largely because while many developing world countries have higher numbers of women in their executives than established democracies, the influence of those women is often heavily constrained. Further, there is no support for the notion that more women at the highest level of

[1] http://www.weforum.org/en/Communities/Women%20Leaders%20and%20Gender%20Parity/GenderGapNetwork/index.htm

TABLE 7.3 *Ministerial portfolios held by women*

	Proportion of total 1998 (%)	Proportion of total 2008 (%)
Foreign affairs	3	5
Finance–treasury	1	2
Home–interior	1	3
Defense	1	1
Health–welfare	14	14
Education	9	7
Labor–employment	6	5
Environment–energy	6	6
Planning–development	5	10
Law–justice	4	5
Communication–information	4	3
Trade–industry–science	4	7
Agriculture–fishing	3	3
Regional–local	3	2
Transport	2	2
Civil service	1	3
Housing	1	3
Women's affairs	13	7
Culture–arts	9	4
Family–children	8	8
Sport	3	2
Tourism	1	2

Note: December 1998 – 180 cases; January 2008 – 190 cases.
Sources: Reynolds (1999) and compiled by author from IPU data for 2008.

government make slippage back from strides toward gender equity less likely. The World Economic Forum's data shows that in forty-three nations the gap between men and women's status on dimension of economic participation, educational attainment, health, and political empowerment actually widened between 2008 and 2009. Those countries had an average of 16.2 percent women in cabinet, compared to the global average of 16 percent.

SEXUAL ORIENTATION

At the executive level there are currently, and have been in the past, a few openly gay cabinet ministers. I have identified seventeen. Guido Westerwelle became Foreign Minister of Germany in October 2009, along with being leader of the German Free Democratic Party. Senator Penny Wong is Australia's first Climate Change and Water Minister, becoming both the country's first openly gay and Asian-born cabinet minister. Chris Carter is New Zealand's Minister of Education, and Gerda Verburg is the Dutch Minister for Agriculture, Nature, and Food Quality. The Italian Green leader, Alfonso Pecoraro Scanio, was appointed by Prime Minister Romano Prodi as Environment Minister in 2006. Gábor Szetey came out as Hungary's first openly gay politician in 2007 after being appointed as Secretary of State for Human Resources in 2006. As of 2009, there were two openly gay or bisexual Ministers in the Swedish cabinet, Tobias Billström (Migration and Asylum Policy) and Andreas Carlgren (Environment and Sustainable Development). In June 2009, Nicolas Sarkozy appointed Frédéric Mitterrand, nephew of the late President François Mitterrand, as culture minister – Mitterrand is openly gay and a columnist in the gay magazine *Tetu*. Former out cabinet ministers include: Chris Smith, who was appointed UK Secretary of State for Culture, Media, and Sport in 1997 (and the first MP to acknowledge he was HIV positive in 2005); Peter Mandelson was the UK Secretary of State for Trade and Industry 1998 and Secretary of State for Northern Ireland 1999–2001. Between 2004 and 2008, he served as the European Commissioner for Trade but returned to the British cabinet as Secretary of State for Business in October 2008. Nick Brown was UK Minister for Agriculture 1998–2001, Scott Brison was Minister of Public Works and Government Service in Canada until 2006, and Per-Kristian Foss, Norwegian Minister of Finance 2001–5, and also Prime Minister briefly in 2002. Jeronimo Saavedra Acevedo was the Spanish Minister of Public Administration 1993–5 and Minister of Education and Science 1995–6, but as noted earlier he did not come out until 2000. In 2007, he was elected mayor of Las Palmas in the Canary Islands. Roger Karoutchi, Minister in Charge of Parliamentary Relations in the French Government, came out while in office in 2009. Karoutchi is currently French Ambassador to the OECD. There are prominent openly gay mayors in Berlin (Klaus Wowereit), Paris (Bertrand Delanoe), Houston (Annise Parker), and Cambridge, England (transsexual, Jenny Bailey). Jóhanna Sigurðardóttir was Minister of Social Affairs in Iceland before becoming Prime Minister in 2009.

Unsurprisingly there is a link between the presence of openly gay cabinet ministers and progressive LGBT public policy, but the causal arrows are not clear. The twelve nations that have, or have had, openly gay executive office holders, score 3.0 on the "gay friendly law" index (which ranges between –2 and 5, see chapter 6). In contrast, the average for all sixty-six cases scored under the index is 1.1. Ten of these twelve cases have enacted either gay marriage or civil partnership provisions. Among these cases, five states had gay cabinet ministers *before* the legislation was passed, while the other five saw the appointment of openly gay cabinet ministers only *after* the progressive legislation had come into force (in the cases of Iceland, the Netherlands, Germany, and Sweden, many years after gay marriage/union laws had been passed) (Table 7.4).

TABLE 7.4 *Open LGBT cabinet ministers (2010)*

Chris Smith	Culture	United Kingdom	1997–2001
Peter Mandelson	Trade and industry	United Kingdom	1998–9
	Northern Ireland		1999–2001
	Business		2008–9
Nick Brown	Agriculture	United Kingdom	1998–2001
Per-Kristian Foss	Finance	Norway	2001–5
	Acting PM		2002
Alfonso Pecoraro	Agriculture	Italy	2000–1
Scanio	Environment		2006–8
Chris Carter	Housing	New Zealand	2004–5
	Building		2005–7
	Education		2007–8
Scott Brison	Public works	Canada	2004–6
Tobias Billström	Migration	Sweden	2006–
Andreas Carlgren	Environment	Sweden	2006–
Gerda Verberg	Agriculture, nature, and food	Netherlands	2007–
Gábor Szetey	Human resources	Hungary	2007–8
Jóhanna	Social affairs	Iceland	2007–9
Sigurðardóttir	Prime Minister		2009–
Penny Wong	Climate change	Australia	2008–
Roger Karoutchi	Parliamentary relations	France	2007–9
Frederic Mitterrand	Culture	France	2009–
Guido Westerwelle	Foreign Minister	Germany	2009–

YOUTH (UNDER 30)

As noted in chapter 6, there are 502 members of parliament under the age of 30 in the seventy-two cases that I have data for (5% of the total), but as of 2009 I have not been able to find a single cabinet minister in the world who is under 30 years of age. The closest is Agatha Sangma, the Minister of State in the Ministry of Rural Development in the Indian government who was 28 when appointed but her executive position is not technically in the cabinet. Kate Jones was 29 in March 2009 when appointed to become the state of Queensland's (Australia) climate change and sustainability minister.

THE USE OF DECENTRALIZATION OF POWER

Devolving power down to regional, local, or village levels is a significant tool of the power-sharing constructor. The benefits for peace and stability in divided societies have been manifest in countless plural nations that use federal states as the building blocks of their national government. Indeed, Stepan argues that to be democratic a plural state *must* be federal (Stepan 1999), while Nancy Bermeo finds that when minorities are geographically concentrated federalism helps to keep the peace (Bermeo 2002). It is true that decentralization can invest a minority group in decisions that directly effect them, particularly when the minority is geographically concentrated. Power over their own affairs, in their own region, can reassure a marginalized group that their rights will be protected. Local leaders deciding local issues may also be a more vibrant form of democracy in any nation. Decentralization is an important aspect of power sharing because power sharing rests on multiple access points to power, allowing for control to be spread out. Giving substantive power to regional, municipal, and village governments is an excellent way of creating many new doorways to real power.

Creating a federal state is an important step to recognizing diversity and creating multiple access points to power, which minority groups can take advantage of. Nowhere is this clearer than in modern Afghanistan. In contrast to the Iraqi model, and in the face of significant geographical concentrations of mutually distrustful Pashtuns, Hazaras, Uzbeks, and Tajiks, Afghanistan chose to adopt a highly centralized system devoid of federalism or significant provincial or local government. The democratic designers diagnosed the ailment of Afghanistan as one of a weak center thwarted in its reform and modernization efforts by a powerful, corrupt, and fragmented periphery. Thus, they chose to give a large amount of power to the central state in Kabul. The logic may have been sound but of course central government needs to be backed up by state power. There must either be a central monopoly of force to subjugate the local strong men or enough resources to leverage the people away from dependence on the traditionally powerful, local elites. Unfortunately, the central Afghan state has neither the resources nor the force to achieve either of these ends; the state is a paper tiger and relies on shifting alliances to maintain some degree of control. Centralization of power in Afghanistan may have been the most dangerous example of wishful thinking.

But there are dangers of decentralization. First, localizing control may merely empower and entrench the existing undemocratic power brokers who hold sway on the ground in war-torn societies. A decentralized power structure in Afghanistan might lessen conflict and reassure minorities in the North and West (Hazaras could happily run the central provinces of Bamyan and Daikondi while Uzbeks would dominate in Faryb and Jozjan in the North), but a federal structure would undoubtedly empower the Taliban in vast swathes of the south and east of the country. Second, the transferring of state resources from the center to the periphery can enrich and finance anti-governmental groups – guerillas, warlords, and ideological paramilitaries. Eaton describes how decentralization in Colombia financed anti-state paramilitaries from both the left and the right and ultimately contributed to the destruction of the central state's monopoly of force (Eaton 2006). Third, the push toward federalism, or confederalism, can spur on the slip toward secessionism and the breakup of the state. Many observers fear that the Sudanese power-sharing agreement of 2005, which devolved significant power to a Government of the Southern Sudan, and scheduled a referendum on independence, in fact precipitates the breakup of that state.

SHARING INFLUENCE OUTSIDE OF THE ELECTORAL SPHERE: JOBS, WEALTH, AND VALUES

While including the key groups and parties in the institutions of government is crucial, true inclusion only comes about through fair representation of all groups in the organizations that administer, police, adjudicate, and defend the nation. Laws may be drafted by an inclusive legislature, but if they are administered by a bureaucracy that is dominated by one ethnic group then the excluded groups have good reason to believe that in their interpretation the laws will be biased. If the police are overwhelmingly of one group (as the Royal Ulster Constabulary (RUC) were in Northern Ireland) then the "other side" will be deeply distrustful that the law is applied equally. When the judiciary is all of one side, the appearance (if not the reality) of bias is terribly destabilizing. Last, if the military represents just one community (or the leadership is from one side and the foot soldiers from another) you have a recipe for anything ranging from the military influencing elected governments to outright coups d'état. Power sharing often requires that the membership of the civil service, military, police, judiciary, be balanced and diverse. This can be according to a particular formula (quotas), group proportionality, multiparty allocations, or a less formal ethos of inclusion and affirmative promotion of minority professionals.

The civil service, military, police, and judiciary might be productively diversified to include minorities and indeed share jobs out proportionally among the main groups but, as with most options, there are dangers to such a strategy. What happens when there is a lack of capacity, skills, or expertise among the previously marginalized groups to fill those reserved positions? Does the government merely let the administrative units of the state collapse or does it maintain institutions with one group dominating as they always have? Clearly, removing majority individuals from their jobs to replace them with minorities will breed huge resentment if handled in an insensitive way. In South Africa, white bureaucrats and military officers were protected from being removed for a five-year period after 1994. In Northern Ireland, nationalist distrust of the police force has made it difficult to try and attract Catholic recruits to integrate the service. In many cases, it is far from sufficient to mandate balance in employment – the state must uplift the marginalized to provide them the skills and experience to fulfill bureaucratic, police, or judicial roles.

One of the most important underlying causes of conflict is the perception (real or imagined) that the wealth of the nation, the resources, and the investments in society are skewed toward the members of one group. To minimize such a source of conflict, a number of strategies can be tried. Public spending can be aimed at addressing historical imbalances. State monies are invested in marginalized communities: their jobs, health care, education, and community infrastructure. Ever since its birth in 1948, India has had a policy of directing state resources to uplift the weakest and poorest.

Wealth sharing can require that resource allocation takes place according to a particular formula or proportionality. The 2005 Comprehensive Peace Agreement in Sudan provides for 50 percent of revenues from oil producing wells in Southern Sudan to go to the South and the other 50 percent to the National Government and the states in Northern Sudan. A small amount of the profits are also reserved for the local areas where the oil is found – in particular, the borderland disputed territories of Abeyei, the Nuba mountains, and the Blue Nile. An alternative strategy is to share the wealth of the nation from a central pot, regardless of where the money, resources, and taxes actually come from. Unitary governments, without significant decentralized power, in theory would be able to share equally on the basis of population or land size. Power sharing after a period of minority rule may see land redistribution as an important element in the broader goal of uplifting a historically disadvantaged group. Redistribution has occurred with varying degrees of success in Southern Africa (South Africa, Namibia, and Zimbabwe) and in Guatemala.

Wealth sharing may be the trickiest part of power sharing of all. There are very few cases of successful wealth sharing where majorities and minorities are satisfied with the way the resources of the nation are allocated. Some of the key challenges are (a) leaving out of wealth sharing those regions who are not blessed with natural resources (e.g., Darfur, Sudan; Sunni areas in Iraq); (b) ensuring that the benefits of wealth sharing trickle down to regular citizens and do not merely fill up the private pockets of corrupt elites (there are already signs of this happening under the North-South oil-wealth-sharing deals in the Sudan); (c) an important aspect of wealth sharing can be land redistribution where marginalized groups reclaim or are given access to land, which has long been monopolized by a hostile group. However, if done poorly such land redistribution can devastate the economy. Farms can be fragmented to such a degree that they become unviable; land may be given to corrupt elites rather than the masses, the repossession of land can generate great fear and resentment on behalf of the minority, and the rule of law may be injured in the process. All of these dangers have been dramatically on show in Zimbabwe.

The building of respect for differing communal values and practices can be encouraged by institutions. Power-sharing regimes usually seek to explicitly protect minority cultural, language, and education rights. There may be state funding for minority communal schools (as in Northern Ireland). A parallel legal system can be established to serve a community with distinct rules (Muslims in India). A specialized consultative body can be appointed/elected, which must review legislation that affects the group members (e.g., house of chiefs in South Africa).

It is probably the case that trying to promote shared respect, mutual understanding, and reconciliation through institutions is the most difficult challenge that any divided society faces. Legal bodies can only do so much to change hearts and minds. Truth and Reconciliation Commissions in Africa and Latin American have been criticized for being weighted in favor of the perpetrators of violence, rather than their victims. Some South Africans felt that their TRC was too quick to give amnesty and too slow to reveal "truths." When the state funds certain minority education rights, it may be advantaging separation over integration and parallel communal legal systems may transgress basic individual rights, which should be ensured by the State as a whole. There is a fine line to be trod between the respect of different cultural values, and practices and the segmentation and polarization of groups.

CHALLENGES TO POWER-SHARING AGREEMENTS

Power-sharing solutions are reached, and endure, when the stars come into alignment – a variety of factors need to be favorable. The timing must be right, the process must have sufficient domestic ownership, and all the groups that matter must be around the negotiating table.

Peace settlements, especially those that revolve around power-sharing provisions, happen when the time is "ripe." Much as though we may wish for conflict and tension to be eased as soon as possible, the leaders and people may just not be ready to abide by a negotiated settlement. If the time is not ripe, then imposing a settlement from outside may be setting up a new government for quick failure. So how do we know that the time is ripe and that real negotiations can begin and succeed? Violence can reach a stage of exhaustion where the leadership of all parties to the conflict come to believe that their future economic and communal well-being is only hurt by *continued* violence. Exhaustion may be a factor of time, number of deaths, or collateral impacts on the everyday lives of people. However, countless cases of ethnic conflict have apparently defied the exhaustion that many predicted – for example, Sri Lanka's impasse continues despite nearly a half century of instability. A few years ago, Sudan and Northern Ireland's vulnerability seemed similarly intractable. Political leaders may make the calculation that they gain more from instability than the formal stability of a political settlement, but even when such incentives to *not* share power exist, there remain cases of noble leadership where pragmatism and accommodation overcomes the desire for short-term gain. The choice to make peace can be encouraged by outside pressure; either neighboring countries with a reason to press for a settlement, or a superpower that is motivated to bring its diplomatic leverage in bear on the problem.

Of course there is a great tension between international intervention to bring about a power-sharing settlement and the likelihood that such an externally promoted agreement will endure once the foreign actors leave the scene. If the locals themselves do not fully accept power sharing, how will they abide by its rules when the mediators leave the country? Even if there is significant local ownership of the peace process, can the fragile new government survive without constant international support and assistance? Sisk and Paris (2009) note three key tensions and contradictions when it comes to international involvement in postwar state building (of any sort). (*a*) Outside intervention is used to foster self-government. A superpower may install a power-sharing government but the weak new administration may rely heavily on the superpower to survive. When the external power goes, has it left a state with enough local support to endure challenges from the extremes? (*b*) Outsiders are involved in defining "legitimate" local leaders. The foreign power inevitably ends up helping to determine who gets a seat at the table – on occasion the interventionists have pushed heavily their "preferred local leaders" even when it was demonstrated that those leaders had very little local support. You can only share power among those who are actually *powerful*. (*c*) "Universal" values are promoted as a remedy for local problems. One of the problems with (the limited) advocacy of formal power sharing, which has been tried over the last decade is that it still resembles a one-size-fits-all construct that may be unsuitable for the needs of the given society at issue. Power-sharing options are sometimes too packaged to be adaptable to very different local conditions.

Even if the peace talks are locally owned, power-sharing agreements are typically negotiated between the armed factions and dominant communal groups. They can limit political participation to a narrow category of actor. Civil society groups, nonviolent leaders, multiethnic leaders, and indeed any group that is too weak to demand a seat at the table will be locked out of the power-sharing bargains which are made. This has implications for the sort of state that is formed by such settlements and the longer term stability of the agreements reached. Few would dispute the fact that the armed groups need to be included in any pact, but limiting negotiations to such groups provides a weak foundation for a democratic future. On occasion, power-sharing negotiations fail to include a certain group or region and that motivates a new armed conflict – such was the case in the Darfur region of Sudan in 2003 as the marginalized Western part of the country felt they had no voice at the North–South peace talks being held in Kenya.

At least three challenges face a grand coalition power-sharing executive: first, the exclusion of others; second, the devil in the details; and third, the danger of paralysis. In Sudan, the Comprehensive Peace Agreement signed in 2005 was neither comprehensive nor a guarantee of peace. Twenty percent of the cabinet in Khartoum (the Government of Sudan) and in Juba (the Government of the Southern Sudan) was reserved for minority groups outside of the big two – the NCP and SPLM, but these positions have been largely directed to complicit leaders rather than authentic opposition leaders. In most other cases, the smaller minorities do not receive any executive representation. The power sharing goes on between the largest and most militarized groups.

When it comes to any power-sharing executive, the devil is in the details. Sometimes the allocation of cabinet positions can be fair and formal (as in Northern Ireland) or informal (as in South Africa in 1994), but often major fights arise over which portfolios each group gets. The specific seats were not set out in the Sudanese CPA and this became a major source of conflict in the appointment of the government. The SPLM wanted the Ministry of Energy and Resources, and had been promised it, but lost it at the last minute when President al Bashir was prevailed upon to maintain the control over oil contracts for the North. Last, as in the legislature, a need for consensus in the cabinet can lead to gridlock; one could allow majority rule in executive decisions but this would fly in the face of the power-sharing principle.

Tull and Mehler (2005) do not merely see challenges in how power sharing is implemented but they argue that the heightened awareness of power sharing as an institutional option has actually *increased* civil strife and induced ethnic elites to conquer state power by violent rather than nonviolent means. As power sharing has become a key component of Western aid for post-conflict reconstruction plans, the rebels see an opportunity. "Providing rebels with a share of power, has important demonstration effects across the continent (Africa). It creates an incentive structure would-be leaders can seize upon by embarking on the insurgent path as well." Tull and Mehler argue this was at work in Burundi, Rwanda, the Democratic Republic of the Congo, Sierra Leone, Liberia, Ivory Coast, Sudan, Central African Republic, and Chad. In sum, air bags make drivers more dangerous and advances in lung cancer treatment make smoking more likely.

LONGER TERM PITFALLS OF POWER SHARING

Even if the short-term benefits of power sharing are manifest, there are a number of longer term potential difficulties and downsides to any power-sharing construct. The key challenges lay in the areas of leadership, entrenching hostile identities, promoting policy deadlock, resourcing the construct, being adaptable to new realities, and striking a balance between international help and domestic ownership. To function well, power sharing requires political leadership that is willing to compromise and build coalitions across ethnic or religious divides. Of course this is rare in post-conflict or divided societies: peace-loving leaders can be a rarity and extremism can catch hold quicker than moderation. Even when elites come to the realization that sharing power is better than fighting, they remain under pressure from firebrand elements within their constituencies who oppose compromise. The initial power-sharing construct is more focused on practicalities than a change in mindset or worldview. Power-sharing arrangements are often the result of agreements between elites over access to power and resources, not real attempts to resolve divisions between ethnic communities. Therefore, the power sharing may be little more than a band-aid over deep social wounds. Without significant reconciliation, the institutions may crumble in the face of the next flashpoint. Robert Kaplan (1997: 60) places the blame for the Rwandan genocide at the feet of their 1992 Hutu-Tutsi power-sharing coalition government, arguing that "the new political parties became masks for ethnic groups that organized murderous militias, and the coalition nature of the new government helped to prepare the context for the events that led to the genocide in 1994." Kaplan offers no causal link between power sharing and the promotion of genocide, but he does point to the fact that simply sharing executive power between representatives of the main ethnic divisions did not dampen the rise of extremists in that case.

Related to this is the conundrum recognizing difference, in a very formal way, without perpetuating the divisions. Power-sharing constructs can freeze the wartime balance of power, advantage those who began the conflict, and preclude the evolution of politics to something different. At their worst, power-sharing institutions entrench the war instigators and shut down the political space for new leaders to emerge and the expression of other, nonsectarian, interests. In many cases, the formal organization of power along identity or ethnic lines seems to entrench the divisions that fueled the conflict, rather than ameliorate them, and divisions appear to become even more radicalized during the power-sharing phase.

At their core, all power-sharing constructs restrain the majority and include the minority so they inherently create substantial potential for political deadlock. Although cooperative behavior may emerge in the long term, that may take decades. Before power-sharing governments evolve into a nonethnic way of politics, they may simply stagnate. Power sharing is designed to make decision making more inclusive, if not consensus based, in order to reassure parties that they will be consulted on matters of importance. However, this reduces the parties' incentives to compromise and hence often leads to deadlock. Power-sharing governments are also especially vulnerable to collapse when one or more parties pull out or threaten to do so. Working through consensus requires substantial commitment and compromise, which is difficult to achieve in highly divided societies. If the power-sharing regime *is* working as it should, then all the significant groups come together to agree on policy and procedures. But this very consensus weakens the crucial role that an opposition plays in democracy.

When everyone is on the same page, who is to check the abuses of power and enrichment of elites that inevitably takes place when leaders become detached and unchecked?

Power-sharing institutions require significant investment. New policies need to be administered, new institutions need to be resourced, and new jobs are created. If the state does not have the resources to fully fund the power-sharing agreement, and share out power meaningfully, popular alienation will quickly follow. Minority leaders may be given cabinet titles, marginalized communities may be promised new investments, the bureaucracy will be diversified and enlarged, and the legal system will be vested with new responsibilities to protect. But without significant monies the fragile pact will collapse under the weight of unfulfilled expectations.

Power-sharing arrangements are put into place often at times of crisis and fragility, but while political realities change it is unusual that democratic institutions are reformed to reflect the new realities. As I noted in chapter 3, the freezing of institutions at the time of emergency medicine sets a dangerous precedent. Constitutions are notoriously difficult to change and power-sharing provisions can be even more frozen. There are two significant ways that divided societies evolve. Either, the groups change in their strength and numbers, or the very nature of political identity changes. The former is more common than the latter, but in either case the power-sharing institutions may become inappropriate for the new politics. The Lebanese government is shared on a rigid 50/50 split between Christians and Muslims, but emigration has reduced the Christian Lebanese population to a figure far below half of the nation. Switzerland took many years to alter its 2:2:2:1 "magic" formula for executive membership of their federal council. From 1959, the Free Democratic Party, Social Democratic Party, and Christian Democratic People's Party received two executive positions and the Swiss People's Party one. But by 1999, the Swiss People's Party had gone from being the smallest vote getter to the largest – however, it took a huge political groundswell to redistribute one seat from the Christian Democrats to the People's Party.

CONCLUSIONS

At their very best, power-sharing institutions promote an ethos of inclusion – bringing minority voices into the conversation and restraining majorities from monopolizing power. At its core, it offers an alternative to simple majoritarian government where minority groups are often permanently excluded from power. The representative institutions are truly that – *representative* – they better reflect the social diversity of the population. Agreed wealth-sharing provisions are key to hopes for stability in most divided societies. Power-sharing structures can include institutions that promote an ethos of toleration of difference. Giving power over their own affairs, in their own region, can reassure a marginalized group that their rights will be protected. One of the most important underlying causes of conflict is the perception that the wealth of the nation is skewed toward the members of one group. Wealth sharing can minimize that source of conflict. Land redistribution is an important element in the broader goal of uplifting a historically disadvantaged group. Power sharing can provide the foundation for a more efficient form of policy making, which puts into place policies that can be sustained for the long run. Power sharing provides groups with incentives to work within the system rather than following an anti-system or violent path. A longer-term goal of power sharing is to breed understanding and compromise through familiarity.

But conversely, if the time is not ripe then imposing a power-sharing settlement from outside may be setting up a new government for quick failure. Power-sharing agreements are typically negotiated between the armed factions and so they limit political participation to a narrow category of actor. The list PR election system used in many power-sharing regimes has problems with geographical and individual accountability. PR systems also rely heavily on political parties as the building blocks of the polity, but what if there are no established or trusted political parties? How does one define and measure ethnic group membership in a power-sharing regime? If you predefine who has a right to representation, you can preclude multiethnic movements. Power sharing is usually introduced at a time of crisis and fragility when swift and effective decision making is at a premium but power sharing can lead to gridlock. There are very few cases of successful wealth sharing where majorities and minorities are satisfied with the way the resources of the nation are allocated. Power sharing requires political leadership that is willing to compromise and build coalitions across ethnic or religious divides, but this is rare in post-conflict or divided societies. Power-sharing constructs can freeze the wartime balance of power, advantage those who began the conflict, and preclude the evolution of politics to something different. Power-sharing institutions can shut down the political space for new leaders to emerge and the expression of other, nonsectarian, interests. If the state does not have the resources to fully fund the power-sharing agreement, and share out power meaningfully, alienation will quickly follow. The institutions imposed during the peace settlement can be counterproductive for the consolidation of a democratic political order in the longer term.

8

Case Treatment Plans

This book has attempted to answer an apparently simple question – what makes for a lasting democracy? Unfortunately, the answer to this simple question proves to be complicated beyond belief. Even if one had perfect command of the interactions of the moving parts of history, economics, sociology, and politics, one would still be mystified about why some nations democratize and stabilize while others collapse into anarchy. Earlier chapters in this book have offered quantitative evidence based on data from over sixty cases which suggested that there are background factors which facilitate stability and promote democracy, and choosing the right institutions can help even in apparently unsuitable cases.

In chapter 3, I offered twenty demographic, sociopolitical, economic, and historical variables that should be considered when diagnosing what ails a state and would help inform the choice of the institutional medicines most appropriate to heal their body politic. Chapter 4 applied that theory to the case pool and found that while stability and democracy were driven by a variety of socioeconomic factors, institutional choices such as the electoral system, inclusion in the executive, the presidential versus parliamentary dichotomy, and the degree of decentralization helped explain more of the puzzle.

To supplement our investigation, I now turn to a more detailed analysis of six paired cases to test whether our quantitative findings have resonance in some of the most important cases of post-conflict democratic design in the world today. Furthermore, what institutions would our theory predict should be used in each case to help promote democracy and stability?

Two are patients in the Intensive Care Unit – Afghanistan and Iraq – who have dominated American and European foreign policy for the last decade. A second pair of cases – Sudan and Zimbabwe – are in the operating theater undergoing *democratic surgery* (transitional elections and constitutional redesign). Both cases are high profile, regionally consequential, and likely to become even more visible as they go through the traumas of elections and government change. Last, I consider two prospective patients – Syria and Burma – dictatorships which show little sign of moving toward democracy, but nevertheless could do so under drastically altered domestic and international conditions. I include Syria and Burma because the theory of constitutional design and practice of democracy support has been particularly ill-prepared for the surprises of state transformation.

Using the rubric of diagnosis and the evidence of the consequences of democratic design laid out in earlier chapters, I assess the prognosis for democratic stability in Afghanistan, Iraq, Sudan, and Zimbabwe: (*a*) What are the political, social, economic, and historical connections between the cases? (*b*) How did their transitions to democracy affect their trajectories? (*c*) In what ways are the challenges similar and how do they differ? (*d*) Specifically in each case, what democratic arrangements have been put in place and are they most appropriate? (*e*) If evidence from elsewhere suggests that the institutions used today are not likely to promote long-term health, well then what would be better? For the future patient cases of Syria and Burma, I will run the diagnosis and offer prescriptions.

CHANCES OF STABILITY

First, let us assess how the six cases do under the methodology of diagnosis developed earlier. Table 4.8 described how six variables were statistically significant in predicting stability in our overall model: (*a*) the degree of nationalism, (*b*) the income level, (*c*) the dependency on natural resources, and (*d*) the nature of those resources, (*e*) the type of *ancien regime*, and (*f*) the electoral system used for multiparty elections in the new dispensation.

Table 8.1 illustrates that our six focal cases are unsurprisingly complex in their background diagnostic characteristics. If each factor was of equal weight across country and time, we could merely add up the pluses and minuses and say country X is most likely to be stable and country Y has no chance. But unfortunately, while we have good evidence to say how each factor matters and in what way, we do not have a grasp on the relative weight of factors within a given case. For example, having a proportional election system may help in a post-conflict state but that positive can be outweighed by the much more powerful blight of a plethora of lootable resources. Alternatively, a nation may have a sleeping but potentially unifying nationalism, but that advantage is subsumed under a crashing economy and polarizing election system.

The patterns in the table do suggest that the least likely cases to be stable in the foreseeable future are Afghanistan and Sudan, while perhaps surprisingly, Syria (even if they began to hold multiparty competitive elections) would have the best chance of stability. The only indicator in which Afghanistan scores positively is its lack of a formal economic dependence on natural resources but of course informally their dependence on opium is overwhelming. At least Sudan's natural resource dependence is on oil (not narcotics) and it uses a proportional election system, but on the remaining diagnostic elements Sudan scores either poorly or very poorly. Burma struggles with almost as much inherent instability as

TABLE 8.1 *Diagnosing prospects for stability*

	Iraq	Afghanistan	Sudan	Zimbabwe	Burma	Syria
Nationalism	×	×	×	√√	×	√√
Income	√	××	×	××	××	√
Natural resources	××	√√	××	√	√√	—
Resource type	√	××	√	√√	××	√
Ancien regime	×	×	×	××	√	×
Electoral system	√	×	√	××	××	××

Notes: √√ = highly favorable, √ = favorable, × = unfavorable, ×× = highly unfavorable. For data measurement, see chapter 3.

Afghanistan (although its military regime makes any future democracy slightly more predisposed to success than if it had minority oligarchy or theocratic ancient regime). Iraq and Zimbabwe, while not quite as well positioned for stability as Syria, are in better shape than the other four cases. Iraq has a higher level of income, the "right" type of resources, and a positive election system. Zimbabweans are fortunate to share a national identity and a lower dependence on natural resources. This is not to say that either case is guaranteed to be any better off than the other cases, but it is true that they have a stronger foundation for stability if other elements can fall into place. The diagnostic model would predict that (if the variables remain the same) Iraq is more likely to stabilize than Afghanistan and Zimbabwe is more likely to survive than Sudan. While some of the variables are givens (such as the *ancien regime* or the type of natural resources a state possesses), others are potentially changeable. It would take many years for Afghanistan to dramatically increase its GDP or Sudan to reduce its dependence on oil revenues, but the model suggests that such a mission would be good for stability. The easiest variable to change (among the six listed here) is the election system and that is why so much attention has been paid to that lever of political pressure.

PROSPECTS FOR DEMOCRACY

When it comes to democracy, twenty variables had a statistical relationship to some aspect of democratic health: executive recruitment, executive constraints, and/or political competition (see Table 4.8). Two of those variables affected component parts in opposite ways. The type of *ancien regime* had a reverse effect on executive constraints than its effect on political competition, and more proportional election systems increased the vibrancy of political competition but lessened executive constraints. As with stability, our six cases vary greatly on their foundational propensities for democratic vibrancy. Again this is unsurprising

TABLE 8.2 *Diagnosing prospects for democracy: executive recruitment*

	Iraq	Afghan	Sudan	Zimbabwe	Burma	Syria
Majority group	√	××	√	√√	√	√√
Income	√	××	×	××	××	√
Inequality	×	√√	√	√	×	×
Antigovernment	√	√√	√√	×	√	××
Ex inclusion	××	√	××	×	√√	√√

Notes: √√ = highly favorable, √ = favorable, × = unfavorable, ×× = highly unfavorable. For data measurement, see chapter 3.

TABLE 8.3 *Diagnosing prospects for democracy: executive constraints*

	Iraq	Afghanistan	Sudan	Zimbabwe	Burma	Syria
Majority group	√	××	√	√√	√	√√
Nationalism	×	×	×	√√	×	√√
Natural resources	××	√√	××	√	√√	˙
Resource type	√	××	√	√√	××	√
Ancien regime	×	×	×	××	√	×
Transition	√	√	×			
Antigovernment	√	√√	√√	×	√	××
Electoral system	√	×	√	××	××	××
Ex inclusion	××	√	××	×	√√	√√
Parliamentary	√√	××	×	××	××	××

Notes: √√ = highly favorable, √ = favorable, × = unfavorable, ×× = highly unfavorable, ˙ = neutral. For data measurement, see chapter 3.

because these cases are among the most fragile and least obviously susceptible to democratization.

POLITY IV scores the democratic strength of a nation's "executive recruitment" by looking at the competitiveness, openness, and regulation of the process that leads to the selection of an executive. Five variables were significant predictors of executive recruitment scores in the overall data model. In this regard, each of our cases demonstrates positive and negative background conditions. Syria has the highest propensity for vibrant executive recruitment if we just look at these five variables (Table 8.2). Surprisingly, Afghanistan is better placed than Iraq to have democratic executive recruitment measures, while Zimbabwe is least well placed on this aspect.

Executive constraints are deemed to be the constitutional requirements and rules that constrain the power of a prime minister or president. In this regard they are more formal articulations of democracy rather than practical applications. Ten of our independent variables were correlated with this part of the POLITY index and Table 8.3 shows each case performance. Iraq does better on predictors for a constrained executive than it did for executive recruitment, while Afghanistan does much worse. Similarly, Sudan's background diagnostic

TABLE 8.4 *Diagnosing prospects for democracy: political competition*

	Iraq	Afghan	Sudan	Zimbabwe	Burma	Syria
Majority Group	√	××	√	√√	√	√√
Fragmentation	×	×	×	×	×	×
Concentration	√	√	√√	×	√√	×
External threat	××	××	×	√	√	××
Income	√	××	×	××	××	√
Inequality	×	√√	√	√	×	×
Resource type	√	××	√	√√	××	√
Colonialism	××	√√	×	×	×	√
Ancien regime	√	√	√	√√	×	√
Military	√	××	××	√√	×	√
Culture			××			
Transition	√	√	×			
Violence	××	××	××	√	×	√
Antigovernment	√	√√	√√	×	√	××
Electoral system	√	×	√	××	××	××
Federalism	××	√√	×	√√	√√	√√
Parliamentary	√√	×>	×	××	××	××

Notes: √√ = highly favorable, √ = favorable, × = unfavorable, ×× = highly unfavorable, ' = neutral. For data measurement, see chapter 3.

characteristics would suggest that it will be more democratic in its recruitment of an executive than the constraints that the President and cabinet operate under.

Table 8.4 shows the seventeen variables that affected political competition. Zimbabwe and Iraq demonstrate a slight balance in favor of positive attributes when it comes to predicting the vibrancy of democratic political competition, but Sudan and Afghanistan remain very poorly positioned for strong political competition. While Burma was somewhat middling on the first two indicators of democracy, Table 8.4 shows it is disastrously placed to demonstrate strong competition if and when multiparty elections do take place.

SUMMARY

In sum, none of the six cases demonstrates an obvious and consistent tendency for democracy but, considering their histories, it would be surprising if they did. Syria scores well on factors that are associated with high levels of democratic executive recruitment and has moderate advantages when it comes to executive constraints and political competition. Zimbabwe is likely to have strong political competition but does less well at the executive level. Sudan, Burma, and Afghanistan have some chance of democratic executive recruitment but are poorly placed in other areas. Iraq has contradictory indicators across the board.

The exercise of considering the case-specific variables that we know matter at a more broadly comparative level has improved our diagnostic capacity and highlighted areas in which it would be productive to invest time and resources to produce stability and democracy. The next step must be to take a much more detailed case history of the patient to be able to pronounce upon the efficacy of the political medicines that have (or about to be) applied in each of our focus cases.

THE INTENSIVE CARE UNIT: IRAQ AND AFGHANISTAN

With burgeoning instability in Afghanistan and a continuing struggle to keep a lid on violence in Iraq, one might pose the question: How central is domestic constitutional design to the future of each case? Is not the need to defeat the insurgencies, eliminate corruption, and rebuild socioeconomic infrastructure much more pressing than the niceties of elections and legislative maneuvers? In fact, the emergence of agreed-upon competitive political structures has been central to both nations' survival since American-led occupation, and without attention to institutional design, democratic slippage will doom both cases to ever-increasing fragmentation, polarization, and violence. A vacuum of legitimate political power always promotes a climate of insurgency and instability.

It is clear that both cases suffered from serious misdiagnosis of their ailments in their initial post-conflict/post-occupation incarnations. Afghans diagnosed the ailment of Afghanistan through the ages as being one of a weak center thwarted in its reform and modernization efforts by a powerful, unaccountable, corrupt, and fragmented periphery. Thus, they choose to give a huge amount of power to the central state in Kabul. Despite the intuition of the diagnosis, the prescription flew in the face of wisdom drawn from other fragmented societies in conflict. When power is manifested in the regions, one either needs a central monopoly of force to subjugate the local strongmen or enough resources to leverage the people away from dependence on those traditionally powerful local elites. The central Afghan state has neither the resources nor the force, so the state is purely a paper tiger and relies on shifting alliances with various warlords and external military force to maintain some degree of control. Even if they had, the diagnosis rests on the assumption that the powerful center is controlled by the "good guys" who will enforce liberal, progressive, democratic, anti-graft policies. That clearly has not been the case in Afghanistan.

The misdiagnosis of what ailed Iraq in 2003 was perhaps less of a misdiagnosis and more of a head-in-the-sand ostrichlike approach to what might come after the ousting of Saddam Hussein and the Baath party. A vacuum of leadership and forethought on both political and security dimensions persisted for at least the first two years of the American-led occupation. Quickly establishing a legitimate domestic government might have constrained the antigovernment and sectarianism violence that quickly grew out of control. In the second half of the 2000s, a multiethnic Iraqi government slowly gathered some legitimacy around itself but its emergence was not quick or comprehensive enough to forestall the initial slide into anarchy, and its leaders *continued* to play both publicly democratic but privately paramilitary games.

Afghanistan and Iraq remain a highly complex mosaic of power plays, age-old ethnic enmities, battles over religion and nation, and struggles over wealth, which teem through their political discourse and in essence these conflicts are expressed through debates about how their democracies are crafted. Who has power, how are they chosen, and how is that power restrained?

Alongside the substance of new constitutions, the process through which new institutions are chosen can be as equally powerful in reducing or exaggerating ethnic polarization. In Afghanistan, the interim and permanent political arrangements were evolved through secretive behind-the-scenes horse-trading between (mostly) unsavory elites. Both Loya Jirgas (to choose an interim government and ratify the new constitution) set antidemocratic precedents which have bedeviled the evolution of multiparty politics ever since. The Loya Jirga (2002) that selected Hamid Karzai as interim president was chaotic and unfocused, with power ceded to strongmen who had been co-opted into the Karzai/US camp. Southern and eastern Pashtuns felt left out of a process they saw as essentially Northern Alliance Tajik/Uzbek driven. The Constitutional Loya Jirga (2004) had a more representative membership, but the delegates only received the constitutional draft on their arrival in Kabul and were precluded from making any significant alterations to the document.

The process of democratic design in Iraq post the war of 2003 was characterized by a series of missteps, misreadings, and errors of judgment made by the occupying Coalition Provisional Authority (CPA). The first Iraqi Governing Council members chosen by the CPA proved to be impotent because they were largely unrepresentative of Iraqis. American "advisers" resisted early calls by Grand Ayatollah Sistani for national elections and wasted fruitless months trying to engineer a parliament selected by elite caucuses in major towns. The vacuum in legitimate leadership expanded along with growing political violence over the next three years – despite the technical handover of sovereignty to Prime Minister Allawi in June 2004, the election of a transitional assembly in January 2005 (virtually devoid of Sunni representatives), and permanent Assembly elections (now with Sunnis) in December 2005. It is true that ultimately an elected assembly drafted the new constitution and the document was approved in a national referendum, but Sunnis were effectively shut out of both processes and the vagueness of the document when it comes to the details of how power is manifested leaves a troubling space for future power grabs by the Shia majority.

The government of Afghanistan is formally presidential and majoritarian, while the Iraqi institutions are parliamentary, more consensual, allow for multi-ethnic government, and a check on unfettered majority rule. But, in practice, President Karzai still has to pay at least lip service to the inclusion of members of the main ethnic groups in his administration, while Shias and Kurds are ultimately dominant over Sunnis in Iraq.

Every new government in Kabul since 2003 has been inclusive on some level but swayed toward the inclusion of the powerful rather than the representative. Warlords were let into the tent but embryonic civil society movements of Afghans – without armies and private agendas – were not deemed to be as essential to governance. Crucially, the multiethnic composition of the Afghan government is not legally mandated and at the whim of the sitting President. There is no guarantee that Hamid Karzai, or any future President, will continue the balancing act. The Pashtun community was the delivery vehicle behind both Karzai's 2004 and 2009 victories. Indeed, his victory on the first round in 2004 would have been in question if Afghans in Pakistan (who were overwhelmingly Pashtun) had not been allowed to vote. Pashtuns celebrated their return to power but in much of the Hazara center and Uzbek and Tajik north, Karzai was roundly defeated by his ethnic opponents.

In Iraq, it is difficult to imagine any government that did not include representatives of the three main ethnic blocks within the country. The President (largely ceremonial) is a Kurd, the Prime Minister a Shia, assisted by Deputy Prime Ministers who are Sunni and Kurdish. The Defense Minister is a Sunni as are eight of his cabinet colleagues (there are twenty-two Shia Ministers, eight Kurds, and one Christian). There is no formal supermajority or Government of National Unity requirement in the constitution but the parliamentary proportional representation system makes coalitions inevitable and the sharing of executive posts goes beyond an informal norm. Nevertheless, the specifics of how power would be divided between the executive and legislature were lacking in the 2005 Constitution – in essence the rules of the democratic game continue to be improvised day by day.

The executive lies in the hands of the largest ethnic group in both countries: Pashtun in Afghanistan, Shia in Iraq. Both President Karzai and Prime Minister Jawad al-Maliki have to work with legislatures that they do not control. The makeup of the Afghan Wolesi Jirga makes the passage of President Karzai's reform agenda exceptionally difficult. Between 2005 and 2010, there were over thirty different factions represented and the largest party had only 10 percent of the seats. At any given time, roughly a third of legislators could be considered "pro-government," a third pro-opposition, and a third nonaligned or have no clear pro- or anti-stance. Such fragmentation and individual-vested interests meant that each bill has to be backed by a majority cobbled together with piecemeal presidential promises. The Iraqi legislature is more powerful and less fragmented. The Council of Representatives can hire and fire Prime Ministers and their cabinets and control legislation. Four main blocks (Shia, Kurdish, Sunni, and secular) hold almost all Assembly seats and while the United Iraqi Alliance is a partnership of the Shia Daawa Party and the Supreme Council for the Islamic Revolution in Iraq (SCIRI), until 2010 they held a near-parliamentary majority.

Iraq and Afghanistan are classic case studies in ethnic polarization, but they have adopted opposite strategies of how to divide power between the center and the regions. The Iraqi constitution allows the space for the creation of powerful "superstate" regions (provinces coming together to form a larger administrative district), which can overwhelm the decisions and authority of the central government in Baghdad. These largely autonomous regions will have tax-raising powers, effective judicial control, and the lion's share of oil revenues from "current" fields in their territory (note the absence of language about future oil-field discoveries). Some have seen the creation of Sunni and Shia regions as an inevitable reaction to the *de facto* Kurdish state that already exists. Indeed, the asymmetrical autonomy of the Catalan and Basque regions of Spain has been cited as a positive example of concentrated minorities being reassured by self-governing powers, but one must not overlook the fact that the Spanish constitution explicitly blocks two or more states coming together as superstates, because the drafters were fearful of the disintegration of the nation-state as a whole. In dramatic contrast, and in the face of significant geographical concentrations of mutually distrustful Pashtuns, Hazaras, Uzbeks, and Tajiks, Afghanistan adopted a highly centralized system, without federalism or significant provincial or local government. Acknowledging this, Abdullah Abdullah campaigned on the basis of introducing a more decentralized system when he ran for President against Hamid Karzai in 2009.

When elections were first envisaged in the post-conflict chaos of both Afghanistan and Iraq, international advisers recommended systems of provincially based proportional representation to elect both the parliaments. Unfortunately, neither country followed through on that advice. Iraq ended up using a national list PR system with disastrous consequences in their transitional Assembly elections of January 2005, while Afghanistan stumbled their way into using the single nontransferable vote (SNTV) for their legislative elections in September of that year.

The national list PR system worked poorly in January 2005 in Iraq because it meant that low Sunni vote turnout resulted in a Constitutional Convention with almost no Sunni representation. In the months that followed, interethnic violence spiraled out of control and a provincial list system (in which Sunnis would gain a "fair" share of the seats regardless of voter turnout in their provinces) was introduced for the December 2005 elections: a case of too little too late. However, getting the system "right," even while late, has provided the space for elites to seek to build multiethnic coalitions. In 2010 general elections, Prime Minister Nuri Kamal al-Maliki crafted his "State of Law" coalition that sought to bring in political and tribal leaders from the Sunni, Kurdish, and Christian communities to ally with his Shia base.

In the case of Afghanistan's election system, a series of unintended consequences were triggered by a widespread distrust of political parties, associated with the Communist era, and a misunderstanding of the implications of having given a single vote for individual candidates in large multimember constituencies. President Karzai changed a provincially-based list PR system to SNTV by simply pronouncing that voters would select a candidate rather than a party/list/block, and that candidates could not show party affiliation on the ballot. In 2006, the system resulted in much voter confusion (in Kabul, there were 400 candidates for the thirty-three spots up for election) and a spoiled ballot rate of 5 percent (it was 1% in Iraq). A highly fragmented parliament contained over thirty, continuously evolving factions with shifting loyalties (as noted above, in Iraq there are only four main blocks). Over two-thirds of all votes were cast for losing candidates and thus were "wasted" (in 2005 in Iraq only 5% of votes were wasted in this way). One of the key reform proposals that Abdullah Abdullah campaigned on in 2009 was to bring in a mixed election system, based on party votes (PR) and individual votes (SNTV).[1]

There were, and are, clearly no constitutional design solutions that would simply neutralize the overwhelming challenges to stability and democratization in either country, but it is clear that substantive changes need to be made in the institutions of both cases to give them a shot at recovery. In Afghanistan, *de jure* power rests in the hands of one man but a more formal recognition of a much more complex reality needs to be considered. A federal system of decentralized power is key to the chances of incorporating democratic elements outside of the capital. When there are more prizes to be won, progressive forces can gain more of a foothold in government structures. Second, there is a need to formalize power-sharing arrangements at the executive level to reassure minority groups that their voice in government is not dependent on the altruism of the majority group. One might recognize regional movements as proxies for ethnic interests while at the same time crafting a space for those identifiers to break down and multiethnic movements to emerge, compete for, and share power. It is also apparent that a stronger legislature, one not so controlled by the executive, might be a crucial constraint on any president bent on domination. Last, there is no doubt that a new electoral system is needed to fairly translate votes cast into seats won. A mixed system, including a proportional element, has been proposed in parliament and by foreign advisers.

Iraq has similar issues with an administration that informally includes majority and minority interests but does not guarantee such power sharing in the future.

---

[1] http://www.drabdullah.af/pdf/Platform_english.pdf

Indeed, the Iraqi constitution remains so vague that the document is silent upon the real details of governance. The powers of the President, Prime Minister, and cabinet, and their interactions, are as murky as the relationship between future federal states and the center. Above all else, the issue of federalism is key in Iraq and getting that balance right will go a long way to providing the foundation for the country to stabilize itself. Iraq needs a system of two magnets that are opposite forces, but complement the whole. Powers given out to regional governments need to be balanced by incentives to compete for power at the national level. Any future federal regions must have a degree of autonomy over their own affairs and wealth; but the center must also retain overarching powers to align the legal system, security affairs, and economic planning. If most of the oil wells are in Shia areas (both current and future), then those regions should get a significant cut of that wealth but at the same time the central state's cut needs to be significant and guaranteed and available for use in the Sunni areas where natural resources are scarce. Last, there should be minority inclusion in regional governments. We tend to forget about minorities within minorities at the local level but their interests and rights need to be protected just as strongly as at the national level.

As noted earlier, a well thought-out democratic design is a necessary, if not sufficient, condition for stability. Among the plethora of lessons that Afghanistan and Iraq can teach us, three issues of process stand out. First, both cases suggest that when democracy is born, the "old" elites, the warlords, and the ethnic strongmen should be marginalized, while space should be created for more democratic leaders to emerge. Using the existing corrupt and violent men as the foundations for the new Afghan and Iraqi states may have appeared unavoidable during the transition but a few years on that base has starved the oxygen from peaceful and representative new leaders. Second, elections and democracy need to be sequenced bottom up rather than top down. Local and regional elections should develop democratic norms and parties before national elections are tried. A vibrant subnational tier of governance will be the nursery for sustainable democracy at the national level. Last, and above all else, both Afghanistan and Iraq shout the lesson that you need a state before you can attempt to prop it up. Without a monopoly of force or the basic elements of a bureaucracy, even a well-designed constitution will do little to promote a belief and investment in the new democracy.

IN SURGERY: SUDAN AND ZIMBABWE

Sudan and Zimbabwe are undergoing "democratic surgery" at the time of writing. In the case of Sudan, it means national, federal, and state elections in 2010, the closest thing to "democratic" elections ever held in Sudan. In the case of

Zimbabwe, democratic surgery is a period of constitutional redesign as mandated by the power-sharing peace agreement of September 2008, a process that has made very little substantive headway in restoring democracy or the rule of law to Zimbabwe. In Sudan, hopes remain that the fragile peace between the Government of Omar al-Bashir and the Southern People's Liberation Movement will be held together by the elaborate power-sharing agreement that was reached in 2005. However, the subdued, but still unsolved, crisis in Darfur, along with burgeoning instability on the border between the North and the South, continues to threaten the "peace."

At first glance, there appears to be some similarity between Zimbabwe and Sudan – both are former Anglophone colonies who in recent times have been cursed with more than their share of violent conflict, economic devastation, and political machination. In both states, politics has been presented to the world as a two-sided battle and power-sharing settlements have been introduced to try and stem the worst of the conflict. However, what separates the two cases is much more profound. Sudan is characterized by a rigid and historically embedded animosity between the North and the South, to say nothing of the West (Darfur) and the East (Beja) (see Reynolds, Saltzman, and Stigant 2011). Politics is over-whelmingly defined by the language you speak, the village you are from, the clan you are loyal too, and the god(s) you worship. Southern Sudan has long endured a Khartoum-promoted policy of economic exploitation, slavery, and Arabization. In Zimbabwe, while ethnicity (Shona and Ndebele) and race (Black and White) was determining throughout the 1970s and 1980s, today the fault lines of politics are much more about authoritarians versus democrats, urban versus rural. Intra-ethnic tensions retain currency but the link between ethnicity, race, and conflict is much murkier. Robert Mugabe's Zimbabwean African National Union is a predominantly Shona party, but the opposition Movement for Democratic Change (MDC) takes the urban Shona vote along with the votes of the minority Ndebele. The breakaway MDC-Mutambara is predominantly Ndebele, but it is dwarfed by Tsvangari's MDC. The fault lines are now much more ideological than ethnic or racial.

There are also differences in the resources at hand, the level of infrastructure, and bureaucracy that can be called upon for rebuilding, the nature and legacy of colonialism, the degree of geographical separation of ethnic groups, and, perhaps key, the overall belief in state. Upon independence in 1980, Zimbabwe was seen by many as one of the best hopes for democracy, growth, and political stability in Africa. It was agriculturally strong – the breadbasket of Africa – it had a robust infrastructure and it appeared to be unified behind a leader who was an inclusive nation builder. Mugabe initially reached out to whites as the comrades who could drive the economy. In 1980, the diagnostic variables outlined in this book would have suggested that Zimbabwe had a comparatively good chance to be both stable and democratic. Indeed, if Zimbabwe 1980 were in Table 8.1, instead of Zimbabwe 2010, it would be the most likely of all six cases to be stable.

Their *ancien regime* would have been no different but in 1980 Zimbabwe had a much higher level of income and they were using a proportional system for national elections. Even after decades of conflict, Zimbabweans retain a shared and unifying belief in their nation-state. Zimbabwe is the case that exemplifies the agency of failed leadership in destroying the hopes for democracy in even positively disposed countries. Specifically, President Mugabe scaled back democratic institutions, effectively suspended the rule of law, emboldened insidious conflict-promoting forces, and brought a thriving economy to its knees through mismanagement and corruption.

In contrast, Sudan has, and had, very little of the inherent advantages of Zimbabwe. The peoples are polarized and separated and share no belief in the integrity of the nation-state. Infrastructure and bureaucracy is almost non-existent throughout much of the South and West and the Khartoum state does not have a monopoly of force within its national boundaries. Sudan is a crushingly poor country, with large marginalized areas vying to be the poorest territory anywhere in the globe (South and West). One glimmer of economic hope are the huge oil fields that lay beneath the border between the North and the South but this prize is already proving to be a poisoned chalice – promoting the corruption, conflict, and bureaucratic fragility that characterizes so many other nations who are cursed by lootable wealth.

While both Sudan and Zimbabwe have introduced power-sharing settlements, the differences between the settlements are also profoundly important. Sudan has the advantage that its power sharing is formal and constitutionally robust. The Comprehensive Peace Agreement of 2005 prescribed power sharing in the executive, a limited minority veto, majority and minority inclusion in the interim legislatures of both the government of Sudan and Southern Sudan and the civil service; wealth sharing between the North and the South; and regional decentralization with power sharing. Crucially, the CPA also scheduled a referendum on Southern independence and the sovereignty of the disputed territory of Abyei.

The medicines may well have been appropriate but they failed to address the body politic as a whole: the settlement was limited to just the North and the South, ignoring the infectious instability of the West (Darfur) and to a lesser degree, the East. It also assumed two parties, two main organs, which has proven to be far from a realistic assessment of political fragmentation in both the North and the South. The CPA also lacked democratic legitimacy and vertical ties of accountability, in both its design and implementation. The public was entirely disconnected from the process and the legitimacy of the National Congress Party (NCP) and Sudan People's Liberation Movement (SPLM) as the sole arbiters of opinion in the North and the South has never been tested. This has resulted in the very worst of an elite cartel where unelected leaders in both the North and the South appear to be monopolizing power and resources, largely for selfish, rather than national purposes.

In April 2010, Sudan held national elections after two postponements.[2] These were an important test of the ability of a power-sharing agreement and a new mixed electoral system to promote accommodation and political stability. If there is one state in Africa that did not need accentuated tension and competition between ethnic groups, it is Sudan.

The elections for the national parliament were held under a mixed (parallel) system of both districts and party lists. This was the product of the negotiated peace settlement between the SPLM of the South and President Omar al-Bashir's Khartoum NCP regime in the North (see details in chapter 5).

While the electoral system had proportional elements, it actually reinforced one-party dominance because there were not enough PR seats in the system to ensure proportionality in the South. Each southern state had either one or two party list seats, and thus any group wishing to challenge the SPLM needed more than a third of the statewide votes to win a seat – a very high bar considering there is no serious opposition to the SPLM in the South.[3] However, the system allowed for higher levels of inclusion and fragmentation in the North. Some states had multiple PR seats – Khartoum (nine), Southern Darfur (seven), and Gezira (six) – and in these districts minority parties were able to pick seats away from the government.

The election system used in Sudan in 2010 was not fine-tuned enough to respond to the tensions that elections will undoubtedly bring to that nation. But the elections are merely one cog in a wheel of many institutional arrangements that need to work together to stop conflicts being processed by the bullet rather than the ballot. Nevertheless, it has been proven beyond a doubt that authoritarian rule does not lead to stability in Sudan – the roof may still be leaky but at least now there is a roof to mend.

The diagnosis of which medicines were needed in Sudan in 2005 were partially on the mark – but they treated only the head and legs; there was significant disease in both arms and the Comprehensive Peace Agreement ignored that illness in the body politic. A more considered diagnosis would have prescribed more inclusive power-sharing institutions, taking in representatives from the West and East of the country along with non-NCP and SPLM members. It would have recommended a more vibrant federalism rooted in states rather than regions. Last, the electoral system had positive elements of inclusion but needed to be more proportional to allow access to new parties and movements.

---

[2] In fact, Sudan held six different elections at the same time: the Presidency of Sudan, Presidency of Southern Sudan (GOSS), the National Assembly, the GOSS Assembly, State Governorships, and State Legislatures.

[3] In June 2009, the former SPLM-nominated Sudanese Foreign Minister, Lam Akol, set up a rival SPLM-DC party but there is scant evidence to show any nascent electoral strength for the new party.

Zimbabwe's peace agreement of 2008 was more broadly inclusive but informal and thus far less robust or enforceable. After decades of declining civil rights, economic instability and democratic atrophy, President Mugabe was finally prevailed upon to offer the crumbs of inclusion to his nemesis Morgan Tsvangari and the MDC. The immediate trigger to the negotiations was the MDC victory in legislative elections and Mugabe's defeat in the first round of presidential elections (March 2008) leading to a reign of state repression which led to Tsvangari withdrawing from the runoff election. The Interparty Political Agreement (IPA) signed on September 11, 2008 was a band-aid applied to a large open wound. Mugabe retained his powerful Presidency, while Tsvangari became (a much less powerful) Prime Minister. The cabinet (still chaired by the President) consisted of fifteen ZANU-PF ministers, thirteen MDC, and three from Arthur Mutambara's breakaway MDC party. A multiparty committee was to be established to review the constitution, and part of its remit was the election system. But the first two years of the power-sharing government saw very little improvement in democracy, human rights, or constraint of the abuse of executive power.

It is reasonable to suggest that the Lancaster House conference diagnosis of what structures would best assist a democratizing Zimbabwe in 1980 was largely on point. The country needed inclusive institutions, majority political control, and minority reassurance and protection, and the PR-Parliamentary-Unitary state institutions introduced under the Lancaster House agreement did provide a positive foundation for the first seven years. Those institutional structures were operating well from 1980 to 1987, until Robert Mugabe dismantled them, changing the electoral system, eliminating decentralization, and monopolizing executive power by transforming himself from Prime Minister to President. The 2008 political construct was a very different treatment plan. The agreement was on the surface inclusive, but in reality unwieldy, unclear, and ultimately unenforceable. The temporary emergency nature of the medicine enabled Mugabe to effectively ignore the power-sharing elements. At the very least, Zimbabwe needs a permanent reformation of its majoritarian political institutions. If power sharing is desired, it needs to be entrenched and enforced. There is little doubt that a more inclusive legislative election system would preclude some of the extreme polarization and shenanigans that have characterized all Zimbabwean general elections since 1990.

FUTURE PATIENTS: BURMA AND SYRIA

If political earthquakes were to occur in either of these cases, they would pose fascinating conundrums and challenges to the democratic designer. Burma is a multiethnic melting pot with a long history of military control but a populace educated in, and in most part enamored by, democracy. Syria's state is reminiscent of the secular authoritarian minority rule of Saddam Hussein's Iraq, but nowadays it grapples more with the internal threat of Islamic fundamentalism and an external desire to throw off its pariah state label. The diagnostic model outlined in this book allows comparison of each nation's socioeconomic historical background factors and informs us on what type of political institutions might be most productive in any hypothetical post-authoritarian regime. As noted earlier in this chapter, in the terms of our model of salient variables, Syria has more favorable background characteristics than Burma for political stabilization and is better predisposed on all three measures of democratization – dramatically so in the case of political competition.

When it comes to the chances for stability, Syria has advantages in its moderately high levels of income and nationalism, low dependence on natural resources, and dearth of dangerous lootable resources. Burma's military regime is more likely than Syria's populist authoritarian/minority rule regime to lead to post-democratization stability, and both cases have majoritarian electoral systems on the books which could destabilize the polity if electoral politics became competitive. Of course, as I note below, the electoral system could be changed.

The chief challenge to democratization in Burma is a single institution – the Tatmadaw (military) – but the chief challenge to democracy taking hold is the tension between the Burmese majority and the "ethnics" who long been marginalized to the periphery of both geography and state psychology. The chief challenge to democratization in Syria is the grip on power of the Alawite Shia minority (15%) who would be fearful of Sunni dominance under a popular majority system of governance. The military plays a significant role in Syria but they rely on the patronage from the Asads, they are not the central figures as in Burma. However, akin to Burma, the chief challenge to the endurance of democracy in Syria is likely to be the open fragmentation of the polity into Sunni, Alawite, Druze, Christians, Turks, Circassians, Armenians, Jews, Maronites, Islamic fundamentalists and secular Baathists – a recipe that makes democracy so problematic in Lebanon.

Neither case has a strong democratic history to fall back on: one was gifted the institutions of Westminster, the other of Paris, neither took. Syria has had very little multiparty, competitive electoral history to look back on. From its creation as an independent nation free of French administration in 1944, Syria only saw very brief periods of civilian rule and no democratic rule to speak of. There were competitive elections in 1947, 1949, and 1953 with the Muslim Brotherhood, Islamic Socialists, the Baath, and a People's Party (opposed to the military) all winning seats in parliament (see Talhami 2001), but these legislators were not the rulers. The subsequent short-lived civilian governments of the 1950s and 1960s were rooted in unelected elites, and the one-party state ethos took root long before Hafiz al-Asad's takeover in 1970. Burma has slightly more of a democratic history but it is an equally distant memory. For most of sixty years of her exist-ence, the contours of politics in Burma have been blurry to locals and virtually indecipherable to foreigners. The founder of modern Burma, General Aung San, drove the British and Japanese out of his land in short order between 1941 and 1945 only to be assassinated by a jealous rival as he discussed a new constitution with his cabinet six months before formal independence from British colonial rule. There were four multiparty elections between 1948 and 1960 but the resulting governments were fragile, fragmented, and self-serving. They stum-bled along, finally to be ousted by the Army chief, General Ne Win, in a coup d'état in 1962. For the next twenty six years, Ne Win led the country with a credo of national socialism wrapped up in an iron fist. At his core was the belief that soldiers were the saviors of the nation, but his bizarre actions stemmed from a kitchen cabinet of mystical astrologers and paranoid thuggish deputies.

Both cases have had sparks of public protest and awakening that briefly raised hopes for democratization. Burma has had such moments in 1977, 1988, and most recently the Saffron revolution, led by monks, in 2007. The closest antigovern-ment forces came to success was in the late 1980s. In July 1988 the number one general, Ne Win, shocked the nation by announcing his resignation and the pres-sure cooker blew. With food and dignity becoming scarce, students saw a window of opportunity for change. By August, they were leading mass nonviolent demon-strations in the streets of Rangoon. But the state reacted with a viciousness which surpassed even the Chinese crackdown in Tiananmen Square ten months later. The Rangoon police left forty-one wounded students in a van to bake to death in the oppressive heat, a truck crushed two schoolchildren under its wheels, and as news of the latest atrocity spread the crowds swelled in size and anger. In Rangoon, and across the country, it is estimated that as many as 10,000 were killed with thousands more being arrested and tortured.

As the charismatic daughter of *the* icon of nationhood, it was almost inevitable that Suu Kyi would become the figurehead of the pro-democracy movement. Five foot four inches tall and weighing 100 lbs, her presence commanded every venue she entered. Two weeks after the massacres of August 8, she spoke to a half million people at the Shwedagon Pagoda. A year later in the Delta, a major rescinded the order to have troops shoot her dead as she spoke to another mass protest. Three months later, on July 20, 1989, she was placed under her first house arrest in the lakeside villa prison where she sits as of 2010. The generals surprised many by honoring a pledge to hold free elections for the unicameral national legislature in May 1990. Most likely, they were counting on a fragmented outcome that would allow them to dominate any new government. However, while she languished in jail, her party, the National League for Democracy (NLD), rode a massive wave of popular support to win 60 percent of the votes in 1990 legis-lative elections. Moreover, thanks to the first-past-the-post (FPTP) system inherited from colonial rule, the NLD won an overwhelming 81 percent of the seats. The military responded to its defeat at the polls by insisting that the new parliament could not meet until a regime-appointed National Convention drafted a new constitution.

After the elder Asad's death in 2000, Syria experienced what became known as the "Damascus spring" (see Landis and Pace 2007). Bashar Asad called for public constructive criticism and political modernization, thousands of political prisoners were released and intellectuals began to call publicly for liberalization, and a democracy rooted in Syria's essence. In January 2001, a thousand activists signed a statement calling for democracy and the revitalization of civil society. A new electoral block, the Movement for Social Peace, was born to challenge the regime. But the crackdown was swift and harsh. Opposition leaders were arrested, the burgeoning civil society was neutered, and political parties were shut down.

Neither country has the nascent building blocks of a vibrant party system. As Landis and Pace note (2007: 49), "civil society in Syria is a wasteland." The remnants of political parties/movements are so discredited – for example, Communists, Baathists, Nasserists – that their capacity to insert themselves into a democratic discussion is unlikely. The Muslim Brotherhood and Kurdish nationalists have been driven underground without being discredited, but their role in multiparty politics may be more as spoilers than institution builders.

Twenty years after their stunning victory, the Burmese National League for Democracy is a faith rather than a party. Only the Rangoon headquarters are allowed to open their doors and spies record all activity within and outside of the building. Thousands of leaders are in jail, underground, or in exile. A Central Executive Committee does exist but the members are mostly in their 80s, known as the "uncles," and have been criticized for being detached from new realities and wary of delegating. Indeed, the ethos of hierarchy, integral to Buddhism, cuts as a double-edged sword for the opposition. Her husband noted that Suu brought "over-whelming unity to a spontaneous, hitherto leaderless revolt" but her isolation has left the second tier of NLD leadership frozen and indecisive. Inside Burma no one wishes to second guess Daw Suu's decisions but no one really knows where precisely she stands on the most important issues of the day. As in Syria, in Burma a highly repressive state has left progressive civil society a wasteland.

While their propensity for democracy and stability vary, if Burma or Syria were to move to democracy, what type of rules would best serve democratic consolidation in each case?

While the Syrian regime has not offered a multiparty template the Burmese junta has, but its constitution (approved by a rigged referendum in the midst of the devastating cyclone Nargis in 2008) is far from democratic. Elections happen but popular will is neutered. The deck is stacked to such an extent that it is impossible to break the army's grip on politics. The generals propose that one-quarter of the seats in the legislature are reserved for their nominees and 166 of the 300-member electoral college that chooses a powerful state president come from the officer ranks. The head of state must be well acquainted with military affairs, have resided in the country for at least twenty years, and not have parents, spouses, or children who are subjects, citizens of, or owe allegiance to, a foreign power. In the Tatmadaw's constitutional nirvana, federalism is on the books but it is hollow – regional assemblies exist but are powerless. But despite their impotence, the generals will still reserve one-third of the seats in state legislatures for their own ranks. State Premiers are to be appointed by the President (who it will be remembered is to be a senior General). And for smaller ethnic groups, there are "bantustans" akin to racist South Africa's homeland policy of the 1970s. If an ethnic minority does not dominate a state, then "self administered areas are to be prescribed for national races who reside together."

This construct of military-run "democracy" is borrowed from Suharto's credo of "guided democracy" that crashed so spectacularly in Indonesia in 1998. The military "will have the right to independently administer all affairs concerning the forces," with the Defense Committee of parliament consisting solely of Tatmadaw members without being subject to oversight. Every citizen will not only undergo military service, but also "have the duty to learn military science."

Historically, what limited experience of electoral competition each case has, has been with Anglophone or Francophone majoritarian institutions – FPTP in the case of Burma and the Two Round System (TRS) in Syria. Between 1948 and 1962, FPTP worked reasonably well in Burma. It allowed for strong opposition parliamentary caucuses (103 seats in 1956 and 93 in 1960, out of a legislature numbering 250 members), and it enabled minority nationalities to achieve representation. Shan parties, for instance, took 8 percent of the seats in the 1956 parliament at a time when they constituted about 10 percent of the population. The 1990 election, however, demonstrated the inherent dangers of plurality voting in the Burmese context. Under any system of proportional representation, the NLD (with almost 60% of the vote) would still have won handily, but the military's party (with 20% support) would likely have gained more than a hundred seats instead of the paltry ten they actually wound up with. This would have meant not only a sizable opposition bloc, but ninety more senior military politicians probably enjoying legal immunity from prosecution as members of parliament. Had Burma used PR instead of plurality voting in 1990, would the military have been so quick to nullify the results and invite more than a decade of international opprobrium and ostracism? In retrospect, many in the NLD now think not. As Stepan, Oo, Levine, and I have noted, a mixed-member proportional (MMP) version of PR might do a much better job of combining geographical-constituency representation with a parliament that reflects nationwide political preferences (2001).

While it may be less obvious to what precise election system a democratic Syria might best need, it is startlingly clear what Syria does not need. That would be the block confessional system of Lebanon, which would polarize and segment Syria just as much as it has done in Lebanon. Nor the Palestinian Authority mix of non-confessional block voting and list PR which enabled Hamas to win an absolute majority on a minority of the vote. Such an event in Syria would be a recipe for disaster. Some degree of proportionality seems to make sense for Syria, at least the alternative is unpalatable.

In both nations, there are intense feelings about borders and the integrity of the state. Suu Kyi and the NLD are clearly the dominant democratic force in the country but Burma is, and has always been, a *ménage à trois* of the military, the Bamar majority, and the "ethnics." The Kachin, Karen, Shan, Mon, Wa, and Chin are groups who together constitute a third of the population and are clustered in large tracts of land on the borders with Thailand, China, and India. The history of relations between the center and periphery has been fractious and in many ways as equal a challenge to democratic stability as the behavior of the military. At independence, the "Panglong" agreement brokered by Aung San with the ethnics cited federalism as the foundation for political unity and alluded to a capacity for states to eventually secede if they so wished but powers to the states never became manifest. Up until the 1990s, Rangoon fought a number of significant civil wars with ethnic insurgent groups who were driven at times by a crusade for political autonomy and at others by baser desires for control of the opium trade and local resources. The Shan, Karen, Kachin, and Wa groups at various times were engaged in warfare with the Burmese military. However, one by one the generals bought off all of the significant ethnic armies outside of the Karen National Union (KNU). This gave the ethnic "ceasefire" groups places in the National Convention and with one of the tripod legs stabilized the military was free to crack down on the NLD. The Tatmadaw's constitution has a centralized unitary state disguised as a federal polity. In one of the sessions of national convention, a delegate from the government asked the ethnic representatives, "why do you want to build seven little houses when we are building one big house where everyone can have a floor?"

In Syria, the fight is not over internal fragmentation but rather over boundary enlargement. Syrians uniformly agree that the colonially imposed borders should be revised and the Golan Heights should be returned from Israeli occupation, but they differ over how far Syria's borders should ultimately stretch or morph. Nevertheless, there are no substantive pressures to break up the Syrian state from inside, while the history of Burma has always been about the center trying to woo, bribe, and threaten the periphery into staying within the national fold. These diagnoses strongly suggest that Burma requires a structure of robust federalism (asymmetrical federalism with distinctive and particular rights for the ethnic states), while Syria would be better served by a unitary state.

Finally, if they did transition to democracy, constitutional designers would have to be cognizant of the temporal nature of constitutional design as discussed in chapter 3. The most likely transition to democracy in Burma (however unlikely that maybe) would be a transformation. The reality is that because of the proven strength of the junta and demonstrated inability of the opposition to marshal enough internal or external pressure to oust them, any new multiparty constitution would be led and dominated by the military's ideas and fears. It is possible that the reins of transformation from authoritarianism to pseudo-democracy led by the regime could slip from their grasp and become more of a pacted transition (transplacement) between the Tatmadaw and NLD, but initially the process is likely to be government driven, an elite trying to extricate themselves while hanging on to significant political power and protections and economic influence. Any new constitution designed under such circumstances would be restraining of the majority and enabling to the military. In Chile, General Augusto Pinochet left power only after he had been granted amnesty from prosecution, he and his generals retained control over the army (for ten years), and after that date he became a senator for life. A pacted (or junta-dominated) transition would be emergency medicine and it would not put in place the type of robust democratic institutions that would be needed for longer-term democratic consolidation in Burma. Therefore, designers would need to ensure that expiration dates and review processes were in place before signing on to a new order.

Syria is also most likely to witness a ruling elite liberalizing power piecemeal in order to hold on to significant influence while trying to placate the pressures from the populace Transplacement institutions in Syria would probably entrench minority (Alawite) influence and military dominance. Again such measures may not deserve the level of permanence in a new "democratic" constitution.

Conclusions:
The Lessons of Designing Democracy

We live our lives forwards, we understand our lives backwards.

Soren Kierkegaard

The concluding chapter of the book pulls together evidence from the previous chapters to offer suggestions for both domestic constitutional engineers and foreign advisers.

DEVELOP A PORTABLE CONTINGENT THEORY OF DESIGN

The evidence in this book does not suggest that cases that cluster in certain ways must use exactly the same institutional prescriptions, but the patterns I have found do suggest that a robust diagnostic method can produce an appropriate treatment plan, especially if it has inbuilt flexibility. Upon study of the individual country-patient, the treatment plan may be adapted in small or large part, but the important thing is that the rubric creates a starting point. All else being equal, a country will be best served using institutions that have proven to have encouraged stability and promoted democracy in similar cases – of course all else is never equal, but a robust diagnosis minimizes the parameters for catastrophic mistakes in democratic design.

A contingent theory of design would have at its heart issues of alignment. (a) Horizontal alignment, that is, across the universe of all the political institutions put into place. For example, when it comes to horizontal alignment electoral systems need to reinforce the legislature's ability to legislate and represent. Federalism needs to pay attention to minorities within minorities in geographical areas and power sharing institutions need to be horizontally checked by other institutions to avoid an elite cartel. (b) Vertical alignment, that is, between the political institutions and the sociopolitical traits of the state. For example, the entire web of political decision-making structures must to be rooted in the nation's cultural-social norms. The way leaders are chosen, and held accountable, should resonate with how the culture(s) view political rule. Election methods need not be familiar to be legitimate but they must be intuitive and understandable. Last, if the society has always operated in a highly decentralized way then one cannot superimpose central institutions and expect them to flourish.

Ultimately, the rationale for developing a contingent theory is that it allows one to craft democratic institutions appropriate to the society in question. There are many varieties of democracy and even more ways of electing leaders, sharing power, and reassuring majorities and minorities that they have a central role. There is perhaps no stronger lesson of twentieth-century democratization than that simply imposing American- or European-style democratic institutions in the developing world is a recipe for disaster. There is a broad menu of electoral and governance arrangements, which can be crafted to the needs of a given society. The menu includes different electoral systems, varieties of federalism, autonomies, and local government; the way power is divided between the executive and legislature; and whether there is mandated multiethnic power sharing or a winner-take-all system.

THE MEDICINES FOR SHORT-TERM STABILITY ARE NOT NECESSARILY THE SAME AS THOSE REQUIRED FOR DEMOCRACY

As noted in chapter 4, the variables that effect and promote stability in a post-conflict state are not necessarily the ones that promote democratization. One might envision that constraining democratic competition could promote short-term stability, or that focusing executive power on a single office might allow effective decision making unconstrained by the niceties of separation of powers. However, my quantitative analysis in chapter 4 found that while it is true that the levers are different, the strategies of how to promote stability and democracy are not necessarily in tension. Ultimately, the choice of which medicines to apply becomes about prioritizing resources – there is a role for sequencing but it is not true that one must wait for wealth and development before bringing in vibrant democratic institutions.

Higher wealth, a reduced reliance on natural resources, and lower lootable resources, all predict increased stability for a given case. Choosing a proportional election system is also correlated with higher chances of stability. Table 4.8 illustrates that elements of democracy are promoted by a variety of other factors, in concert with the ones that promote stability. There appears to be no real downside to getting the institutions right early on, even as the polity is in the midst of trying to stabilize itself. If anything, choosing pseudo-democratic institutions at the start merely entrenches an ethos of majoritarian exclusion, which becomes difficult to break away from as the society tries to become more participatory and democratic down the road.

PRE-PLAN THE TRANSITION

Without a short- to medium-term plan of treatment for the transition, a power vacuum will take hold quickly and eat away at future stability. If there is heavy external involvement in the transition, external powers should partner with local leaders who are legitimate, respected, and representative – even if they may not be the occupiers' first choice. In Iraq in 2003, the better partner was the Grand Ayatollah Ali al Sistani, and not the chancer Ahmed Chalabi. It is a truism that the transition will be smoother and more likely to endure if there is the perception of local ownership – in this case, process becomes as important as the institutions that are ultimately introduced. Additionally, much better information about institutional choices must be made available to domestic political designers – politicians, civil society groups, academic institutions, and the bureaucracy. The United States and United Nations have made tentative steps toward developing organizations that can coordinate, consolidate, and package such information effectively. Experts who *know* the country and region, such as anthropologists, historians, political scientists, and public policy experts should be included alongside the military specialists. The key is to find a way to marry participatory democratic ideals with deeply rooted local customs and governance traditions.

FACILITATE EXIT STRATEGIES FOR THE ANCIEN REGIME

If the authoritarian regime is not removed by force but by a negotiated transition, then history has shown that the remnants of the dictatorship need to be given an exit route limiting their role as spoilers of the nascent democracy. The forces of democracy have to buy off the men in uniform, despite how distasteful that will be to victims and their advocates. There are many examples of successful strategies that have allowed authoritarian regimes to leave power peacefully. In parts of Southeast Asia, military rulers were either moved into think tanks and upper houses of parliament (Singapore, Thailand); given protection of business and personal interests (Korea, Philippines); or were offered reserved seats for a time in legislatures (Indonesia). In Latin America, a variety of these methods were employed, along with more robust prosecution of crimes once the threat of military re-intervention had waned (Chile, Argentina). Innovative thinking about how the military can be encouraged to extricate themselves from power is the key to transformation in Burma, among other cases.

TAKE INTO ACCOUNT WHERE THE STATE HAS COME FROM

Democrats often have a clear idea of where they want the state to go – that is, to become an open, human rights abiding, free market democracy – but planners often fail to appreciate that the trajectory is heavily dependent upon the nation's past. The type of transition, whether peaceful or bloody, internally or externally driven, and the nature of the former regime determine what needs to be done to facilitate the transition to a fledgling democracy. The institutions and party system that exist under a personalized dictatorship (e.g., Iraq or Syria) are very different to those that underlie a military regime (e.g., Burma or Togo) or a theocratic state (e.g., Iran). In those countries where civil society is at the forefront of change (e.g., Ukraine), supporting democracy from the outside is often about promoting political development and institutional strength. Conversely, when change emanates from the violent overthrow of the sitting regime (either from without or within), supporting democracy will require investment in civil society and space for new, participatory forms of politics to flourish.

CREATE THE SPACE FOR A NEW TYPE OF LEADER TO EMERGE

One of the most common pitfalls inherent in transitions to multiparty competition is locking in power the powerful players who were in control during the time of conflict. Those power brokers are often far from the most democratic or even the most representative of leaders. Allowing the carryover of the old elites may also entrench the insidious divides of identity politics – freezing politics into a detached cartel of leaders drawn from divided cultural segments of society. One might think of this as *the Liberia Problem*, which has only been partially weakened with the election of President Ellen Johnson-Shirleaf. Weak states are often controlled by the same small number of powerful players, whether it is a dictatorship or fledgling democracy – they may be family, tribe, or secret society (as in West Africa). The players rotate in and out of power, sometimes in elected office, sometimes behind the scenes, but always pulling the strings. These dominant groups (corrupt businessmen in Liberia, warlords, and religious conservatives in Afghanistan) restrict the space for new forms of leadership based on popular social movements.

While the power sharing regime should include elected leaders and popular communal leaders, it may have to also include paramilitary leaders, "traditional" leaders, and those responsible for previous conflict or abuses (Rashid Dostum in Afghanistan (Chief of Army) and Riek Machar (Deputy President of the South) in Sudan immediately spring to mind). How are those elites balanced against the inclusion of previously marginalized groups who may not have been party to the conflict? These may include women and other cultural and civil society groups. The key in democratic design in the short term is to allow the space for more democratic leaders to emerge through election systems, which allow for a level playing field and easy entry and the creation of multiple access points to political power.

REDUCE THE INFLUENCE OF PRIVATE ARMIES AND MILITIAS

The successful disarmament, demobilization, and reintegration (DDR) of para-military groups almost always comes late (or not at all) but almost all experts argue that removing private armies needs to come first, not last. There have been examples of DDR strategies that allowed newly elected governments in very violent politics to consolidate their authority and promote the rule of law. Years of brutal civil war in Sierra Leone left society dominated by heavily armed and chaotic militias. However, by 2002 an ambitious DDR program demobilized 72,000 combatants, and over 40,000 weapons were destroyed. Despite its distinctly inauspicious state of affairs, Sierra Leone held successful national elections in 2002 and 2007, the comprehensive DDR program of the 1990s being integral to this progress. Conversely, DDR was never seriously implemented in Afghanistan. As a result, the central state was hamstrung by warlords with private militias, a plethora of easy access weapons, and a drug trade, which ate away at any steps toward the rule of law.

ENGAGE THE DIASPORA EARLY

Laboring under dictatorship, the brightest and best educated often flee their homelands to find opportunities in the West, or pro-democracy activists are forced abroad through fear of imprisonment or worse. Thus, when it comes to rebuilding a nation along democratic lines, engaging the diaspora is key. They not only bring the obvious benefits of money and foreign investment but they – judges, doctors, teachers, engineers – possess skills that often have been deci-mated in chaotic states. Some members of the diaspora return to their homelands while others contribute significantly through remittances. However, the returning diaspora are the most crucial as they bring new ways of thinking, which can invigorate civil society and electoral politics in their home countries. Skilled returnees provide the foundation building, which is lacking in simple remittances. This is particularly true of women's movements: in southern Sudan and Afghanistan, some of the most dramatic changes on the ground have come from women's groups energized by returnees. Of course, foreign policy must not be hitched to any diaspora group that simply presents itself. A full stocktaking of the group's internal legitimacy is crucial before empowering a visible group with monies and influence over the design of the new state.

THE SEQUENCING OF DEMOCRACY

As I have noted earlier in this book, in a number of nations the shock of national general elections has often thrown fragile patients into trauma. There are a host of reasons why it is better to hold lower-level elections first and then build up to national polls. First, village, municipal, and provincial elections provide a nursery of sorts for new politics to take root. Administrators learn how to conduct elections in somewhat less-pressurized circumstances, parties learn how to campaign and deal, voters are educated in the nuances of elections and strategic behaviors. Second, such "training ground" elections create a space for new actors to gain a foothold – actors who may be shut out in the early days of democratization. If new parties win seats in local governance, they will have a better ability to compete as the scale of elections grows. Last, sequencing de-emphasizes the national election as the "moment" of democracy – reminds all that democracy is a process, not a moment. The comprehensive peace agreement in the Sudan spelled out the most detailed electoral sequencing of any recent process. Local elections were to be held first, legislative elections for the Governments of Sudan and Southern Sudan to be held after three years, presidential elections after five, and a referendum on the secession of the South after six years. Unfortunately that well-crafted sequence was never kept to and all elections (outside of the referendum) happened on the same day in April 2010.

YOU NEED A STATE BEFORE YOU TRY TO PROP IT UP

The challenges of democracy promotion are vastly increased in cases of state failure, in those *worst* cases where scarce monopoly exists over the exercise of power within a state's territory. In cases such as Somalia, DR Congo, or Southern Sudan, the priorities differ substantially from cases in which some semblance of a state already exists. Before they can concentrate on building democracy, in other words, external actors must first help resuscitate the state. Rushing to elections too quickly, before the nation is logistically and psychologically ready for competitive campaigning and choice, can quickly delegitimize democratization efforts. If elections fail, it is a huge step back toward authoritarianism and instability. It is also true that emphasis needs to be placed on early and substantive local-level involvement, to provide some insurance against national bureaucratic dependency, encourage local ownership, and underwrite the institutional stability essential to the departure of foreign assistance. State rebuilding – the delivery of public services and enforcement of the rule of law – is most visible at the local level and that is where perceptions of the state's competence will be formed. Without the local will to build the state, external efforts can be futile.

Bibliography

Acemoglu, Daron and James Robinson (2006). *Economic Origins of Dictatorship and Democracy*. New York: Cambridge University Press.

Aristotle (trans. C Lord 1984). *The Politics*. Chicago, IL: University of Chicago Press.

Asmal, Kader (1990). *Electoral Systems: A Critical Survey*. Bellville, TX: Centre for Development Studies, University of the Western Cape.

Baldez, Lisa (2003). "Women's Movements and Democratic Transition in Brazil, Chile, East Germany and Poland," *Comparative Politics*, 35:3: 253–72.

Bennett, C (1998). "Bosnia-Herzegovina," in Peter Harris and Ben Reilly (eds.) *Democracy and Deep Rooted Conflicts*. Stockholm: International IDEA.

Bermeo, Nancy (2002). "The Import of Institutions," *Journal of Democracy*, 13:2: 96–110.

Bloomfield, David and Ben Reilly (1998). "Characteristics of Deep Rooted Conflict," in Peter Harris and Ben Reilly (eds.) *Democracy and Deep Rooted Conflicts*. Stockholm: International IDEA.

Boix, Carlos (2003). *Democracy and Redistribution*. New York: Cambridge University Press.

Bratton, Kathleen (2002). "The Effect of Legislative Diversity on Agenda Setting," *American Politics Research*, 30:2: 115–43.

——and Kerry Haynie (1999). "Agenda Setting and Legislative Success in State Legislatures: The Effects of Gender and Race," *Journal of politics*, 61:3: 658–80.

Bremer, Ian (2006). *The J Curve*. New York: Simon and Schuster.

Buhaug, Halvard and Scott Gates (2002). "The Geography of Civil War," *Journal of Peace Research*, 39:4: 417–33.

Bunce, Valerie (2008). "Reflections on Elections," *APSA-CP Newsletter*, 19:2: 1–5.

Carey, John and Simon Hix (2009). "The Electoral Sweet Spot: Low Magnitude Proportional Electoral Systems," http://web.mit.edu/polisci/research/wip/Carey_Hix_Jan_2009.pdf

Carothers, Thomas (1999). *Critical Mission: Essays on Democracy Promotion*. New York: Carnegie.

Childs, Sarah and Mona Lena Krook (2009). "Analysing Women's Substantive Representation: From Critical Mass to Critical Actors," *Government & Opposition*, 44:2: 125–45.

——(2004). *Critical Mission*. New York: Carnegie.

——(2006). Confronting the Weakest Link: Aiding Political Parties in New Democracies. Washington D.C.: Carnegie.

Cohen, Joshua and Joel Rogers (1992). "Secondary Associations and Democratic Governance." *Politics and Society*. 20:4: 393–472.

Collier, Paul (2008). "Naïve Faith in the Ballot Box," *The Guardian*, Monday, November 3, 2008.

——(2009). *Wars, Guns, and Votes*. New York: Harper.

Crowley, Jocelyn Elise. (2004). "When Tokens Matter," *Legislative Studies Quarterly.* 24:1: 109–36.

Cutler, Paul (1998). *Problem Solving in Clinical Medicine: From Data to Diagnosis*, 3rd edition. Philadelphia, PA: Lippincott Williams and Wilkins.

Deng, Francis M (2008). *Identity, Diversity, and Constitutionalism in Africa.* Washington D.C.: USIP Press.

Diamond, Larry (2007). *Squandered Victory.* New York: Times Books.

——(2008). *The Sprit of Democracy.* New York: Times Books.

Dryzek, John (1996). "Political Inclusion and the Dynamics of Democratization," *American Political Science Review.* 90:1: 475–87.

Eaton, Kent. (2006). "The Downside of Decentralization: Armed Clientelism in Colombia," *Security Studies*, 15:4: 533–62.

Eisinger, Peter (1982). "The Economic Conditions of Black Employment in Municipal Bureaucracies," *American Journal of Political Science*, 26:4: 754–72.

Elklit, Jørgen and Palle Svensson (1997).'"What Makes Elections Free and Fair?," *Journal of Democracy*, 8:3: 32–46.

Fearon, Fearon and David Laitin (2003). "Ethnicity, Insurgency, and Civil War," *American Political Science Review*, 97:1: 75–90.

Fetzer, Joel (2008). "Election Strategy and Ethnic Politics in Singapore," Taiwan, *Journal of Democracy*, 4:1: 135–54.

Fish, Steven (2001). "The Inner Asian Anomaly: Mongolia's Democratization in Comparative Perspective," *Communist and Post-Communist Studies*, 34: 323–38.

Frankel, Jon (2001). "The Alternative Vote System in Fiji: Electoral Engineering or Ballot-Rigging?," *Journal of Commonwealth and Comparative Politics*, 39:2: 1–31.

Fritz, Verena (2008). "Mongolia: The Rise and Travails of a Deviant Democracy," *Democratization*, 15:4: 766–88.

Fukuyama, Francis (2006). *Nation-Building: Beyond Afghanistan and Iraq.* Baltimore, MD: Johns Hopkins University Press.

Garcia-Montalvo, J and M Reynal-Querol (2005). "Ethnic Polarization, Potential Conflict and Civil War," *American Economic Review*, 95:3: 796–816.

Gerring, John and Strom C Thacker (2004). "From Political Institutions and Corruption: The Role of Unitarism and Parliamentarism," *British Journal of Political Science*, 34:2: 295–330.

Ghada Hasham Talhami (2001). "Syria: Islam, Arab Nationalism and the Military," *Middle East Policy*, VIII:4: 110–27.

Goodin, Robert (2008). *Innovating Democracy: Democratic theory and practice after the deliberative turn.* Oxford: Oxford University Press.

Grey, Sandra (2002). "Does size matter? Critical mass and New Zealand's women MPs." *Parliamentary Affairs* 55:1: 19–29.

Grove, William and Paul Meehl (1996). "Comparative Efficiency of Informal (Subjective, Impressionistic) and Formal (Mechanical, Algorithmic) Prediction Procedures: The Clinical Statistical Controversy," *Psychology, Public Policy, and Law*, 2: 293–323.

Guinier, Lani (1992). "Voting Rights and Democratic Theory: Where do we go from here?" in Bernard Grofman and Chandler Davidson (eds.) *Controversies in Minority Voting.* Washington D.C.: Brookings.

Haass, Richard (2005). "Regime Change and Its Limits," *Foreign Affairs*, 84:4: 66–78.

Haider-Markel, Donald P (2007). "Representation and Backlash: The Positive and Negative Influence of Descriptive Representation," *Legislative Studies Quarterly*, XXXII, February.

——, Mark R. Joslyn and Chad J. Kniss (2000). "Minority Group Interests and Political Representation: Gay Elected Officials in the Policy Process," *Journal of Politics* 62:2.

Hall, Peter and Daniel Gingerich (2009). "Varieties of Capitalism and Institutional Complementarities in the Macroeconomy: An Empirical Assessment," *British Journal of Political Science*, 39: 449–82.

Hanf, Theodor (1993). *Coexistence in Wartime Lebanon: Decline of a State and Rise of a Nation*. London: I.B. Tauris.

Harris, Peter and Ben Reilly (eds.) (1998). *Democracy and Deep Rooted Conflicts*. Stockholm: International Institute for Democracy and Electoral Assistance.

Hastie, Reid and Robyn Dawes (2001). *Rational Choice in an Uncertain World*. Thousand Oaks, CA: Sage.

Hegel, GWF (trans. L Rauch 1988). *The Philosophy of History*. Indianapolis, IN: Hackett.

Hemmer, Jort (2009). *Ticking the Box: Elections in Sudan*. Netherlands: Clingendael Institute.

Horowitz, Donald L (1985). *Ethnic Groups in Conflict*. Berkeley, CA: University of California Press.

—— (1991). *A Democratic South Africa: Constitutional Engineering in a Divided Society*. Berkeley, CA: University of California Press.

—— (2002). "Constitutional Design: Proposals Versus Processes," in Andrew Reynolds (ed.) *The Architecture of Democracy*. Oxford: Oxford University Press.

Huntington, Samuel T, (1993). *The Third Wave: Democratization in the Late Twentieth Century*. Norman, OK: University of Oklahoma Press.

Jamal, Amaney and Mark Tessler (2008). "Attitudes in the Arab World," *Journal of Democracy*, 19:1: 97–110.

Jung, Courtney and Ian Shapiro (1995). "South Africa's Negotiated Transition: Democracy, Opposition, and the New Constitutional Order," *Politics and Society*, 23: 269–308.

Kaplan, Robert B (1994). "The Coming Anarchy," *Atlantic Monthly*, February.

—— (1997). *The Ends of the Earth*. New York: Random House.

Karl, Terry L (1997). *The Paradox of Plenty. Oil Booms and Petro-States*. Berkeley, CA: University of California Press.

Kaspin, Deborah (1995). "The Politics of Ethnicity in Malawi's Democratic Transition," *Journal of Modern African Studies,* 33: 595–620.

Lal, Brij (2002). "Constitutional Engineering in Post Coup Fiji," in Andrew Reynolds (ed.) *The Architecture of Democracy*. Oxford: Oxford University Press.

Lal, Brij and Peter Larmour (eds.) (1997). *Electoral Systems in Divided Societies: the Fiji Constitutional Review*. Canberra: National Centre for Development Studies.

Landis, Joshua and Joe Pace (2007). "The Syrian Opposition," *The Washington Quarterly*, 30:1: 45–68.

Lijphart, Arend (1971). "Comparative Politics and the Comparative Method," *American Political Science Review*, 65:3: 682–93.

—— (1977). *Democracy in Plural Societies*. New Haven, CT: Yale University Press.

—— (1985). *Power Sharing in South Africa*. Berkeley, CA: University of California.

Lindgren, Karl-Oskar, Magdalena Inkinen and Sten Widmalm (2009). "Who Knows Best What the People Want: Women or Men?: A Study of Political Representation in India," *Comparative Political Studies*, 42:1: 31–55.

Locke, John (trans. P Laslett 1960). *Two Treatises of Government*. Cambridge: Cambridge University Press.

Machiavelli, Niccolo (trans. Q Skinner 1988). *The Prince*. Cambridge: Cambridge University Press.

Mansfield, Edward G and Jack Snyder (2005). *Electing to Fight: Why Emerging Democracies Go to War*. Cambridge, MA: MIT Press.

Mill, John Stuart (1865). *Considerations on Representative Government*. London: Longman, Roberts & Green.

Milner, Helen V and Keiko Kubota (2005). "Why the Move to Free Trade? Democracy and Trade Policy in the Developing Countries," *International Organization*, 59: 107–43.

Moore, Mick (2001). "Political Underdevelopment. What Causes 'Bad Governance?'," *Public Management Review*, 3:3: 385–418.

Mosley, Layna and Saika Uno (2007). "Racing to the Bottom or Climbing to the Top? Economic Globalization and Collective Labor Rights," *Comparative Political Studies*, 40:8: 923–48.

Munck, Geraldo and Jay Verkuilen (2002). "Conceptualizing and Measuring Democracy," *Comparative Political Studies*, 35:1: 5–34.

Nadje, Al-Ali and Nicola Pratt (2008). "Women's Organizing and the Conflict in Iraq since 2003," *Feminist Review*, 88.

Nolutshungu, Samuel C (1993). "Constitutionalism in Africa: Some Conclusions," in Katz Greenberg et al. (eds.) *Constitutionalism and Democracy: Transitions in the Contemporary World*. New York: Oxford University Press.

Norlinger, Eric (1972). *Conflict Regulation in Divided Societies*. Cambridge: Harvard University Press.

Norris, Pippa (2008). *Driving Democracy: Do Power-Sharing Institutions Work?* Cambridge: Cambridge University Press.

O'Donnell, Guillermo (2004). "In partial defense of an Evanescent Paradigm," in Thomas Carothers. *Critical Mission*. New York: Carnegie.

O'Higgins, Niall (2007). "The Challenge of Youth Unemployment," *International Social Security Review*, 50:4: 63–93.

Phillips, Anne (1993). *Democracy and Difference*. University Park: Penn State University Press.

——(1999). "Exporting Democracy: German Political Foundations in Central-East Europe," *Democratization*, 6:2: 70–98.

Pitkin, Hanna (1967). *The Concept of Representation*. Berkeley, University of California Press.

——(1969). (ed.) *Representation*. New York, Atherton Press.

Plato (trans. GMA Grube 1992). *Republic*. Indianapolis, IN: Hackett.

Pomper, Gerald (2008). "The Wisdom of the Masses: A Philosophical Case for Elections," *Harvard International Review*, XXIX:1: 34–8.

Przeworski, Adam (1991). *Democracy and the Market*. Cambridge: Cambridge University Press.

——, Michael Alvarez, Jose Antonio Cheibub, and Fernando Limongi (2000). *Democracy and Development*. Cambridge: Cambridge University Press.

Reid, Ann (1993). *Conflict Resolution in Africa: Lessons from Angola*. INR Foreign Affairs Brief. Washington D.C.: Bureau of Intelligence and Research, US Department of State.

Reilly, Benjamin (2001). *Democracy in Divided Societies*. Cambridge: Cambridge University Press.

Reingold, Beth (2008). "Women as Officeholders: Linking Descriptive and Substantive Representation," in Wolbrecht, Beckwith and Baldez (eds.) *Political Women and American Democracy*. Cambridge, Cambridge University Press.

Reynolds, Andrew (1993). *Voting for a New South Africa*. Cape Town: Maskew Miller Longman.

——(1999). "Women in the Legislatures and Executives of the World: Knocking at the Highest Glass Ceiling," *World Politics*, 51:4: 547–72.

——(2006). "The Curious Case of Afghanistan," *Journal of Democracy*, 17:2: 104–17.

——(2007). "The State of Play: Minority MPs in National Legislatures," in *State of the World's Minorities: Events of 2005–6*. London: Minority Rights Group International.

——, Alfred Stepan, Zaw Oo, and Stephen Levine (2001). "How Burma Could Democratize," *Journal of Democracy*, 12:4: 95–108.

——, Jeffrey Saltzman, and Susan Stigant (2011). "Can Power Sharing Bring a Democratic Peace to the Sudan?," in Kaare Strom and Scott Gates (eds.) *Fragile Bargains: Power Sharing in Africa*. Oslo: PRIO.

Ross, Michael (2001). "Does Oil Hinder Democracy?," *World Politics*, 53:3: 325–61.

——(2004). "How Do Natural Resources Influence Civil War? Evidence from Thirteen Cases," *International Organization*, 58: 35–67.

——(2006). "A Closer Look at Oil, Diamonds and Civil War," *American Review of Political Science*, 9: 265–300.

Rousseau, Jean-Jacques (1985). *The Government of Poland*. Indianapolis, IN: Hacket.

Sackett DL, Straus SE, Richardson WS, Rosenberg W, Haynes RB (2000). *Evidence-Based Medicine: How to Practice and Teach EBM*, 2nd ed. Edinburgh & New York: Churchill Livingstone.

Saint-Germain, Michelle (1989). "Does their difference make a difference? The impact of women on public policy in the Arizona legislature." *Social Science Quarterly* 70:4: 956–68.

Saltzstein, Grace Hall (1986). "Female Mayors and Women in Municipal Jobs," *American Journal of Political Science*, 30:1: 140–65.

——(1989). "Black Mayors and Police Policies," *Journal of Politics*, 51:3: 525–45.

Samuels, Kirsti and Vanessa Hawkins Wyeth (2006). *State-Building and Constitutional Design after Conflict*. New York: IPA.

Sen, Amartya (1999). *Development as Freedom*. New York: Knopf.

Sherover, Charles M (1974). *The Development of the Democratic Idea*. New York: Mentor.

Shilts, Randy (1982). *The Mayor of Castro Street: The Life and Times of Harvey Milk*. New York: St. Martin's Press.

Sisk, Timothy D (1995). *Democratization in South Africa: The Elusive Social Contract*. Princeton, NJ: Princeton University Press.

——(1996). *Power Sharing and International Mediation in Ethnic Conflicts*. Washington, D.C.: USIP Press.

——and Roland Paris (2009). *The Dilemmas of Statebuilding: Confronting the Contradictions of Postwar Peace Operations*. London: Routledge.

Smith, Raymond A and Donald Haider-Markel (2002). *Gay and Lesbian Americans and Political Participation.* Santa Barbara, CA: ABC-CLIO.

Stepan, Alfred (1999). "Federalism and Democracy: Beyond the U.S. Model," *Journal of Democracy*, 10:4: 19–34.

Suberu, Rotimi and Larry Diamond (2002). "Institutional Design, Ethnic Conflict Management and Democracy in Nigeria," in Andrew Reynolds (ed.) *The Architecture of Democracy.* Oxford: Oxford University Press.

Trier, Shawn and Simon Jackman (2008). "Democracy as a Latent Variable," *American Journal of Political Science*, 52:1: 201–17.

Tull, Denis and Andreas Mehler (2005). "The Hidden Costs of Power-Sharing: Reproducing Insurgent Violence in Africa," *African Affairs*, 104:416: 375–98.

Varshney, Ashutosh (2002). *Ethnic Conflict and Civic Life: Hindus and Muslims in India.* New Haven, CT: Yale University Press.

Vollan, Kaare (2008). "The System of Representation for the Constituent Assembly Elections in Nepal," Unpublished paper, Kathmandu.

Wald, Kenneth D, James Button and Barbara Rienzo (1996). "The politics of gay rights in American communities: Explaining antidiscrimination ordinances and Policies," *American Journal of Political Science*, 40:4: 1152–78.

Walzer, Michael (1994). "Multiculturalism and Individualism," *Dissent* 41:2: 185–191.

Wolbrecht, Christina, Karen Beckwith, and Lisa Baldez (eds.) (2008). *Political Women and American Democracy.* Cambridge: Cambridge University Press.

Wordsworth, Anna (2007). "A Matter of Interests: Gender and the Politics of Presence in Afghanistan's Wolesi Jirga," Kabul: Afghan Research and Evaluation Unit.

Young, Iris Marion (1989). "Polity and Group Difference: A Critique of the Ideal of Universal Citizenship." *Ethics* 99:2: 250–74.

Zakaria, Fareed (1997). "The Rise of Illiberal Democracy," *Foreign Affairs*, 76:6.

——(2003). *The Future of Freedom: Illiberal Democracy at Home and Abroad.* New York: Norton, 22–43.

Data Sources

United Kingdom: The Report of the Independent Commission on the Voting System
http://www.archive.official-documents.co.uk/document/cm40/4090/4090.htm

The Global Gender Gap Report
http://www.weforum.org/en/Communities/Women%20Leaders%20and%20
Gender%20Parity/GenderGapNetwork/index.htm

Openly Gay Elected and Appointed Officials
http://www.glli.org/out_officials

Inter Parliamentary Union—Women in Politics
http://www.ipu.org/wmn-e/world.htm

UN Human Development Report
http://hdr.undp.org/en/statistics/

The Fund for Peace
http://www.fundforpeace.org/web/index.php?option=com_content&task=view&id=99
&Itemid=140

World Bank: Governance Statistics
http://info.worldbank.org/governance/wgi/index.asp

Global Peace Index
http://www.visionofhumanity.org/gpi/home.php

Peace Research Institute of Oslo Datasets
http://www.prio.no/Data/

Minority Rights International: Peoples Under Threat
http://www.minorityrights.org/464/peoples-under-threat/table-1-peoples-most-under-threat--highest-rated-countries-2008.html

Internal Displacement Monitoring Center
http://www.internal-displacement.org/8025708F004CE90B/(httpPages)/22FB1D4E2B1
96DAA802570BB005E787C?OpenDocument&count=1000

Transparency International Corruption Index
http://www.transparency.org/news_room/in_focus/2008/cpi2008/cpi_2008_table

Polity IV Project
http://www.systemicpeace.org/polity/polity4.htm

Freedom House Democracy Scores
http://www.freedomhouse.org/template.cfm?page=274

Voter Turnout: International IDEA
http://www.idea.int/vt/index.cfm

World Institute for Development Economics Research
http://www.wider.unu.edu/research/Database/en_GB/wiid/

UN Human Development Report
http://hdrstats.undp.org/indicators/147.html

GINI Inequality Index
http://earthtrends.wri.org/text/economics-business/variable-353. html

Global Employment Trends for Youth. ILO. Geneva
http://www.ilo.org/public/english/employment/strat/download/gety08.pdf

Index

DATE DUE

BRODART, CO.

Cat. No. 23-221